The International Criminal Court and Peace Processes in Africa

The book investigates how involvement by the International Criminal Court (ICC) affects efforts to negotiate peace. It offers an interpretive account of how peace negotiators and mediators in two peace processes in Uganda and Kenya sought to navigate and understand the new terrain of international justice, while also tracing how and why international decision-making processes interfered with the negotiations, narrated the conflicts and insisted on a narrow scope of justice. Building on this interpretive analysis, a comparative analysis of peace processes in Uganda, Kenya and Colombia explores a set of general features pertaining to the judicialisation of peace.

Line Engbo Gissel argues that the level and timing of ICC involvement is key to the ICC's impact on peace processes and explains why this is the case: a high level of ICC involvement during the negotiation phase of a peace process delegates politico-legal and discursive authority away from peace process actors, while a low level of ICC involvement during the negotiation phase retains such forms of authority at the level of the peace process. As politico-legal authority enables the resolution of sticking points and discursive authority constructs the conflict and its resolution, the location of authority is important for the peace process. Furthermore, judicialisation also affects the negotiation and implementation of a justice policy, with a narrowing scope for justice accompanying increasing levels of ICC involvement.

Line Engbo Gissel is an Associate Professor in the Department of Social Sciences and Business at Roskilde University, Denmark.

Routledge Studies in Peace, Conflict and Security in Africa
Edited by Cyril Obi
African Peacebuilding Network

The International Criminal Court and Peace Processes in Africa
Judicialising Peace
Line Engbo Gissel

The International Criminal Court and Peace Processes in Africa

Judicialising Peace

Line Engbo Gissel

Routledge
Taylor & Francis Group
LONDON AND NEW YORK

First published 2018
by Routledge

2 Park Square, Milton Park, Abingdon, Oxfordshire OX14 4RN
52 Vanderbilt Avenue, New York, NY 10017

Routledge is an imprint of the Taylor & Francis Group, an informa business

First issued in paperback 2020

British Library Cataloguing in Publication Data
A catalogue record for this book is available from the British Library

Library of Congress Cataloging in Publication Data
A catalog record for this book has been requested

ISBN: 978-1-138-10401-3 (hbk)
ISBN: 978-0-367-59335-3 (pbk)

Typeset in Times New Roman
by Wearset Ltd, Boldon, Tyne and Wear

Contents

Illustrations

Figures

Tables

Acknowledgements

The idea for this book developed a decade ago, when I moved to Apac in Northern Uganda to work for a small umbrella NGO, the NGO Link Forum Apac, seconded by ActionAid Denmark. At the time – and seemingly all the time – friends and colleagues attended the ICC's sensitisation workshops and other justice-related events. The LRA was in the DRC and thus some distance away, but there was a sense that the rebels could move quickly and easily to anywhere they wanted. In the evenings, when we would discuss the ICC intervention, the LRA and the government, the dilemmas of peace and justice were real and concrete. It is appropriate therefore to begin this book by thanking Sam Jamara, Julie Cherukut, Jimmy Ogwal, Susan Apio, Brenda Otika and Christopher Odic for their friendship and willingness to share their knowledge and experiences.

The book owes its existence to all those who agreed to be interviewed or helped me during field research in Kenya and Uganda. I am grateful to my anonymous or named interviewees for their time, insights and opinions, and for the assistance of David Ebong MP and librarian Andrew Bayunga at the Parliament of Uganda. Professionals in Nairobi, who shall remain unnamed for security reasons, greatly helped me with contacting high-profile interviewees in Kenya. Thomas Winkler and David Kendal of the Danish Ministry of Foreign Affairs kindly included me in the Danish delegation to the 2010 ICC Review Conference in Kampala, which provided invaluable observation of the world of ICC diplomacy and a crash course on the Rome Statute.

The book has a previous incarnation as a PhD dissertation written at Aarhus University's Department of Political Science, where Jørgen Elklit and Anne Mette Kjær supervised and nurtured my research by asking difficult questions while believing in the project. I am grateful to them for providing a supportive space within which to find my feet in (Danish) academia after a professional career outside and to develop my thinking on the politics of international justice in Africa.

Roskilde University's Department of Social Sciences and Business has been my happy home during the writing process, which has benefitted from stimulating discussions in the research groups on global political sociology and globalisation and Europeanisation. A research stay at the Makerere Institute of Social Research contributed greatly to the overall framing of the argument.

I would like to thank Ben Schiff, Adam Branch, Barney Afako, Peter Brett, Helena Flam, Christian Lund, Sarah Nouwen, Phil Clark and Lisbet Christoffersen for their interest in my research for this book. I am grateful to my mother for practical and emotional support and childminding, all my parents and my Indian family for cheering me on, and Maya and Milan for being forgiving of my absences and long working hours. I dedicate this book to Devapriyo, my better half, who makes our everyday life possible while pursuing his own busy career.

August 2017

Timelines of the Uganda and Kenya cases

Uganda case: The Juba Peace Talks

14 June 2002	**Membership stage:** Government of Uganda ratifies the Rome Statute
16 June 2003	**Preliminary Examination stage:** The OTP begins to look into the Uganda situation
16 December 2003	Government of Uganda refers the northern situation to the ICC
29 January 2004	**Investigation stage:** OTP and government of Uganda hold joint press briefing
September 2004	The LRA moves to Garamba Forest, Haut Uele Province, DRC
Early 2005	Betty Bigombe meets LRA officers
6 May 2005	**Indictment stage:** OTP submits a sealed request for arrest warrants for five LRA leaders: Joseph Kony, Vincent Otti, Okot Odhiambo, Dominic Ongwen and Raska Lukwiya
8 July 2005	PTC II authorises sealed arrest warrants for the five LRA leaders
August 2005	SPLA/M leader Salva Kiir calls on UPDF and LRA to negotiate, leave Sudan or be attacked by SPLA
13 October 2005	PTC unseals the arrest warrants following a request from the OTP
30 November 2005	**Pre-Negotiation phase:** LRA articulates a desire to talk peace
February 2006	Southern Sudan regional government and LRA sign pre-negotiation agreement
May 2006	President Museveni is presented with a film recording of Kony expressing a wish to negotiate peace. He agrees to enter peace negotiations
16 May 2006	Museveni offers security guarantee to LRA leaders
14 July 2006	**Negotiation phase:** Juba Peace Talks launched
26 August 2006	Parties sign the Cessation of Hostilities Agreement

December 2006	Joachim Chissano appointed as the UN Secretary-General's Special Envoy for LRA-Affected Areas
January 2007	The LRA/M delegation leaves the Talks, citing multiple grievances against the SPLM
26 April 2007	A new round of talks is launched
2 May 2007	The parties sign the Agreement on Comprehensive Solutions
29 June 2007	The parties sign the Agreement on Accountability and Reconciliation
October 2007	Vincent Otti is killed
19 February 2008	The parties sign the Annexure to the Agreement on Accountability and Reconciliation
22 February 2008	The parties sign the Implementation Protocol to the Agreement on Comprehensive Solutions
23 February 2008	The parties sign the Agreement on Permanent Ceasefire
29 February 2008	The parties sign the Agreement on Disarmament, Demobilisation and Reintegration
10 April 2008	Planned ceremony to sign the Final Peace Agreement. Kony refuses to appear
30 November 2008	Final deadline for Kony to sign the Final Peace Agreement
14 December 2008	Launch of Operation Lightning Thunder in Garamba Forest
15 December 2008	**Implementation phase:** The Negotiation phase ends
23 May 2012	The Minister of Internal Affairs lapses Part II of the Amnesty Act (2000)
15 May 2013	Parliament reinstates Part II of the Amnesty Act (2000)

Kenya case: the Kenya National Dialogue and Reconciliation

15 March 2005	**Membership stage:** Government of Kenya ratifies the Rome Statute
30 December 2007	**Pre-Negotiation phase:** Regional and international actors arrive in Kenya to obtain the conflict principals' commitment to enter into dialogue
22 January 2008	Kofi Annan arrives in Nairobi and begins to assemble the mediation office
24 January 2008	Mwai Kibaki and Raila Odinga shake hands on the steps of Harambee House
29 January 2008	**Negotiation phase:** Formal launch of the Kenya National Dialogue and Reconciliation
1 February 2008	The parties sign the Public Statement to Immediately Halt the Violence
4 February 2008	The parties sign the Public Statement on Immediate Measures to Address the Humanitarian Crisis

5 February 2008	**Preliminary examination stage:** The OTP announces it will monitor the Kenyan situation
14 February 2008	The parties sign the Agreement on agenda Item 3: How to Resolve the Political Crisis
28 February 2008	The parties sign Acting Together for Kenya: Agreement on the Principles of Partnership of the Coalition Government
4 March 2008	The parties sign the Agreement on the Commission of Inquiry on Post-Election Violence; the Agreement on the Independent Review Committee: Terms of Reference; the Agreement on the Truth, Justice and Reconciliation Commission; and the Agreement on Longer-Term Issues and Solutions: Constitutional Review
13 March 2008	**Implementation phase:** The government establishes IREC
18 March 2008	Parliament approves the National Accord and Reconciliation Act
23 May 2008	The parties sign Statement of Principles on Long-Term Issues and Solutions
30 July 2008	The parties sign the Long-Term Issues and Solutions: Matrix of Implementation Agenda
16 October 2008	CIPEV releases a report on the post-election violence
17 October 2008	CIPEV hands potentially incriminating evidence, including an envelope of names of alleged perpetrators, to PEAP
12 February 2009	Vote on the Constitution of Kenya (Amendment) Bill 2008
9 July 2009	PEAP hands CIPEV's incriminating evidence to the OTP
26 November 2010	The OTP applies for authorisation of a *proprio motu* investigation of the Kenyan post-election violence
31 March 2010	**Investigation stage:** The PTC authorises an investigation into the situation in Kenya between 1 June 2005 and 26 November 2009
15 December 2010	**Indictment stage:** The OTP issues summons to appear for William Ruto, Henry Kosgey, Joshua Arap Sang, Uhuru Kenyatta, Francis Muthaura and Mohammed Hussein Ali
31 March 2011	The government challenges admissibility of the Kenyan cases
January 2011	The AU Assembly endorses Kenya's deferral request to the UN Security Council
March and April 2011	The UN Security Council conducts informal discussions of Kenya's deferral request and drops the issue because of internal disagreement

23 January 2012	Confirmation of charges against Ruto, Sang, Kenyatta and Muthaura
4 March 2013	General elections in Kenya. The Jubilee Alliance wins the Presidency. Kenyatta and Ruto become president-elect and vice-president-elect, respectively

Abbreviations and acronyms

AU	African Union
CAR	Central African Republic
CIPEV	Commission of Inquiry into the Post-Election Violence
DDR	Demobilisation, disarmament and reintegration
DPA	UN Department of Political Affairs
DRC	Democratic Republic of Congo
EU	European Union
FARC	The Revolutionary Armed Forces of Colombia
GNU	Government of National Unity
ICC	International Criminal Court
ICD	International Crimes Division of the High Court of Uganda
ICTR	International Criminal Tribunal for Rwanda
ICTY	International Criminal Tribunal for the Former Yugoslavia
IDP	Internally displaced persons
IGAD	Inter-Governmental Authority on Development
ILC	International Law Commission
IREC	Independent Review Committee
LRA	Lord's Resistance Army
LRA/M	Lord's Resistance Army/Movement
NGO	Non-Governmental Organisation
NRA	National Resistance Army
NRM	National Resistance Movement
OCHA	UN Office for the Coordination of Humanitarian Affairs
ODM	Orange Democratic Movement
OTP	Office of the Prosecutor
PEAP	Panel of Eminent African Personalities
PNU	Party of National Unity
PRDP	Peace, Recovery and Development Plan
PTC	Pre-Trial Chamber
SCSL	Special Court for Sierra Leone
SJP	Special Jurisdiction for Peace
SPLA	Sudan People's Liberation Army
SPLA/M	Sudan People's Liberation Army/Movement

SPLM	Sudan People's Liberation Movement
STK	Special Tribunal of Kenya
TJRC	Truth, Justice and Reconciliation Commission
UN	United Nations
UNSC	United Nations Security Council
UPA	Uganda People's Army
UPDA	Uganda People's Democratic Army
UPDF	Uganda People's Defence Forces
US	United States

1 Introduction

International justice and the problem of peace

When it comes to peace and justice, we are living in a new world.
Ban Ki-moon, UN Secretary-General, Security Council open debate, 'Peace and Justice with a Special Focus on the Role of the International Criminal Court', New York, 19 October 2012

It is a new world of mediation when amnesties are not an option. We don't have a lot of experience of peace processes without amnesty options.
James LeMoyne, Mediator, Rome Statute Review Conference plenary debate, 'Stocktaking on Peace and Justice', Kampala, 2 June 2010

For UN Secretary-General Ban Ki-moon and mediator James LeMoyne, peace-making practices and justice norms co-habit 'a new world'. In this world, perpetrators of atrocity are held to account, unable to 'trade their power for amnesty and then slip away, unpunished, to some safe haven' (Secretary-General in UN Security Council 2012). Its novelty springs from the fact that an emerging international criminal law regime claims relevance for conflict resolution. Until recently, peace processes were fairly independent of the formal rules that frame ordinary politics. Mediators had discretionary power to choose which legal obligations to bring into the negotiations. As Väyrynen *et al.* (1995, 68) observed in 1995:

> Third parties may introduce issues to the process of conflict resolution the parties prefer to leave out. The fact that third parties can draw on international legal standards to do so (or ignore these in handling a dispute) can both enhance and limit the possibilities for a mediated solution.

As a result of this approach, engagement with armed groups was characterised by the 'relative neglect' of accountability issues (Whitfield 2010, 7). In contrast, in contemporary conflict resolution, negotiators and mediators are now likely to be under 'considerable pressure' to comply with international principles and international law if the conflict parties have committed gross human rights abuses (Hayner 2009, 9).

This 'new world' is a tense terrain where the pursuit of justice may collide with that of peace, a staggering situation made possible by three characteristics of contemporary conflict and international normativity. First, atrocity usually takes place within a context of political conflict. War crimes, crimes against humanity and genocide are committed against persons perceived as enemies, understood as such within a context of violent political contestation. Of Harff's (2003, 62) 37 cases of genocide and mass political murder between 1955 and 1997, all but one occurred during or immediately after political upheavals. International criminal law's timeless prosecution of atrocity catapults the International Criminal Court (ICC) and other international criminal tribunals into the field of conflict.

Second, armed conflicts can be ended militarily or politically. Military victory will stop the violence, but may not solve its underlying incompatibility. When there is insufficient capacity on either side to secure a military victory, war may last for decades. The only way to end this type of protracted conflict is by means of a negotiated settlement, where the conflict parties agree to accept each other's continued existence as parties (Wallensteen 2012). Political solutions presuppose rehabilitation, while military solutions rest on capitulation. Settlements that end internal conflicts therefore often include arrangements for the integration of former insurgents into the national army and the rehabilitation of their group. This solution has led to different degrees of societal improvement in countries such as El Salvador, Mozambique, South Africa and Spain and it is, therefore, on its own, insufficient for creating a 'positive peace', meaning the absence of structural violence. While in many cases a peace settlement may not prevent a later return to war (Högbladh 2012), it remains the only alternative to military victory.

Last, the pursuit of criminal justice requires the capitulation, cooperation or arrest of alleged perpetrators prior to their trial. This brings the conflict status to the fore. While international criminal law does not distinguish between terminated or ongoing conflicts, this context clearly matters to a justice intervention and its impact on the context. Where conflict has ended, there is no a priori contradiction between the pursuit of justice and that of 'negative peace', meaning the absence of direct physical violence. In contrast, in situations of ongoing conflict, where alleged perpetrators command armies, international judicial interventions inevitably interact with efforts to negotiate an end to war.

To conflict mediators, the 'new world' of peace and justice is difficult to navigate – there are many prescriptions for ensuring that a criminal accountability process is part of the peace, but very few peace processes have succeeded in achieving this. To stay in the geographical metaphor, the maps are there, but few have followed them. To many countries and international organisations, including the United Nations (UN) and the European Union (EU), this lack of experience is less of a concern. What matters is, instead, the promulgation and consolidation of the new, progressive norms and rules. By insisting on maps not drawn from experience, it is possible to chart a new path, to force a change in practice.

This book speaks to these two different concerns by asking how and why ICC involvement in situations of ongoing conflict affects the conditions of possibility for a political settlement. To answer this question, it investigates the relationship between peace and justice empirically, comparatively and interpretively. The analysis is empirical because claims by proponents and critics of judicialised peacemaking are based 'mainly on normative grounds and … deductive reasoning' (Skaar and Malca 2015, 14). It is comparative because comparisons enable a level of generalisation that allows us to understand the judicialisation of peace as a general phenomenon, abstracted from the particularities of specific processes of conflict resolution. Finally, the analysis is interpretive because the interaction between justice actors and peacemakers needs to be approached as concept-dependent and meaningful in order to be understood. The practices, rules, roles and relations of judicialised peacemaking depend on what they mean to its actors (Maxwell 2004).

To understand how and why international justice interventions affect peacemaking processes, this book analyses two peace processes that have taken place in the context of ICC involvement: the Juba Peace Talks between the Ugandan government and the Lord's Resistance Army (LRA) rebel group, which sought to end the protracted insurgency in Northern Uganda, and the Kenya National Dialogue and Reconciliation process between two political parties, the Party of National Unity (PNU) and Orange Democratic Movement (ODM), who used violence to claim the presidency following the 2007 general elections. These two peace processes are purposefully selected from a universe of cases defined by the scope condition of active ICC involvement. Peace processes without active ICC involvement are considered too causally heterogeneous to enable the research.

The cases are selected on the basis of their peace process outcomes and the nature of the conflicts. A successful and an unsuccessful peace process represent the two possible outcomes. Selecting one of each outcome type prevents the conclusion that ICC involvement per se dooms the resolution of judicialised conflicts. It also ensures that the findings are not exclusive to peace processes that could be argued to have been always failure-prone. This is an important point, as international justice proponents tend to brush off mediators' ICC critiques as a strategy to avoid blame for having failed to secure a settlement.[1] The failure of the Juba process to end a protracted conflict was never seen as inevitable. The Northern Ugandan conflict was not more immune to resolution than the civil wars in Mozambique, South Africa and Sudan, which were all settled politically.

The variation in conflict types ensures that the findings are robust across different contexts of conflict resolution. It is more likely that the ICC is the cause of important patterns of judicialisation if these patterns are shared across peace processes that tackle different types of conflict. The selection for maximum variation enables findings 'that cut across cases and derive their significance from having emerged out of heterogeneity' (Patton 2002, 235).

The selected cases are a successful and an unsuccessful peace process: the Juba Peace Talks failed to achieve a political solution to conflict, while the Kenya Dialogue managed to end the post-election violence by means of a power-sharing agreement. These two peace processes also dealt with different types of conflict: the Juba Peace Talks sought to end a long-standing insurgency, while the Kenya Dialogue aimed to end violent civil unrest that derived from long-standing land-based conflicts. The comparison of peace processes with such different conflict contexts does not focus on the specific content of the proposed solutions, but studies how participants arrived at these solutions and how and why ICC involvement affected the latter and the negotiations.

By comparing these two processes of conflict resolution, the book identifies a set of general characteristics pertaining to judicialised peace processes. These characteristics relate to the delegation of politico-legal and discursive authority, the shaping of sticking points and the decontestation of the meaning of justice. Given the importance of both authority and meaning-making for the achievement of a political solution to conflict, these characteristics do not lend themselves to a simple reconciliation between peace and justice in situations of ongoing conflict. However, they do encourage a reconsideration of the temporality of each process and enable a deep understanding of judicialised peace processes that can help practitioners and policy-makers navigate in the 'new world'.

The book presents a theory about how ICC involvement during ongoing conflict impacts upon peace processes that seek to end the conflict. Contrary to received wisdom in many UN agencies, governments and non-governmental organisations (NGOs), peace and justice do not always 'go hand in hand'. Whether they do this depends on the level of ICC involvement during the Negotiation phase. A high level of ICC involvement shapes the nature of the sticking points of the peace process, transfers politico-legal authority to the international level and seeks to decontest justice. In contrast, a low level of ICC involvement allows for conflict-specific sticking points, retains politico-legal authority at the level of the peace process and allows for broad notions of justice. A low level of involvement also delegates discursive authority from domestic actors to the ICC, but whether ICC discourses are accommodating of peacemaking depends on the indictment mode: warranted suspects compel the ICC to promote a discourse of marginalisation and capture, while summoned suspects allow for a Court discourse of assistance and conflict prevention.

The remainder of the chapter situates the investigation in its ideational, institutional and discursive context. It first discusses how the 'new world' of justice and peace came about through multiple global processes of practice, normative change and institution-building in the domains of conflict resolution, transitional justice and international criminal law. The chapter then zooms in on the peace-versus-justice debate (hereafter the peace/justice debate), conceptualising it as a meeting between two global discourses which shaped Ugandan and Kenyan peacemaking. This section maps three sets of discursive narratives about the effects of ICC involvement on peacemaking, which later chapters show as being influential in the exercise of agency over the two peace processes.

Origins: The 'new world' of judicialised peacemaking

The story of international justice has been told in several ways, with most accounts beginning with the Nuremberg trials. This section combines different developments in a narrative through which judicialised peacemaking emerges as the central *problematique*. These developments are the post-Cold-War practice of political conflict resolution, the norm of a duty to prosecute serious international crimes, the establishment of the ICC and the global and general legalisation of politics.

The political resolution of conflict

The post-Cold-War field of conflict has been characterised mainly by internal wars, involving insurgent and separatist armies, sometimes with foreign support from patronage states or diaspora groups. After 1946, conflict prevalence peaked in the early 1990s (Themnér and Wallensteen 2014).[2] There were 53 armed conflicts in 1992, after which they declined in number to reach an annual average of 34 in the 2000s (Wallensteen and Themnér 2012). Since 2010, war has increased, with 2015 seeing as many as 50 armed conflicts.

The post-Cold-War rise in internal conflict was initially accompanied by an increased use of political negotiations to end conflicts. Although negotiations did not always lead to a sustained peace, the 1990s represented 'a larger shift from confrontation toward accommodation' (Gurr 2000, 52), signified by 'a proliferation' of peace processes (Darby and Rae 1999, 46). Between 1990 and 2008, there was an average of almost ten peace agreements per year, with peaks of 19 and 18 agreements in 1990 and 1993 (Högbladh 2012, 49). Since 2008, there has been a marked decline in the number of peace agreements, even matching the Cold War levels of zero to two agreements per year. It is not clear why the past decade has seen this decline in peacemaking, but Högbladh (2012, 50) suggests it is explained by a change the international community's attitudes.

The end of the Cold War led to greater international involvement in conflict resolution. Most major powers, the UN and regional organisations in Europe and Africa supported the principle of settling armed conflicts by negotiation (Gurr 2000). There was a 'broad acceptance' that it was the mandate of the UN Secretary-General or other peacemakers to establish contact with groups formerly considered pariahs but now acknowledged as potential partners for peace (Whitfield 2010, 7). According to one count, the UN brokered 60 per cent of the agreements signed from 1988 to 1992, and 36 per cent of agreements between 1993 and 1998 (Darby and Rae 1999, 46).

During the 1990s, it was common to agree on a non-criminal solution to the problem of accountability: there was a prevalent use of truth commissions and de facto or *de jure* amnesties. Accountability issues were left unaddressed while ex-rebels joined the national army or returned to civilian life. Insurgent movements were rehabilitated and transformed into political parties. Since then, the tendency to offer insurgents and other armed opponents a process of political rehabilitation has dropped, while the criminalisation of these actors has emerged on a greater scale (Vinjamuri and Boesenecker 2007).

A watershed year for the new world of peace and justice came in 1999. The UN Secretary-General's Special Representative appended a disclaimer to his endorsement of the Lomé Peace Agreement between Sierra Leone and the Revolutionary United Front, which contained a broad amnesty provision. Stating 'The United Nations does not recognize amnesty for genocide, crimes against humanity, war crimes, and other serious violations of international humanitarian law' (Office of the UN High Commissioner for Human Rights 2009a, para. 17), the disclaimer represents a break with the UN's practice of supporting the negotiation of agreements that include amnesty provisions for atrocities that are common to internal conflict. Since then, UN officials have appended similar reservations to agreements in Angola and Sudan.

The divergent fates of Alfonzo Dhlakama of Mozambican rebel group RENAMO and Thomas Lubanga Dyilo of the Union of Congolese Patriots serve to highlight the change in international approaches to accountability. Both rebel leaders commanded armies that committed atrocities and used child soldiers, with RENAMO pioneering the latter strategy in the mid-1980s when it had difficulties obtaining adult recruits (Young 2004, 45). However, Dhlakama was rehabilitated as a national politician and RENAMO's presidential candidate after the 1992 peace accords, while Lubanga was arrested in the Democratic Republic of Congo (DRC), prosecuted and convicted of war crimes by the ICC. Two decades after Mozambique's 'pacted peace', Lubanga was held accountable for recruiting and training child soldiers in eastern DRC.

The duty to prosecute

The period between the Mozambican settlement and the arrest of Lubanga in 2006 saw significant institution-building in international law in general and international criminal law in particular, to the extent that the demand for individual criminal responsibility became perceived as both reasonable and realistic. International lawyers working with questions of transitional justice and human rights debated in the early 1990s whether international law warranted a duty to prosecute certain international crimes (Nino 1991; Orentlicher 1991; Scharf 1996). In the human rights community, the dominant position was at the time that if 'prosecutions threatened to imperil a transition to democracy, their potential value was outweighed by their attendant risks' (Orentlicher 2007, 13). Nino (1991, 2620) argued:

> Though it is true that many people approach the issue of human rights violations with a strong retributive impulse, almost all who think momentarily about the issue are not prepared to defend a policy of punishing those abuses once it becomes clear that such a policy would probably provoke, by a causal chain, similar or even worse abuses.

The transitional norm, shaped by the Latin American transitions from dictatorship, was to support victims' right to hear the truth about what happened to them. However, the end of the Cold War created a window of opportunity for giving international criminal law a 'renaissance' (Pensky 2016, 487).

The international criminal law renaissance had been under way in the General Assembly and the International Law Commission (ILC) since the Assembly's discussion of the Genocide Convention in 1948 and, later, the Apartheid Convention in 1973. These treaties provide states parties with a duty to prosecute genocide and apartheid crimes, but do not create an international jurisdiction. During the 1980s, however, the ILC developed an emerging consensus on the idea of establishing an international criminal court and in 1989 the General Assembly directed the ILC to consider the subject of such a court within the context of its ongoing work on the Draft Code of Crimes against the Peace and Security of Mankind (Schabas 2011). In response, the ILC submitted a draft ICC statute to states in 1994, which was negotiated until July 1998 when 120 states formally established the ICC.

Building on the experiments of the Nuremberg and Tokyo Tribunals and benefitting from the post-Cold-War 'eclipse' of prior schemes of global justice (Moyn 2012), the immediate post-Cold-War period saw a willingness to revisit and institutionalise the idea of holding individuals responsible for state crimes. The human rights community supported the call to 'end impunity', forming coalitions to shape the international law-making process. Having just 'won' the Cold War, major liberal powers were open to the idea of international justice, indicated by the 1991 UK and US proposal to try Saddam Hussein for aggression against Kuwait (Schabas 2006, 422). In 1993 and 1994, failing to provide military action to halt the atrocities in Rwanda and the Balkans, the UN Security Council established the ad hoc International Criminal Tribunals for Rwanda (ICTR) and the Former Yugoslavia (ICTY). These courts were important precursors to the ICC because they institutionalised the idea of international individual accountability, showing the world, as it were, what international justice could look like on the cusp of the twenty-first century. They gave a material expression to the claim that judicial responses to violence were a useful innovation.

The new international criminal law codified a duty to prosecute war crimes, crimes against humanity and genocide and gave jurisdiction over these crimes to purpose-built institutions of enforcement, chiefly the permanent ICC. This development was revolutionary because it institutionalised the idea of holding leaders responsible as individuals for crimes committed by states or state-like organisations. It was also innovative because it fused international humanitarian law, international human rights law and international criminal law by drawing on the Geneva, Genocide, Apartheid, and Torture Conventions and the Nuremberg, Tokyo and ICTY statutes (Teitel 2011). However, by identifying with the legal example of the Nuremberg Tribunal – a court that was possible because it was imposed on a defeated and occupied Germany – the new international criminal law developed a blind spot with regard to the political contexts of its crimes.

The ICC

The Rome Statute institutionalises the idea that states and the international community have a duty to prosecute war crimes, crimes against humanity and genocide and establishes the ICC to implement this duty when states are 'unwilling or unable' to genuinely do so.[3] States parties affirm in the preamble that 'the most serious crimes of concern to the international community as a whole must not go unpunished and that their effective prosecution must be ensured'. The Statute is constitutive of our 'new world' because it gives a mandate to the ICC to prosecute the crimes regardless of their context; what matters is the fact of their punishment, not their immediate relationship to an actual political reality. In the words of the Court's first Prosecutor, the mandate of the ICC 'requires that we engage in judicial proceedings in relation to conflicts even before they have ended' (Moreno-Ocampo 2007, 8). As such, the context within which an ICC process takes place may not be transitional, but could be characterised by protracted conflict or stable dictatorship, a development that Human Rights Watch has termed 'real-time justice' (Dicker 2008). Importantly, the Statute's timeless duty to prosecute is widely interpreted as a corresponding 'ban' on amnesties (Hayner 2009; Office of the UN High Commissioner for Human Rights 2009a; but see Schabas 2012, chap. 7).

When negotiating the Statute, some states were concerned with the implications of this 'real-time justice' for political transitions. The blind spot was identified, but could it be remedied? The South African delegates, in particular, were concerned that the Statute would encroach upon an amnesty granted as part of a democratic transition. At the Rome Conference, however, views on the appropriateness of the South African model of amnesty conditional upon truth-telling 'were simply too divergent' to enable a common position (Schabas 2012, 175). States therefore included a provision for the 'interests of justice' in Article 53, although they left it to the Court to define its meaning (Greenawalt 2009). According to this Article, the Prosecutor may stay an investigation or prosecution because it will not serve the interests of justice. As a result of their debate on transition, many delegates in Rome 'seemed to believe that an amnesty like that of South Africa would be effective to block prosecution by the Court' either in the interests of justice or due to inadmissibility rulings on the grounds of gravity (Schabas 2012, 176). Others argued that a transition like that of South Africa would no longer be possible. As we shall see in later chapters, the ICC's interpretation of the Statute supports the latter position.

Besides providing in principle for the interests of justice, the Rome Statute grants discretionary powers to the UN Security Council to request that the ICC defer its investigation or prosecution for 12 months, subject to renewal (Article 16). This request has to fall within the mandate of Chapter VII of the UN Charter and therefore must relate to international peace and security. To ensure its independence, the Court does not have to comply with this request. According to Unger and Wierda (2009, 270), the provisions for an interests of justice withdrawal and a Security Council deferral provide the Statute with a more explicit recognition of the tensions between peace and justice compared to the statutes for the ad hoc tribunals and the Special Court for Sierra Leone (SCSL). However, as we shall see, the way in which the ICC Prosecutor and the Security Council mediate the peace/justice dilemma centres on their particular, situated understandings of their own roles and the interpretive scope of these articles.

Legalisation of politics

The legalisation of the duty to prosecute and the establishment of a permanent court for serious international crimes is part of a general global 'move to law' (Goldstein *et al.* 2000, 385). Thickening their international legal commitments, states have signed nearly 3,600 new multilateral interstate agreements between 1951 and 1995 (Simmons 2008, 188). The immediate post-Cold-War period saw a rapid proliferation of international courts and multilateral agreements, with 19 of the world's 25 permanent international courts established after 1989 (Alter 2014). With jurisdiction over issues such as trade disputes, human rights violations and atrocity crimes, these new judiciaries are regional or global, ranging from the Community Court of Justice of the Economic Community of West African States and the Inter-American Court of Human Rights to the World Trade Organization Appellate Body and the ICC. In the field of international justice, ad hoc and hybrid courts include the ICTY, ICTR, East Timor Tribunal (established 2000), SCSL (2002), Iraq High Tribunal (2003), Khmer Rouge Tribunal (2006), Special Tribunal for Lebanon (2007) and the African Extraordinary Chambers (2012).

The legalisation of world affairs has not only taken the form of a deepening of law, but has also entailed the enlargement and differentiation of law: the codification of new laws or the application of particular laws to new or previously non-legalised domains (Blichner and Molander 2008). The domain of peacemaking represents this development, in the sense that it used to be thinly legalised: the perceived exceptionalism of peace negotiations shielded them from the standards of ordinary society. Along with the development of 'hard' international criminal law, the UN sought to de-exceptionalise peacemaking by means of 'soft' law. In 1999, inspired by the 'Lomé moment', the Secretary-General issued guidelines for mediators, which sought to tackle 'the tensions between the urgency of stopping fighting, on the one hand, and the need to address punishable human rights violations on the other' (UN 1999).

A decade later, the US Supreme Court, in *Holder* v. *Humanitarian Law Project*, upheld the constitutionality of a 1996 federal law that criminalises the provision of 'material support' to foreign terrorist groups (Margulies 2010). As this support includes expert advice or assistance, training, service and personnel, the decision outlawed non-violent engagement with terrorist-designated groups by US citizens or others on US territory, such as mediators and humanitarian activists (Schwartz 2010). The peacemaking field may be further legalised as part of its normalisation. According to Whitfield (2010, 27), it is 'logical that prosecutors (including the ICC) may one day try to subpoena mediators'. They may be asked to testify or provide information about armed groups (such as mobile phone numbers, structure and hierarchy) or defence counsel might ask mediators to provide information relevant to a case against a group member.

The legalisation of peacemaking represents a new way of thinking about political problems in general. Although such problems, whether trade disputes or ethnic cleansing, are basically political, they are delegated to the realm of international law, courts and judges. This is a realm where formal rules apply and where decision-making is largely non-negotiable. Little is known about how this delegation to the legal realm impacts political efforts to solve conflict, although plenty of unsubstantiated claims abound. Beyond a minimum of agreement on Articles 16 and 53, states were not overly concerned with conflict resolution when creating the ICC. Since the Rome Statute entered into force in 2002, however, a 'thin' theory of judicialised peace has been elaborated and critiqued in the peace/justice debate, which discusses whether ICC interventions constitute a help or hindrance to peacemaking.

A global debate: Two discourses on peace and justice

The relationship between peace and justice has been the focus of high-level deliberation in the General Assembly, Security Council, Assembly of the African Union, and ICC Assembly of States Parties. When the ICC became involved in the violent internal conflicts of Uganda and Kenya, ordinary citizens, civil society and politicians as well as foreign donors and diplomats began to debate the difficulties of pursuing both criminal justice and peace. The peace/justice debate produces a series of arguments about the relationship between justice interventions and peace. Justice proponents claim that justice processes help the achievement of peace in the short or long term, while peace proponents argue the opposite. As this book demonstrates, the answer is more nuanced: justice may hinder peace when it takes place at a high level prior to or during the Negotiation phase of a peace process but, at the same time, it is possible to achieve a commitment to peace when it is negotiated in the context of a low level of international judicial intervention.

Proponents of peace and justice provide answers largely based on normative commitments, ideology, anecdotal evidence and human rights advocacy (Hazan 2006; Skaar and Malca 2015; Vinjamuri and Snyder 2004), but it would be wrong to dismiss their debate. Rather, it should be understood as an argument that connects two distinct and asymmetric discourses. As discourses, the ideas, concepts and categories of peace and justice give meaning to physical and social entities and are produced, reproduced and transformed by practices (Hajer 1993). They frame the understanding of conflict and inform policies and action that react to its violence. Because the discourses shape agency, they are intimately related to the two cases analysed in this book.

The justice discourse informed the nature and timing of ICC involvement in Uganda and Kenya, the ideas and compromises generated by conflict parties and mediators, and the role of international bodies. In the case of Uganda, the international community was initially hostile to engagement with the LRA, subscribing to the ICC Prosecutor's marginalisation narrative. In Kenya, parliament was divided over whether a hybrid tribunal would incentivise the rejection of political violence. Rather than treating the claims in the peace/justice debate as sets of hypotheses to be tested, they are understood as narratives that shape the implementation of international justice. They are thus endogenous to the international judicialisation of conflict and to its study. This approach to the peace/justice debate makes the framework for empirical analysis independent of the two discourses and their respective ideological projects to strengthen international justice or liberate peacemaking from hard law.

The two discourses exist in an argumentative context and thus position themselves in relation to each other (Hajer 1993). Where the justice discourse is proactive and currently hegemonic, the peace discourse is reactive and critiques justice interventions on consequentialist grounds. The justice discourse is reproduced by most UN bodies, Western and some non-Western states, international NGOs and international lawyers, while the peace discourse tends to be represented by mediators, diplomats and political scientists. The two discourses produce three sets of opposing narratives about the relationship between peace and justice, centring on incentives, marginalisation and deterrence. As we shall see in the empirical chapters, these narratives shaped the Juba Peace Talks and the Kenya National Dialogue and Reconciliation.

Incentives

The first set of narratives focuses on the impact of justice in the short term. The justice discourse posits that arrest warrants motivate rebel groups to enter negotiations, which increases the possibility of settling the conflict. This is the most widely accepted reason for the beneficial impact of justice processes on conflict resolution, cited by academics, researchers, ICC and government officials, and NGO campaigners and journalists (see, e.g. Bensouda 2013; House of Commons 2007; International Crisis Group 2007; Lanz 2008; Martin 2007). Given the non-negotiable nature of arrest warrants, it is not clear how peace negotiations would move forward after the parties have been brought to the negotiation table, unless they find a justice process acceptable. This narrative therefore assumes a shared consensus among the conflict parties on the acceptance of criminal accountability.

The peace discourse posits that the threat of prosecution removes any incentives for state leaders, rebels or other perpetrators to enter negotiations. In the short term, such individuals fear they may be arrested and, in the long term, they have nothing to gain from a peace agreement that sends them to court. This argument draws on the 'security dilemma', the idea that a non-state or paramilitary army only demobilises if its security is guaranteed (Walter 2002). Once leaders have been indicted by an international court, their security is not guaranteed and they will therefore not demobilise. For example, for peace negotiators in Uganda, 'the LRA process … has effectively broken down over the indictment of Joseph Kony' (Centre for Humanitarian Dialogue 2010, 13). In contrast, for members of the justice community, LRA participation in the Juba Peace Talks proves their point as the LRA became interested in negotiations after they were indicted.

Marginalisation

A second narrative by the justice discourse holds that arrest warrants delegitimise, marginalise and remove spoilers in peace processes, which is helpful to those who want to reach an agreement (Hayner 2009). This position is underpinned by three assumptions: that a negotiation benefits from asymmetries in legitimacy and power, that spoilers are external to the problem that is causing the conflict, and that their interests and preferences against peace are fixed and cannot be changed by persuasion or other means.

Proponents of the peace discourse claim that attempts to delegitimise powerful actors may lead them to commit more violence so as to increase their leverage in the bargaining process or signal strength to domestic constituencies. Mediators argue that hostilities may escalate after an indictment both as a protest and as a means to raise the indictee's profile or to 'increase political pressure to suspend an indictment or to prevent [the conflict principal's] arrest' (Centre for Humanitarian Dialogue 2010, 13). In fact, rather than marginalising hardliners, peace negotiators want to bring them into a political process. Engagement with dangerous groups is preferable since it provides the possibility of influencing and learning about them. It offers the possibility of building trust, making them limit their violence or grant access to humanitarian organisations, developing a channel of communication that can defuse a crisis and reveal more about the group so as to better analyse the risks pertaining to its existence and identify issues for common ground (Whitfield 2010, 9–10).

The debate on marginalisation is often illustrated by the example of the ICTY's indictment of Bosnian Serb leaders Radovan Karadzic and Ratko Mladic six months before the successful 1995 Dayton peace negotiations (e.g. Brubacher 2010, 265). In the justice discourse, the ICTY's indictment of hardliners Karadzic and Mladic ensured their exclusion from the Dayton process, which therefore secured a peace settlement. The peace discourse understands the role of Karadzic and Mladic differently. It highlights that the Bosnian Serb leaders agreed to let Milosevic negotiate on their behalf (Bass 2000). Karadzic and Mladic were therefore only dispensable to the peace process because the Bosnia Serb Army was under the overall control of the Milosevic government. By comparison, ICC indictees such as Kony and al Bashir do not need to defer to a higher authority and thus resemble Milosevic more than Karadzic. The latter did sign the Dayton agreement without being physically present, but only because Milosevic 'delivered' his signature (Holbrooke 1998, 310).

Deterrence

Moving from short to long-term impact, a third set of narratives centres on deterrence. The justice discourse holds that punishment of atrocities can deter future crimes. Thus, 'if we bring perpetrators of the worst violations to justice, future horrors could be prevented' (Song 2009, 7). The reverse is also claimed when the Office of the UN High Commissioner for Human Rights (2009b) states, 'By its nature, impunity invites further abuse.' This position assumes that criminality is perpetrated for private reasons based on rational calculations of opportunity costs. Prospective insurgents are thus understood to weigh the risks of punishment against their perceived need to inflict suffering. Amnesty policies are therefore dangerous: 'If you give an amnesty, you are simply asking for more [atrocities].'[4]

Within the peace discourse, conflict is understood as a broader social and political phenomenon (Mamdani 2009, 2015). The discourse therefore questions whether punishing a limited number of individuals will end conflict and deter future warriors. It also highlights that some countries have achieved lasting peace without undergoing a justice process (Branch 2010). To that end, frequently mentioned examples are Spain after Franco, Mozambique after the civil war and South Africa after Apartheid. These cases show, it is argued, that it is empirically false to claim that impunity always leads to a recurrence of conflict or repression. Table 1.1 provides examples of claims made within the two discourses.

The book

The next chapter constructs a theoretical understanding and analytical framework to enable the empirical analysis in Chapters 3 to 6 and the comparison in Chapter 7. It discusses the relationship between law and politics from liberal institutionalist, constructivist and critical perspectives to obtain a theoretical understanding of judicialised political processes and argues that law regulates and produces politics both interactively and constitutively. The analytical framework disaggregates ICC involvement into five stages in order to distinguish between high and low levels of involvement and divides a peace processes into three phases.

Chapters 3 and 4 analyse the Juba Peace Talks and the impact that ICC involvement had on this peace process. The first Uganda chapter traces the processes of ICC involvement and peacemaking chronologically and according to the various intervention stages and peace process phases. Chapter 4 analyses the constitutive and interactive impact of ICC involvement on the Juba process and explains why it failed to settle the conflict. The two subsequent chapters are devoted to the Kenya Dialogue and take the same format: Chapter 5 traces the processes of ICC involvement and peacemaking chronologically and in the relevant stages and phases, while Chapter 6 analyses the impact of ICC involvement on the Kenyan peace process and explains why it succeeded.

Chapter 7 compares the two cases, analysing the effects of ICC involvement in the light of the temporalities and modalities of ICC involvement and peacemaking in Uganda and Kenya. This chapter identifies the pattern that constitutes the book's central argument pertaining to when and how ICC involvement affects peace processes. The conclusion in Chapter 8 tests these findings on a third case study: the Havana Peace Process (2010–2017) between the Colombian government and the Revolutionary Armed Forces of Colombia (FARC). Thereafter the chapter discusses the book's theory about judicialised peace processes. It ends with a consideration of the main policy advice stemming from the study: the sequencing of justice and peace processes.

Table 1.1 Justice and peace discourses

	Justice discourse	*Peace discourse*
Incentives	**Indicted perpetrators will join the negotiation table** '[A]rrest warrants have brought parties to the negotiating table' (Moreno-Ocampo 2009, 12).	**Indicted perpetrators have no incentive to negotiate peace** 'There would have been no negotiated settlement and so no new democratic South Africa had the negotiators on one side insisted that all perpetrators be brought to trial.... We could very well have had justice, retributive justice, and had a South Africa lying in ashes' (Archbishop Tutu, quoted in Bass 2008, 236).
Marginalisation	**Spoilers will be marginalised** 'One immediate effect international arrest warrants have is to marginalize the target politically and increase the costs associated with supporting or harbouring that individual' (Brubacher 2010, 265). 'In the short term ... indicting war criminals has helped move forward peace processes by marginalizing detrimental actors' (International Criminal International 2010, 1).	**Perpetrators may commit more atrocities** 'It is perhaps immoral, but it is most often wise, to spare the leaders of the enemy state, for otherwise these men will sacrifice the lives and wealth and possessions of their fellow citizens or their subjects in the vain hope of saving themselves. If war as such is criminal, it will be inexpiable' (Aron, quoted in Bass 2008, 235). **Spoilers need to be engaged** 'The best way for Washington to proceed, moreover, is not by confronting Khartoum but by engaging it, even in the face of likely objections from the Darfur advocacy community. However much one may despise Sudan's regime for committing atrocities, moral outrage is no substitute for practical policies aimed at saving lives and promoting stability' (Natsios 2008, 78).
Deterrence	**Future violence will be deterred** 'By laying bare the truth about violations of the past and condemning them, prosecutions can deter potential lawbreakers and inoculate the public against future temptation to be complicit in state-sponsored violence' (Orentlicher 1991, 2542). 'In fact, impunity often contributes to renewed cycles of violence; accountability, on the other hand, may yield positive benefits for long-term stability and for development of rule of law' (Dicker 2008, 4). '[H]istory has taught us that the peace achieved by ignoring justice has mostly been short-lived, and the cycle of violence has continued unabated' (Bensouda 2013, para. 4).	**Peace has occurred without justice** After independence from South Africa, Namibia '[repealed the Apartheid laws and] embraced reconciliation by choosing not to open old wounds.... This policy has served Namibia well to date and the country is enjoying peace, stability and democracy and continues to reform its laws' (Government of Namibia 2013, para. 4).

Notes

1 This counter-critique by proponents of international justice was observed during the Rome Statute Review Conference, Kampala, 31 May–10 June 2010 (participant observation by the author).
2 Armed conflicts in this paragraph are defined by having caused a minimum of 25 battle-related deaths.
3 The crime of aggression is listed in the Statute, but is presently not functional.
4 Participant observation, Rome Statute Review Conference, Kampala, 1 June 2010.

References

Alter, Karen J. 2014. *The New Terrain of International Law: Courts, Politics, Rights*. Princeton, NJ: Princeton University Press.

Bass, Gary Jonathan. 2000. *Stay the Hand of Vengeance: The Politics of War Crimes Tribunals. Princeton Studies in International History and Politics*. Princeton, NJ: Princeton University Press.

Bass, Gary Jonathan. 2008. 'War Crimes Tribunals.' In *The Oxford Handbook of Law and Politics*, edited by Keith Whittington, R Daniel Kelemen and Gregory A Caldeira, 229–244. Oxford: Oxford University Press.

Bensouda, Fatou. 2013, March 19. 'International Justice and Diplomacy.' *New York Times*.

Blichner, Lars Chr, and Anders Molander. 2008. 'Mapping Juridification.' *European Law Journal* 14 (1): 36–54.

Branch, Adam. 2010. 'No Peace without Justice?' Keynote address delivered at 'The Politics of Peace and Justice' panel in the NGO wings of the Rome Statute Review Conference, Kampala, Uganda, 3 June. www-rohan.sdsu.edu/~abranch/Publications/Branch-No Peace without Justice.pdf.

Brubacher, Matthew. 2010. 'The ICC Investigation of the Lord's Resistance Army: An Insider's View.' In *The Lord's Resistance Army: Myth and Reality*, edited by Tim Allen and Koen Vlassenroot, 262–277. London and New York: Zed Books Ltd.

Centre for Humanitarian Dialogue. 2010. *Meeting Report, Oslo Forum 2010 Annual Mediators' Retreat*. Geneva: Centre for Humanitarian Dialogue.

Darby, John, and James Rae. 1999. 'Peace Processes From 1988–1998: Changing Patterns.' *Ethnic Studies Report* XVII (1).

Dicker, Richard. 2008. 'Commemoration of the 10th Anniversary of the Rome Statute of the International Criminal Court, July 17 2008.' Coalition for the ICC. http://coalitionfortheicc.org/?mod=rome&lang=en.

Goldstein, Judith O, Miles Kahler, Robert Keohane, and Anne-Marie Slaughter. 2000. 'Introduction: Legalization and World Politics.' *International Organization* 54 (3): 385. doi:10.1162/002081800551262.

Government of Namibia. 2013. *Statement by Hon. Utoni Nujoma, Minister of Justice, at the High-Level Thematic Debate on Role of International Criminal Justice in Reconciliation*. Windhoek: Government of Namibia.

Greenawalt, Alexander K A. 2009. 'Complementarity in Crisis: Uganda, Alternative Justice, and the International Criminal Court.' *Virginia Journal of International Law* 50 (1): 107.

Gurr, Ted Robert. 2000. 'Ethnic Warfare on the Wane.' *Foreign Affairs* 79 (3): 52.

Hajer, Maarten A. 1993. 'Discourse Coalitions and the Institutionalization of Practice: The Case of Acid Rain in Practice.' In *The Argumentative Turn in Policy Analysis and Planning*, edited by Frank Fischer and John Forester, 43–76. Durham and London: Duke University Press.

Harff, Barbara. 2003. 'No Lessons Learned from the Holocaust? Assessing Risks of Genocide and Political Mass Murder since 1955.' *The American Political Science Review* 97 (1): 57. doi:10.1017/S0003055403000522.

Hayner, Priscilla. 2009. *Negotiating Justice: Guidance for Mediators*. Geneva: Henry Dunant Centre for Humanitarian Dialogue.

Hazan, Pierre. 2006. 'Measuring the Impact of Punishment and Forgiveness: A Framework for Evaluating Transitional Justice.' *International Review of the Red Cross* 88 (861): 19–47. doi:10.1017/S1816383106000038.

Högbladh, Stina. 2012. 'Peace Agreements 1975–2011 – Updating the UCDP Peace Agreement Dataset.' In *States in Armed Conflict, 2011*, edited by Therése Petterson and Lotta Themnér, 39–56. Uppsala: Uppsala University, Department of Peace and Conflict Research Report 99.

Holbrooke, Richard C. 1998. *To End a War*. 1st edn. New York: Random House.

House of Commons. 2007. *Prospects for Sustainable Peace in Uganda. International Development Committee. Report, Together with Formal Minutes and Oral and Written Evidence*. London: The Stationery Office Limited.

International Criminal Court. 2010. *The Importance of Justice in Securing Peace. Review Conference of the Rome Statute*. The Hague: International Criminal Court.

International Crisis Group. 2007. *Northern Uganda: Seizing the Opportunity for Peace. Crisis Group Africa Report*. Vol. 124. Brussels: International Crisis Group.

Lanz, David. 2008. 'Northern Uganda, Juba Negotiations.' In *Unpacking the Mystery of Mediation in African Peace Processes*, edited by Annika Åberg, Sabina Laederach, David Lanz, Jonahan Litscher, Simon J A Mason, and Damiano Sguaitamatti, 60–65. Zurich and Bern: Center for Security Studies and Swisspeace.

Mamdani, Mahmood. 2009. *Saviours and Survivors: Darfur, Politics and the War on Terror*. London: Verso.

Mamdani, Mahmood. 2015. 'Beyond Nuremberg: The Historical Significance of the Post-Apartheid Transition in South Africa.' *Politics & Society* 43 (1): 61–88.

Margulies, Peter. 2010. 'Accountable Altruism: The Impact of the Federal Material Support Statute on Humanitarian Aid.' *Suffolk Transnational Law Review* 34 (3): n.p.

Martin, Harriet. 2007. *Power in Mediation: Does Size Matter?* Oslo: The Oslo Forum. www.osloforum.org/retreats/oslo-forum-07-annual-mediators-retreat.

Maxwell, Joseph A. 2004. 'Causal Explanation, Qualitative Research, and Scientific Inquiry in Education.' *Educational Researcher* 33 (2): 3. doi:10.3102/0013189X033002003.

Moreno-Ocampo, Luis. 2007. 'Transitional Justice in Ongoing Conflicts.' *The International Journal of Transitional Justice* 1 (1): 8–9.

Moreno-Ocampo, Luis. 2009. 'Building a Future on Peace and Justice: The International Criminal Court.' In *Building a Future on Peace and Justice: Studies on Transitional Justice, Peace and Development*, edited by Kai Ambos, Judith Large and Marieke Wierda, 9–13. Berlin and Heidelberg: Springer-Verlag.

Moyn, Samuel. 2012, February 29. 'Of Deserts and Promised Lands: The Dream of Global Justice.' *The Nation*. www.thenation.com/article/166516/deserts-and-promised-lands-dream-global-justice#.

Natsios, Andrew S. 2008. 'Beyond Darfur: Sudan's Slide toward Civil War.' *Foreign Affairs* 87 (3): 77.

Nino, Carlos S. 1991. 'The Duty to Punish Past Abuses of Human Rights Put into Context: The Case of Argentina.' *The Yale Law Journal* 100 (8): 2619–2640.

Office of the UN High Commissioner for Human Rights. 2009a. *Analytical Study on Human Rights and Transitional Justice*. New York: United Nations.

Office of the UN High Commissioner for Human Rights. 2009b. *Rule-of-Law Tools for Post-Conflict States: Amnesties*. New York: United Nations.

Orentlicher, Diane F. 1991. 'Settling Accounts: The Duty to Prosecute Human Rights Violations of a Prior Regime.' *The Yale Law Journal* 100 (8): 2537.

Orentlicher, Diane F. 2007. '"Settling Accounts" Revisited: Reconciling Global Norms with Local Agency.' *The International Journal of Transitional Justice* 1 (1): 10–22.

Patton, Michael Quinn. 2002. *Qualitative Research and Evaluation Methods*. Newbury Park: SAGE.

Pensky, Max. 2016. 'Two Cheers for the Impunity Norm.' *Philosophy and Social Criticism* 42 (4/5): 487–499.

Schabas, William A. 2006. 'International Justice for International Crimes: An Idea Whose Time Has Come.' *European Review* 14 (4): 421. doi:10.1017/S1062798706000469.

Schabas, William A. 2011. *An Introduction to the International Criminal Court*. 4th edn. Cambridge: Cambridge University Press.

Schabas, William A. 2012. *Unimaginable Atrocities: Justice, Politics and Rights at the War Crimes Tribunals*. Oxford: Oxford University Press.

Scharf, Michael P. 1996. 'Swapping Amnesty for Peace: Was There a Duty to Prosecute International Crimes in Haiti? (Symposium on Humanitarian Intervention and International Justice).' *Texas International Law Journal* 31 (1): 1.

Schwartz, Stephanie. 2010. 'When Is International Peacemaking Illegal? Implications of the 2010 Supreme Court Decision in *Holder* v. *Humanitarian Law Project*.' *Peacebrief* 65, United States Institute of Peace.

Simmons, Beth. 2008. 'International Law and International Relations.' In *The Oxford Handbook of Law and Politics*, edited by Keith Whittington, R Daniel Kelemen, and Gregory A Caldeira, 187–208. Oxford: Oxford University Press.

Skaar, Elin, and Camila Gianella Malca. 2015. 'Transitional Justice Alternatives: Claims and Counterclaims.' In *After Violence: Transitional Justice, Peace, and Democracy*, edited by Elin Skaar, Camila Gianella Malca, and Trine Eide, 1–28. Abingdon and New York: Routledge.

Song, Sang-Hyun. 2009. 'Judge Sang-Hyun Song.' In *Assembly of State Parties to the Rome Statute of the International Criminal Court, Seminar on International Criminal Justice: The Role of the ICC*, 7–9. The Hague: Secretariat of the Assembly of State Parties.

Teitel, Ruti G. 2011. *Humanity's Law*. New York: Oxford University Press.

Themnér, Lotta, and Peter Wallensteen. 2014. 'Armed Conflicts, 1946–2013.' *Journal of Peace Research* 51 (4): 541–554. doi:10.1177/0022343312452421.

UN Security Council. 2012. *6849th Meeting*. UN Document S/PV.6849. New York: United Nations.

Unger, Thomas, and Marieke Wierda. 2009. 'Pursuing Justice in Ongoing Conflict: A Discussion of Current Practice.' In *Building a Future on Peace and Justice: Studies on Transitional Justice, Peace and Development*, edited by Kai Ambos, Judith Large, and Marieke Wierda, 263–302. Berlin and Heidelberg: Springer-Verlag.

United Nations. 1999. *Secretary-General Comments on Guidelines Issued to Envoys*. UN Press Release. UN Meetings Coverage and Press Releases, UN.

Väyrynen, Raimo, and Janie Leatherman. 1995. 'Conflict Theory and Conflict Resolution.' *Cooperation and Conflict* 30 (1): 53. doi:10.1177/0010836795030001003.

Vinjamuri, Leslie, and Aaron P Boesenecker. 2007. *Accountability and Peace Agreements: Mapping Trends from 1980 to 2006*. Geneva: Henry Dunant Centre for Humanitarian Dialogue.

Vinjamuri, Leslie, and Jack Snyder. 2004. 'Advocacy and Scholarship in the Study of International War Crime Tribunals and Transitional Justice.' *Annual Review of Political Science* (1): 345–362. doi:10.1146/annurev.polisci.7.012003.104755.

Wallensteen, Peter. 2012. *Understanding Conflict Resolution*. 3rd edn. London: SAGE Publications.

Wallensteen, Peter, and Lotta Themnér. 2012. 'Armed Conflicts, 1946–2011.' *Journal of Peace Research* 49 (4): 565. doi:10.1177/0022343312452421.

Walter, Barbara F. 2002. *Committing to Peace: Successful Settlements of Civil Wars*. Princeton: Princeton University Press.

Whitfield, Teresa. 2010. *Engaging with Armed Groups: Dilemmas and Options for Mediators. Mediation Practice Series*. Geneva: Centre for Humanitarian Dialogue.

Young, Crawford. 2004. 'The End of the Post-Colonial State in Africa? Reflections on Changing African Political Dynamics.' *African Affairs* 103: 23–49. doi:http://dx.doi.org/10.1093/afraf/adh003.

2 Studying ICC involvement

An analytical framework

The peace and justice discourses draw remarkably little on scholarship on international legalisation and conflict resolution, although these fields of study produce relevant theories and arguments. This chapter builds an analytical framework from theories about the relationship between law and politics and the nature of peacemaking. For practical purposes – to enable systematic, empirical investigation – the framework conceptualises ICC involvement and peacemaking as two separate but intertwined processes: ICC involvement is the independent variable that may or may not affect the conditions of possibility for a political settlement (the dependent variable). The framework therefore consists of two models, one for each variable. Studies that ask how ICC involvement affects, say, reconciliation, state resilience or democratisation may wish to pair the present model of ICC involvement with a different model of those dependent variables.

This chapter has two parts, reflecting the two parts of the analytical framework. The first part draws on three bodies of scholarship to build an understanding and model of ICC involvement: liberal institutionalism, constructivism and critical studies. The second part reflects theory on conflict resolution to conceptualise a peace process and its important contextual and internal elements.

Part 1 ICC involvement as judicialisation

Legalisation takes place within a legal order or a legal order in the making, whether at national, international or supranational levels. Also termed 'juridification', legalisation denotes the process of bringing something into the domain of law: legal categories and rules are extended to cover an area of social life that was previously situated outside specific laws (Blichner and Molander 2008), such as peacemaking and mediation. As politics is legalised, politicians conceive of their policy and legislative options as 'bounded by what is legally allowed' while citizens, organisations and businesses see law as 'conferring on them rights that others may not abrogate' (Alter 2011, 1377). This process by which 'people increasingly tend to think of themselves and others as legal subjects' is also termed legal framing (Blichner and Molander 2008, 39).

Judicialisation is the process of bringing societal affairs into the realm of courts and judges. Signifying the judicial aspect of legalisation, it occurs when courts gain authority to define and decide on a matter. Judicialisation of politics happens when societies rely on courts and judicial means for addressing political problems (Hirschl 2008, 94). International judicialisation relates to the activities of international courts. As a result of the rapid post-Cold-War expansion of international judicial reach, many aspects of domestic and international politics have been internationally judicialised (Alter 2011; Alter 2014; Hirschl 2008).

Three theoretical approaches to judicialisation

ICC involvement is understood as a process of international judicialisation. An international court, the ICC extends its judicial realm to domestic and international political processes within its area of jurisdictional coverage. Active ICC involvement in a specific crisis judicialises the relevant political activities that take place within or in relation to that crisis. To complicate things further, as an 'international judicial intervention', ICC involvement straddles the boundaries of law and politics and the domains of the national and international (Kerr 2000; Scheffer 1996). Three bodies of theory offer their perspectives on what this means: liberal institutionalist, constructivist and critical theories study the legalisation and judicialisation of politics and the politicisation of law.[1]

Liberal institutionalism

Liberal institutionalists approach international legalisation through the lens of domestic politics and logics of consequences. Starting from the assumption that states are rational utility-maximising actors who ensure a correspondence between their legal commitments and national interests, they see legalisation as a self-interested response to a range of problems: future uncertainty, transaction costs, interstate disputes and non-compliance with international institutions. Legalisation occurs 'when the benefits of reducing future political uncertainty outweigh the "sovereignty costs" of membership' (Moravcsik 2000, 220). States may, however, withdraw from a regime if the costs begin to outweigh the benefits, such as when courts 'overlegalise' (Helfer 2002).

State preferences are reflected in formal institutional design. Legal regimes can have self-binding or other-binding 'logics' (Alter 2008; 2014) or 'key characteristics' of obligation, delegation and precision (Abbott *et al.* 2000, 402). Design features such as compulsory jurisdiction and private access enable international courts to enforce law and regulate governments; this makes them self-binding from the perspective of states. Other-binding rules, in contrast, apply to others and therefore extend state authority; their creation is therefore less of a puzzle. To measure the degree of an institution's legalisation, a different body of scholarship studies the obligations derived from an institution's rules, the precision of those rules and the extent to which rule application and enforcement are delegated to judicial bodies (Abbott *et al.* 2000, 402; Kelley 2007).

Delegation is a key characteristic of judicialisation, as it involves the granting of authority to courts. The act of granting authority is a deliberate and formal one, specified in constitutional texts such as treaties. Informal forms of authority are not deliberately granted and are therefore excluded from the liberal concept of delegation (Bradley and Kelley 2008, 15). Furthermore, the delegated relationship is often hierarchical, as the principal has 'hard control' over the agent (Abbott *et al.* 2015, 721).

Because law is seen as primarily constraining on states, compliance becomes a key focus. States comply with their international legal commitments because it is in their interest to do so. For instance, Simmons (2000) argues that states comply with treaties to preserve their reputation for predictable behaviour. Compliance may be endogenous, as states only invest time and resources in those international agreements with which they plan to comply (Chapman and Chaudoin 2013; Von Stein 2005, 611).

Due to their rationalist methodology, liberal institutionalists infer state interaction with international law from observable entities such as treaties, formal ratification instruments, litigation, judgements and government positions (Alter 2014; Chapman and Chaudoin 2013; Simmons 2000). However, as reality comprises tangible objects and unchanging, objective interests, this approach is indifferent to the role of law in processes of social constitution.

Constructivism

To constructivists, the liberal institutionalist approach relies on too narrow a conception of law and its interaction with politics. As it defines law as a constraint, the approach does not see law's 'creative or generative powers in social life' (Finnemore and Toope 2001, 745). Furthermore, lacking an ontology of law's normativity, it cannot explain why legal rules are considered obligating or account for law's legitimacy. Adopting a broader conception of both politics and law, constructivists argue that law and politics continually shape each other (Teitel 2000). Moreover, states' identity, purpose and other normative commitments are ontologically prior to their strategic pursuit of interests.

Constructivists agree with liberal institutionalists that law is constraining, but they also conceive of it having enabling qualities (Brake and Katzenstein 2013; Finnemore and Sikkink 1998; Reus-Smit 2007). Law regulates agency by changing actors, identities, interests or categories of action through diffuse social processes of norm institutionalisation: discourse, issue framing, legal interpretation, persuasion, shaming, imitation, emulation, socialisation and internalisation. These processes often involve governments, international organisations, NGOs and 'norm entrepreneurs'.

Where liberal institutionalists infer compliance from co-variation between a formal legal commitment and behavioural indicators, constructivists rely on empirical evidence of rule internalisation. As norms generate moral justifications for action, they leave behind 'an extensive trail of communication among actors' (Finnemore and Sikkink 1998, 892; see also Deitelhoff 2009). Non-internalised rule commitment – states who ratify a treaty that they consistently violate – is seen as a 'tactical concession' to international or NGO pressure (Risse *et al.* 2013; Sikkink 2011).

Power is often an under-theorised aspect of constructivist scholarship. For instance, Sikkink (2011, 233) associates power with efforts to undermine international justice but not with its ascent: '[Power] can't tell us how it became possible in the first place to hold foreign human rights trials in French courts.' Such an account stems from Sikkink's narrow conceptualisation of power, which ignores more productive kinds of power and the way in which normative structures are themselves infused by relations of power (Barnett and Duvall 2005, 41). This is one of the central insights of the critical approach.

Critical studies

Critical approaches to the interplay between law and politics take their starting point in the social relations within and among states, in particular the inequality of means and power. As law cannot be separated from the power relationships that are inherent to its context, any analysis must begin with power. This move reveals what is really going on in the legal sphere: legalisation 'mystifies the working of structural power and hegemony' (Brütsch and Lehmkuhl 2007, 10) and the 'invisible background' of international law creates 'a whole world order, a system of empowering some and disempowering other institutions and dividing resources between human groups' (Koskenniemi 2011, 324). In this system, formal sovereign equality is a 'fiction' that 'masks' unequal social relations (Hartmann 2011). By pretending that law and power are separate, scholars, officials and citizens are reproducing inequality.

To critical scholars, power is both 'coercive' and 'productive' (Barnett and Duvall 2005), which means it can fashion relations and identities. This concept inspires questions about how social relations and identities create a particular legal interpretation, how legal discourse creates particular social relations, and which hierarchies and distributive choices are mobilised in particular legal claims. Such questions focus the analysis on discourses of difference and their legal codification (Campbell 1998; Mamdani 2001). To critical scholars, law reflects, solidifies and fixates social relations in a diffuse process of internalisation. Qua constructivists, this internalisation process involves rules that codify not only ideas and practices, but also dominant identities and representations.

Law's capacity to serve the powerful stems from its inherent indeterminacy; it oscillates between different norms (Koskenniemi 1989). Law is indeterminate because it is characterised by the absence of a set interpretation and reading; thus, the same rules can be interpreted to mean different and even incompatible things. The constructivist model of a trajectory from norm emergence to internalisation is thus too simple: the process of institutionalisation is fraught with ambiguity, negotiation and coercion. The concept of legal indeterminacy has been adopted by some constructivists, who suggest that it is necessary to distinguish between a rule and its interpretation once it is 'out in the world' (Howse and Teitel 2010; 2011).

The liberal institutionalist, constructivist and critical approaches differ in their understanding of the judicialisation of politics. Liberal institutionalists view law as a negotiated product of politics, but, once codified, the legal sphere is assumed to be autonomous. They understand law to affect politics by changing the structure of incentives and preferences of political actors and articulate a logic of consequences that shapes responses to law. In contrast, critical scholars see law and politics as mutually constitutive, with both reflecting the social relations of a given society. Judicialisation therefore serves partisan interests. Constructivists identify the symbolic and constitutive aspects of law and focus on how judicialisation shapes behaviour by becoming appropriate and legitimate. These insights are all useful for understanding how ICC involvement affects political processes in its sites of intervention.

A broader concept of judicialisation

The conceptualisation of legalisation and judicialisation has been conducted primarily by rationalists, who infer these processes from observable entities such as formal negotiation positions, treaties, instruments of ratification and court cases (Abbott *et al.* 2000; Alter 2011; 2014; Bradley and Kelley 2008; Hirschl 2006; Sikkink 2011; Simmons 2013). This is useful, insofar as it makes an abstract process of judicialisation tangible and enables documentation of the fact of judicialisation. However, this operationalisation does not capture the constitutive aspects of the process, such as how legal definition and judicial involvement alter the way in which subjects think about and act on an issue.

To study judicialisation as both observable and subtle, it is useful to combine the rationalist toolbox with reflectivist insights on processes of constitution and forms of power. This does not preclude arguments about the impact of ICC involvement, but it does require a broader concept of causation (Kurki and Suganami 2012). Causation is conceptualised as bringing something about, whether indirectly or directly, deliberately or unintentionally. It may imply forcing, compelling, making, persuading, urging, inducing and enabling (Kurki and Suganami 2012, 405). Causation is also contextual. The context within which a causal process occurs is intrinsically involved in that process and 'often cannot be "controlled for" in a variance-theory sense without misrepresenting the causal mechanism' (Maxwell 2004, 6).

The notion of 'constitutive causality' expands how we understand both the nature of judicialisation and its effects. Constitutive causality means that constitutive ideas, relations and practices are understood to have causal implications because they are '"significant" in producing or influencing an effect, result or consequence' (Ruggie, quoted in Lebow 2009, 213). Identities and cognitive frameworks such as legal categories or peace and justice discourses have constitutive effects because they shape agency, while also influencing the kind of information to which people pay attention and how they interpret it (Lebow 2009, 215).

'Effect' is an abstract term for something that is generated by something else. It is therefore related to power, understood here as 'the production, in and through social relations, of effects that shape the capacities of actors to determine their circumstances and fate' (Barnett and Duvall 2005, 42). Drawing on Barnett and Duvall's (2005) taxonomy of compulsory, institutional, structural and productive power, a broad concept of judicialisation is a process with both interactive and constitutive effects. This means that legal categories and judicial activities affect politics through relations of direct and indirect interaction and constitution.

A model of ICC involvement

The broader notion of judicialisation inspires an analytical model to guide the empirical study of specific ICC interventions and their effects. The model is a linear, five-step trajectory of an ICC intervention on top of which sits a layer of interactive and constitutive effects derived from the three theoretical approaches to the relationship between law and politics. The model ensures that the investigation systematically explores decisions and developments pertaining to all stages of involvement and enables the comparison of different processes of ICC involvement. Furthermore, by formulating effects, it helps to develop an understanding of whether and how ICC involvement transforms politics.

Five stages of involvement

The Rome Statute is a penal code that defines the basic principles of ICC law and the crimes within its jurisdiction as well as a criminal procedure code that regulates how the jurisdiction of the Court is to be exercised (Olásolo 2003, 88). These functions detail and delimit the Court's justice process, a cumulative trajectory with up to five stages that are separated by trigger or control mechanisms.

Stage 1 is the Membership stage and the first step of ICC involvement. It occurs when a state ratifies the Rome Statute, thereby giving the ICC jurisdiction over certain crimes. Stage 1 involvement is a form of inactive involvement: the country is obliged to comply with ICC rules by virtue of its membership, but the Court has at most a very general monitoring role. This role derives from the ICC prosecutor's *proprio motu* authority to initiate an investigation of a situation in a state party, provided this investigation is approved by the Pre-Trial Chamber (PTC).

Stage 2 involvement takes place when the Office of the Prosecutor (OTP) conducts a preliminary examination. At this stage the OTP considers information about alleged ICC crimes, which may be submitted by individuals, organisations and states. Although a low level of involvement, Stage 2 marks the beginning of an active form of involvement on the part of the ICC. Stage 3, the Investigation stage, is when the ICC is conducting a formal investigation in a particular situation with a view to prosecuting those allegedly responsible for international crimes. The Investigation stage is triggered by a referral by a state party or the UN Security Council. Alternatively, the Prosecutor may seek PTC authorisation to conduct an investigation on his or her own initiative (*proprio motu*); this PTC control is designed to prevent investigations on spurious grounds.

Stage 4 is reached when the Prosecutor issues arrest warrants for a suspect or summons him or her to appear before the Court. Warrants may initially be sealed. Stages 3 and 4 are separated by the creative formation of a case against an individual. The OTP creates a narrative of culpability that can be supported by evidence. The deepening of involvement from Stage 3 to 4 is subject to judicial control because the issuing of warrants or summons requires approval by the PTC.

Stage 5 involvement is the Trial stage. Trials cannot be held in the absence of the accused and this stage is therefore triggered by the defendant's arrest or voluntary appearance. The stage ends with a conviction or acquittal (potentially after appeal). Involvement at the Indictment and Trial stages is at a high level because it targets particular individuals who are likely to be politically powerful, given the Court's mandate of prosecuting 'those most responsible' for crimes against humanity, war crimes and genocide. In contrast, Stages 1 and 2, Membership and Preliminary Examination, signify a low level of involvement because they occur at the most general level. At the medium level of involvement, the ICC process investigates alleged crimes and is thereby becoming more specific. The conceptualisation of a five-stage process of ICC involvement is depicted in Figure 2.1.

In deciding whether to ratify, refer, investigate or indict, and thus whether to stall or move the ICC up the trajectory of an involvement process, actors engage in interpretation. Discourses, logics of consequences and appropriateness, and power relationships shape this interpretation. Legal interpretation is the most obvious kind, as each international rule or legal regime entails a spectrum of interpretive possibilities (Koskenniemi 1989). Law is situated by practices and cultures of interpretation and application (Kelsall 2009). Due to the 'law-in-action' of the Rome Statute, its meaning evolves in ways that may differ from what its drafter intended (Arsanjani and Reisman 2005).

Political and strategic considerations by Court actors also shape the trajectory of ICC involvement. Institutional interests or professional biases may cause 'quick and dirty' investigations (Kambale 2012) or a case selection that picks the 'low-hanging fruit' (Graf 2012, 946). The Prosecutor may behave in apolitical, pragmatic or strategic ways in relating to powerful states, and he or she may even be 'captured' by them (Bosco 2013). In its approach to situation countries, the OTP has fostered both adversarial and cooperative relationships (Peskin 2009a; Rodman 2014).

	1	2	3	4	5
Stages	Membership	Preliminary examination	Investigation	Indictment	Trial
Levels	Low		Medium	High	

Figure 2.1 Stages and levels of ICC involvement: A trajectory.

Interpretation is, however, not limited to Court actors. International judicial interventions are situated within wider national, regional and international contexts, which influence their trajectories (Bosco 2013; Branch 2011; Nouwen 2013; Peskin 2009b). In relating to a process of ICC involvement, contextual actors are guided by ideas, norms and interests. The importance of these actors to understanding a particular trajectory of ICC involvement varies from case to case.

Interactive and constitutive dimensions of involvement

Each stage of ICC involvement may activate legal and political resources with interactive and constitutive effects on politics; ICC involvement thus has interactive and constitutive dimensions. Both dimensions regulate action, but they do so in different ways. For instance, the Membership stage may interactively empower state executives to refer a situation to the ICC and grant monitoring authority to the OTP. Constitutively, it may introduce criminal accountability into public debates about justice and frame the country as a rule-of-law-respecting state. As this example shows, the two kinds of effects do not necessarily entail ICC officials creating the effects directly. Rather, ICC involvement enables ICC or non-ICC actors to create a direct or indirect effect. This is to say that ICC involvement is the structure rather than the agent, while agents are the officials, offices or organisations that are involved in the justice intervention: officials, executives, prosecutors, defendants, the ICC, the Security Council and so on, depending on the particularities of a case.

The interactive dimension of ICC involvement denotes how the Rome Statute and the ICC affect political processes by shaping, through direct interaction, the positions, circumstances or actions of political actors. If arrest warrants lure rebels to the negotiation table or remove spoilers from a peace process, ICC involvement has this direct, compulsory interactive effect. The same would apply if the Prosecutor used the threat of a *proprio motu* investigation to coerce a change in government policy. Interactive effects may also be generated by persuasion or incentives.

The interactive dimension also captures indirect effects, such as when one political actor indirectly affects another through institutional rules and procedures. If major countries use the UN Security Council's referral powers to effect regime change or if NGOs use ICC norms to shame national policies or practices, then ICC involvement has an indirect interactive effect. The same applies if powerful countries marginalise indicted peace process spoilers. Scheingold (1974, 7) invites us to think of the symbolic power of law as 'a resource of uncertain worth which is relative to its context, but which is like other political resources such as money, numbers, status, etc.'. In this connection, the Security Council's discretionary authority to refer and defer ICC investigations may be such a political resource of contingent and contextual worth.

The effects of ICC involvement on political processes may also be constitutive in the sense of working through processes of structuration or discursive construction of social relations, identities and systems of knowledge. The constitutive dimension of law may fix options for action, not by outlawing alternatives (which is an interactive mechanism), but by defining social relations or 'decontesting' alternative meanings (Freeden 1996). This dimension may also affect the notions of appropriate behaviour, not by means of persuasion (again, an interactive mechanism), but by changing the way we see and make sense of the world (Howse and Teitel 2010).

Discursive action is central to constitution because of the ability of discourse to 'define the (im)possible, the (im)probable, the natural, the normal, [and] what counts as a problem' (Hayward, quoted in Barnett and Duvall 2005, 55). Hence, a particular discursive event shapes and is shaped by the situations, institutions, objects of knowledge and social structures which frame it. Through discourse, social identities are produced in a process of 'materialisation' that stabilises over time (Butler, quoted in Campbell 1998, 25). For instance, Branch (2011, 182) argues that ICC interventions 'personalize political violence' and reduce its complexity to 'the criminal plots of a few individuals'. Proponents of the justice discourse make a constitutive argument when linking individual ICC trials to rule-of-law development. The model of ICC involvement combines the five stages of involvement with the two kinds of involvement effects. It is summarised in Figure 2.2.

Part 2 Peacemaking as politics

Most contemporary armed conflicts in Africa end with a negotiated settlement. This second part of the chapter theorises the political process that leads to such settlements and proposes a three-phase model of a peace process.

Peace processes

A peace process is 'a political process that facilitates negotiated solutions to long-standing differences' (Ramcharan 2009, 231). It entails a broad variety of tailor-made efforts to tackle the manifestations and causes of conflict and to help re-establish peace. It is also deeply political, politics being a 'generative, indeterminate process, which is inherently unstable, complex, value-laden, contested

Effects	**Interactive**	Coercion, Instrumentalism, Incentivisation, Persuasion, Imitation, Internalisation				
	Constitutive	Materialisation, Meaning-making, Signification, Decontestation				
Stages		1 Membership	2 Preliminary examination	3 Investigation	4 Indictment	5 Trial
Levels		Low		Medium		High →

Figure 2.2 Model of ICC involvement.

and, ultimately, concerned with agency' (Jenkins 2011, 159). As politics occurs where actors can make a difference, it cannot be found in the realm of necessity and is the 'antithesis' of fatalism and resignation (Hay 2007, 67). When a peace process is characterised by inevitability, it is depoliticised.

Three aspects of the nature of peace processes make them political: they are open-ended, agential and contested. Peace processes have an open-ended character because there is no way of knowing a priori the form of its outcome. While some protracted conflicts have ended with a political settlement, other conflicts, which appear less entrenched, fail to generate a sustainable political settlement. Indeed, social psychologists maintain that 'neither the occurrence nor the outcome of conflict is completely and rigidly determined by objective circumstances ... Whether conflict takes a productive or a destructive course is thus open to influence even under the most unfavourable objective conditions' (Deutsch 1973, 11). Open-endedness is related to the capacity for agency. Although acting within local, national and international constraints, peace negotiators, implementers and third parties are endowed with agency to steer a peace process closer to or away from a political solution, in a direction that fits their interests and conflict narrative. They 'make decisions that could be made differently, often with consequential results' (Jung *et al.* 2005, 280). This agency produces, reproduces and reshapes the negotiation table 'whose form and constitutive parameters frame the bargaining of what "peace" might mean' (Srinivasan 2012, 197).

The third political characteristic of a peace process is the essential contestability of that which is negotiated. In political disputes, people disagree not only about a particular matter 'but about what that matter in fact is and about what a resolution might look like' (Finlayson 2007, 550). The 'undecidability' of peace negotiations derives from the fact that those involved understand different things by fundamental concepts, such as fairness and justice, whose meaning can only be established through contestation (Finlayson 2007). Another source of contestability derives from their exclusive and exceptional character. They are conducted by appointed and formally unaccountable negotiators, whose involvement may derive only from their capacity to inflict suffering. Moreover, they rely on a sovereign government bypassing its constitutional law-making processes to sign a contract with an unlawful party (de Waal 2014, 17). As a result, peace process outputs have to be legitimised (Gissel 2017).

As a minimum requirement, peace processes aim to establish a 'negative' peace, defined as the absence of direct, physical violence (Galtung 1969; 1996). A fuller notion of peace, a 'positive' peace, goes beyond security in a narrow sense and aims to provide a variety of social needs such as education, democratic participation and socio-economic development (Lee *et al.* 2016). Negative peace processes are often criticised for delivering 'poor quality peace' because they do not tackle the underlying causes of conflict (Mac Ginty, quoted in Srinivasan 2012, 200). However, negative peace arguably precedes its positive counterpart: survival and physical security are the foundation upon which society can implement policies to meet broader developmental needs. Criticising a peace process for achieving only a negative peace thus puts the proverbial cart before the horse.

Three phases of a peace process

Although often empirically a non-linear phenomenon, peace processes can be analytically divided into three phases: the Pre-negotiation, Negotiation and Implementation phases (Bell 1999, 8; Hartzell and Hoddie 2003, 324; Walter 2002). Research often focuses on the Negotiation phase, although its thinking and discussions may be shaped by the pre-negotiation meetings, principles and agreements (Campbell 1998). An understanding of the Pre-Negotiation phase is thus indispensable to making sense of the two subsequent phases.

The Pre-Negotiation phase aims to get the parties to enter into peace negotiations. In spite of its name, this phase is a process of negotiation about the terms of a prospective formal negotiation. Typical issues include the return or release of exiled or incarcerated negotiators, the safeguarding of future physical integrity and the conduct of the war during the negotiations (Bell 1999, 8). This phase may result in a pre-negotiation agreement as well as an agenda for the Negotiation phase, but these documents are often more akin to declarations. What is important to the parties is 'the fact of having met and having established a joint commitment to future negotiations' (Bell 2006, 377).

The notions of 'mutually hurting stalemate' (Zartman 1995a) and 'coerced compromise' (Cousens 2002, 538) theorise why conflict parties explore pre-negotiations. A mutually hurting stalemate is the point reached when all parties have determined that they cannot win the conflict despite the heavy costs already endured. They become 'ripe for negotiation' (Zartman 1995a). A 'coerced compromise' denotes an alternative way into the Pre-Negotiation phase, when conflict parties are brought to the negotiation table by means of diplomatic and/or military coercion. Proponents of international justice suggest a related route into the peace process, when they argue that criminal charges bring the parties to the negotiation table. The Indictment stage thus induces 'ripeness' or a coerced compromise.

The Negotiation phase is the actual peace negotiations about substantial issues that gave rise to the conflict and ways to address them. In this phase, the parties discuss, design and agree on a framework for solving the underlying incompatibility, often assisted by mediators. The commencement of the Negotiation phase is often formally marked, while its completion is symbolised in the signing of a final peace agreement, overseen and witnessed by relevant third-party actors. The final peace agreement is usually preceded by substantive or part agreements (Call 2002, 389).

The Implementation phase begins once the peace agreement has been signed; it is essentially a process of policy implementation (Stedman *et al.* 2002). It includes the implementation of the various agreed-upon aspects that would secure the ending of the conflict, including the ceasefire, demobilisation, disarmament and agreed reforms. This stage may also include further negotiations on

	Phases	
Pre-negotiation	Negotiation	Implementation

Figure 2.3 Model of a peace process.

issues that were not sufficiently addressed during the previous phase. The Implementation phase has a fuzzy end-point, since some agreements may take decades to implement. It is necessary therefore to distinguish between immediate and long-term goals. Figure 2.3 shows the three-phase model of a peace process.

Political settlements

Political settlements and negotiated solutions are terms used interchangeably to mean a negotiated and shared agreement to end armed conflict. This aims, ideally, to solve the conflict's underlying 'incompatibility' and thus remove the need for violence. Importantly, the settlement implies the acceptance of the continued existence of the other party as a party; a settlement is thus incompatible with capitulation (Wallensteen 2012, 8). This also means that a political solution is contrasted with a military defeat, the two solutions that exhaust the ways of ending a violent conflict.[2] Political solutions aim to end a violent conflict, but may have other, related goals as well, such as the reform of a country. Alternatively, they may end the fighting but fail to establish a positive peace, in which case the conflict may be reignited. Settlements may even incentivise the future use of violence, building a negative peace only in the short term (Keen 2012).

Political solutions are most often agreed between elites: power-holders and conflict principals, which tend to be male. Peacebuilding professionals and scholars therefore call for the inclusion of non-elite actors, such as women and civil-society representatives. They associate elite pacts with negative peace, while more inclusive processes imply a positive peace (Lee *et al.* 2016). This dichotomised approach, however, overlooks that women and civil-society actors generally have a greater need for narrow security than do elites, because they have less capacity for self-protection.

The goal of the Negotiation phase is a political settlement. Often formally agreed at the end of this phase, it needs to be substantiated and carried out in the Implementation phase (Stedman *et al.* 2002). In this latter phase, the settlement is affected by centripetal and centrifugal factors: factors that work to keep the settlement together, and factors that pull it apart. These factors relate to the nature of the settlement as well as to the wider political context.

Peace agreements

Political solutions are documented in peace agreements between the conflict parties. In spite of widespread agreement on what they are and the similar forms they assume, their legal status is disputed because it is unclear from where they derive their legal authority (Bell 2006; Kastner 2012). This is important insofar as peace agreements share constituency with international judicial interventions. In *Kallon* at the SCSL, the appeals chamber ruled that the amnesty-granting Lomé Peace Accords was a purely political agreement because its signatories had insufficient treaty-making ability (Bell 2006). The Accord could therefore not protect individuals against prosecution.

Two features, meanwhile, suggest that conflict parties and mediators perceive peace agreements as legal documents: their 'legal-looking structure', which is indicated by their preambles, numbered sections and articles, dated signatures, and annexes, and their 'legal-type language' that speaks of parties, signatories and binding obligations (Bell 2006, 378). The frequent use of lawyers to assist the negotiation or drafting processes also suggests that peace agreements are considered legal. Some conflict parties have sought to legalise their agreements either by having treaty status conferred on them by patron states or by entrenching them in the constitution. The South African peace agreement was incorporated into the country's interim constitution, while the Kenyan 2008 power-sharing agreement became an act of parliament. In the topography of law, however, national law cannot legitimise violation of international obligations such as the duty to prosecute ICC crimes.[3]

Peace agreements need to be legitimised in order to prevail over supporters of the continuation of conflict, such as extremists within the conflict parties or in wider society (Gissel 2017). This imperative derives from the contestable nature of peace processes and the undecidability of the issues at stake in the conflict. To legitimise their agreements, peace processes may rely on 'brokers' because they can 'frame settlements in ways that resonate across multiple coalitions' within the conflict network (Goddard 2012, 505).

The language of peace agreements is important. A lack of precision or specificity in the wording of the agreement expands the scope for interpretation. Vague language contains an opportunity for flexibility, confusion or disagreement during the Implementation phase. Most peace agreements contain 'important silences, some points of agreement that are described in banal language open to multiple interpretations and, in worst cases, contradictory dictates' (Stedman 2002, 9). Hampson (1996) finds that a good settlement is both specific and flexible.

Internal dynamics

Inside a peace process, a number of social relations and processes shape the conditions of possibility for the outcome: relationships of power, authority and legitimacy, as well as perceptions, narratives and discourses pertaining to the conflict and its resolution. Often originating outside the peace process and straddling its different contexts, these factors play out among those involved and affect their identification and negotiation of issues and solutions.

Power, legitimacy and authority

Various power relationships affect the conditions of possibility for a political settlement. There are multiple, dynamic relationships of power among and between individual and institutional actors involved in a peace process, such as negotiators, conflict parties, conflict principals, mediators and third-party actors. These relationships of power stem from both coercive and economic capabilities and relate to actors' differentiated legitimacy. Both legitimacy and coercive or economic power are translated into power at the negotiation table. For example, an insurgent army that enjoys popular legitimacy will have a degree of authority in the negotiations. An illegitimate conflict party will have less authority at the negotiation table, but can offset this relative weakness by coercive capacity.

Struggles over authority and power occur within conflict parties, and not just between them. Negotiators are therefore concerned to maximise power along two dimensions: in relation to the other conflict party and vis-à-vis extremists or hardliners within their own party (Jung and Shapiro 1995, 278; Oberschall 2007, 33). Moderates on both sides of a conflict:

> can signal to each other their intention to continue in the process, but to do so they must take decisive steps in facing down opposition within their own ranks even before it is clear that an enforceable agreement will be reached
>
> (Jung *et al.* 2005, 284)

In the Northern Ireland peace process, Sinn Féin's Gerry Adams felt that the most difficult negotiation was with his own side (Martin 2007, 41). In South Africa, moderates within the National Party delegitimised the internal opposition to a transition when a whites-only referendum provided de Klerk with a mandate to negotiate. This intra-party dimension of negotiations to end conflict is overlooked by 'dyadic' conflict analysis which focuses on inter-party relations.

In internal conflicts and their resolution processes, relationships of power and legitimacy are asymmetric. In most internal conflicts, governments have legitimacy, sovereignty, allies, armies and access to resources, while insurgents have to fight for all these (Zartman 1995b, 8). Rebels compensate for these deficiencies by being motivated and ideologically driven, or by enlisting foreign support. The contestation involved in a peace process sits within its various power relationships: if one party's narrative is legitimised by a significant external actor, it might succeed in decontesting concepts central to the peace agreement.

Perceptions and narratives

Peace process dynamics also derive from conflict parties' perceptions and narratives. Mediators highlight the importance of perceptions and framing processes. Concepts such as 'mutually hurting stalemate', 'underlying incompatibility' and 'spoiler' do not refer to objective entities, but to inter-subjective evaluations, which only exist following their narrative construction. Violent conflict requires that a situation has been first problematised and then narrated in a way that makes violence an appropriate response. Likewise, a political settlement requires that the conflict parties find this outcome meaningful and appropriate. Narratives are central to such a process of meaning-making.

Narratives are the means by which human experience is translated into structures of meaning, with narration being the process of translation and transmission. Narratives arise 'between our experience of the world and our efforts to describe that experience in language' (White 1989, 1–2). A narrative discourse is a narrative without a narrator. In a discourse, 'events are chronologically recorded as they appear on the horizon of the story'; they seem to tell themselves (Benveniste, in White 1989, 3). As events are narrated without a subject, they seem more objective and come to appear as 'the way things are'. According to Srinivasan (2012, 205), narrative frames were 'active ingredients in the institutional practices of the negotiations' to end the conflict in Southern Sudan: they 'allowed for some possibilities of peace and foreclosed others'.

The concept of a 'spoiler' forgets these narrative insights. A spoiler is an actor that is fundamentally opposed to any agreement and therefore attempts to wreck it: he or she may sign a peace agreement, but that does not necessarily imply a desire for peace (Stedman 1997). Although widely applied and used to justify the utility of indictments during peace processes, the spoiler concept assumes that actor narratives and preferences are static and immune to change. However, peace processes involve learning and second-order learning, with the conflict parties gradually discovering what they are prepared to accept and accommodate (Ramsbotham *et al.* 2011, 186). The spoiler label may furthermore be a tool with which to delegitimise an actor's objectives, narratives or peace process critique.

Third-party involvement

A third-party actor is a person, organisation or state which is not party to the conflict in any direct sense, but is nevertheless involved in conflict resolution, typically in the role of mediator. Third parties tend to be external to the country of conflict and are often seen as useful. For instance, Sisk (2010, 237) argues that transitions 'are more likely to succeed if a robust third-party force helps consolidate the peace'.

Third-party engagement may be coercive, incentivising or facilitative. Coercive strategies entail the use of threats, force or sanctions, and may be of a military, diplomatic, legal or symbolic nature. When third parties deploy militarily without consent, impose sanctions, withhold aid, designate a group as a terrorist organisation, or when they threaten to do any of those things, they act coercively. As it does not address conflict causes or facilitate dialogue, coercive engagement is insufficient for solving a conflict, although it may deter escalatory behaviour or weaken a party's strategic position (Griffiths and Barnes 2008, 11). Terrorist listings are designed to punish or isolate an actor, but seal off choices and avenues for dialogue, sometimes emboldening hardliners (Nadarajah and

Sriskandarajah 2005). Indeed, the third party is 'typically perceived by the proscribed group as an attempt to delegitimise their goals rather than their methods' (Griffiths and Barnes 2008, 11).

Incentivising strategies are measures that provide or withhold rewards for compliance or non-compliance. Rewards can respond to financial needs, to political needs for legitimacy and recognition and to security needs, and may level the playing field by compensating for a perceived asymmetry. External security guarantees are often imperative for a successful settlement; in their absence, insurgents are likely to shun the risk of disarming (Walter 2002). In general, however, the assumptions of rational cost calculations involved in incentivising behaviour may not work in a context of political violence. The conflict parties may hold value-based goals that are not subject to cost–benefit calculations or they may be trapped by their prior investment of resources and commitment (Wood 2003).

Rather than reward and threaten, facilitative strategies seek to enable. They involve confidence and capacity-building, dialogue and the injection of ideas, finances or security. Facilitative tools depend upon the parties' readiness to change. They are slow yielders, yet are 'typically crucial' for success (Griffiths and Barnes 2008, 12).

Turning points, sticking points and zones of possible agreement

Peace processes may experience two kinds of moments that take the negotiations in a new direction: turning points and sticking points. Turning points in peace processes are moments when the conflict parties see a way forward through the negotiations. This realisation may come about because they redefine their goals, open new political space or find a new basis for agreement, or 'because the conjunction of political leaders and circumstances are favourable' (Ramsbotham *et al.* 2011, 186). Turning points can arise because of procedural, substantive or external changes or events and may occur in either of the three peace process phases (Druckman 2001; Druckman and Rosoux 2016).

Sticking points, by contrast, are obstacles to agreement. They are encountered when elites are unfavourable to the process, when parties to agreements defect or 'when political space is closed or conditions are attached to negotiations which prevent forward movement' (Ramsbotham *et al.* 2011, 186). When facing a sticking point, negotiators and/or mediators must find ways around it by drawing on internal and external support, establishing procedures and learning from the flaws of previous agreements. The peace/justice debate implicitly draws on the metaphors of turning and sticking points: arguing that arrest warrants motivate rebels to enter negotiation, proponents of the justice discourse conceptualise high-level ICC involvement as a turning point, while critics of international justice view the issuing of arrest warrants as a sticking point.

The concept of a zone of possible agreement refers to the area of overlap between the conflict parties' range of acceptable outcomes (Druckman and Rosoux 2016, 129). To overcome a sticking point or an impasse, conflict parties may succeed in defining the range of possible solutions or the range of elements that a possible solution would include. As ICC involvement from the Membership stage onwards provides state parties with a duty to prosecute ICC crimes, this may affect the zone of possible agreement in judicialised peace processes.

Contexts

The discussion has so far been limited to the form and content of a peace process, but its context also matters (Skaar *et al.* 2015, 40), in particular the conflict, national politics, and regional and international dynamics. The conflict is the immediate context within which the peace process takes place. Its dynamics give rise to the Pre-Negotiation phase and shape the dynamics of the entire peace process (Schomerus 2012). Conflict dynamics relate to the narratives of conflict causes and the relations between the conflict parties, and between them and the population. The national context consists of social relations and informal and formal political processes. This context produces discourses about the conflict and the peace process, which are brought into the peace process by negotiators, observers and the media. Often, parliaments and government ministries are involved in the Implementation phase.

The regional and international contexts also have a direct or indirect bearing on the peace process. Regional countries may have an interest in a particular outcome and may get a third-party role; alternatively, they may be conflict patrons. Regional organisations such as the Inter-Governmental Authority on Development (IGAD) and the African Union (AU) may take a mediator role. The international level includes the international community, which is often represented by international organisations. Often, Western states claim to represent the international community, although non-Western countries make up a larger proportion of the world. Furthermore, convergence between the norms and interests of Western states and those of the UN may bias conflict parties against organisations of global governance. At other times, UN involvement indicates non-biased mediation.

Process tracing of judicialised peace processes

Srinivasan (2012, 197) argues that the Sudanese peace process had many possible futures and this point would apply to most of its counterparts. To understand how a particular settlement or a return to war came to be, it is useful to trace how the contingent combination of the above peace process aspects produce the conditions for its possibility. Process tracing of individual cases allows scholars to infer causation, going beyond describing a historical sequence (Druckman 2001; George and Bennett 2005). Furthermore, as peace process outcomes have few, if any, necessary and sufficient single causes, the step-wise, process-orientated case approach enables identification of the contingent convergence of diverse factors that produce the outcome (e.g. Call 2002; Khadiagala 2002).

Process tracing of judicialised peace processes combines this chapter's two models, illustrated in Figures 2.2 and 2.3. The approach entails analysis of events and developments relating to the relevant stages of ICC involvement and the three phases of a peace process. To that end, it must identify and understand any interactive and constitutive effects of ICC involvement on the peace process. These effects must furthermore make sense in relation to an interpretation of why the peace process failed to or succeeded in achieving a political settlement.

By taking a point of departure in theories of judicialisation and conflict resolution, the analytical framework differs from other frameworks for impact assessment of transitional justice processes. Hazan (2006) builds a framework for assessing trials on a sort of positive peace associated with norm internalisation or collective catharsis. His indicators are at a highly aggregate level, concerned with penal effectiveness, recipient impact and deterrence. To assess such effects, the analyst would need a number of more-intermediate indicators, but Hazan does not develop those. The framework developed by Skaar *et al.* (2015) suffers from the opposite problem. They build a complex framework to investigate the relationship between different transitional justice mechanisms and peace and democracy in Angola, Peru, Rwanda and Uruguay. To assess the impact of trials on peace, they build a broad framework that takes into account nine contextual variables, ten 'instrumental variables' relating to the establishment and implementation of transitional justice, as well as qualitative and quantitative impact measurements (Skaar *et al.* 2015, 56–57). Their analyses operationalise a positive concept of peace, measuring it by means of human rights violations. This approach complements the present study, which focuses on getting to peace. Over the next four chapters, it will build an understanding of why the Ugandans failed to reach a negotiated end to conflict, while the Kenyans succeeded in this, and it will identify which role ICC involvement played in producing these two outcomes.

Notes

1 For other literature reviews of the dominant approaches to the legalisation or judicialisation of politics, see Alter (2014, 42–52), Blichner and Molander (2008), Deitelhoff (2009), Hirschl (2006) and Schiff (2008, chap. 1).

2 The petering out of conflict when one side gradually loses momentum is akin to military defeat, as the diminishing of a conflict party is likely to stem from the increased capacity of its opponent.

3 See the Vienna Convention on the Law of the Treaties.

References

Abbott, Kenneth W, Philipp Genschel, Duncan Snidal, and Bernhard Zangl. 2015. 'Two Logics of Indirect Governance: Delegation and Orchestration.' *British Journal of Political Science* 46: 719–729.

Abbott, Kenneth W, Robert O Keohane, Andrew Moravcsik, Anne-Marie Slaughter, and Duncan Snidal. 2000. 'The Concept of Legalization.' *International Organization* 54 (3): 401–419.

Alter, Karen J. 2008. 'Delegating to International Courts: Self-Binding vs. Other-Binding Delegation.' *Law and Contemporary Problems* 71 (2): 37.

Alter, Karen J. 2011. 'Judicialization of International Relations.' In *International Encyclopedia of Political Science*, edited by Bertrand Badie, Dirk Berg-Schlosser, and Leonardo Morlino, 1378–1383. SAGE Publications Inc.

Alter, Karen J. 2014. *The New Terrain of International Law: Courts, Politics, Rights.* Princeton NJ: Princeton University Press.

Arsanjani, Mahnoush H, and W Michael Reisman. 2005. 'The Law-in-Action of the International Criminal Court.' *American Journal of International Law* 99 (2): 385–403.

Barnett, Michael, and Raymond Duvall. 2005. 'Power in International Politics.' *International Organization* 59 (1): 39–75.

Bell, Christine. 1999. 'Foreword: A Comparative Perspective on Peace Agreements.' *Accord 7*, 6–9. London: Conciliation Resources.

Bell, Christine. 2006. 'Peace Agreements: Their Nature and Legal Status.' *The American Journal of International Law* 100 (2): 373–412.

Blichner, Lars Chr, and Anders Molander. 2008. 'Mapping Juridification.' *European Law Journal* 14 (1): 36–54.

Bosco, David. 2013. *Rough Justice: The International Criminal Court in a World of Power Politics*. Oxford: Oxford University Press.

Bradley, Curtis A, and Judith G Kelley. 2008. 'The Concept of International Delegation.' *Law and Contemporary Problems* 71 (1): 1–36.

Brake, Benjamin, and Peter J Katzenstein. 2013. 'Lost in Translation? Non-Stake Actors and the Transnational Movement of Procedural Law.' *International Organization* 67 (4): 725–757.

Branch, Adam. 2011. *Displacing Human Rights: War and Intervention in Northern Uganda*. New York: Oxford University Press.

Brütsch, Christian, and Dirk Lehmkuhl. 2007. *Law and Legalization in Transnational Relations*. Abingdon: Routledge.

Call, Charles T. 2002. 'Assessing El Salvador's Transition from Civil War to Peace.' In *Ending Civil Wars: The Implementation of Peace Agreements*, edited by Stephen John Stedman, Donald S Rothchild, and Elizabeth M Cousens, 383–420. Boulder and London: Lynne Rienner Publishers, Inc.

Campbell, David. 1998. *National Deconstruction: Violence, Identity, and Justice in Bosnia*. Minneapolis, MN: University of Minnesota Press.

Chapman, Terrence L, and Stephen Chaudoin. 2013. 'Ratification Patterns and the International Criminal Court.' *International Studies Quarterly* 57 (2): 400. doi:10.1111/isqu.12005.

Cousens, Elizabeth M. 2002. 'From Missed Opportunities to Overcompensation: Implementing the Dayton Agreement on Bosnia.' In *Ending Civil Wars: The Implementation of Peace Agreements*, edited by Stephen John Stedman, Donald S Rothchild, and Elizabeth M Cousens, 531. Boulder and London: Lynne Rienner Publishers, Inc.

de Waal, Alex. 2014. 'Violence and Peacemaking in the Political Marketplace.' In *Legitimacy and Peace Processes: From Coercion to Consent, Accord 25*, edited by Alexander Ramsbotham and Achim Wennmann, 17–20. London: Conciliation Resources.

Deitelhoff, Nicole. 2009. 'The Discursive Process of Legalization: Charting Islands of Persuasion in the ICC Case.' *International Organization* 63 (1): 33–65.

Deutsch, Morton. 1973. *The Resolution of Conflict*. New Haven, CT: Yale University Press.

Druckman, Daniel. 2001. 'Turning Points in International Negotiation: A Comparative Analysis.' *Journal of Conflict Resolution* 45 (4): 519–544.

Druckman, Daniel, and Valerie Rosoux. 2016. 'Focal Points and Turning Points in Negotiation: A Comparative Analysis.' *Negotiation Journal* 32 (2): 127–150. doi:10.1111/nejo.12151.

Finlayson, Alan. 2007. 'From Beliefs to Arguments: Interpretive Methodology and Rhetorical Political Analysis.' *The British Journal of Politics & International Relations* 9 (4): 545. doi:10.1111/j.1467-856X.2007.00269.x.

Finnemore, Martha J, and Kathryn Sikkink. 1998. 'International Norm Dynamics and Political Change.' *International Organization* 52 (4): 887. doi:10.1162/002081898550789.

Finnemore, Martha J, and Stephen Toope. 2001. 'Alternatives to "Legalization": Richer Views of Law and Politics.' *International Organization* 55 (3): 743. doi:10.1162/00208180152507614.

Freeden, Michael. 1996. *Ideologies and Political Theory: A Conceptual Approach*. Oxford: Clarendon.

Galtung, Johan. 1969. 'Violence, Peace, and Peace Research.' *Journal of Peace Research* 6 (3): 167–191.

Galtung, Johan. 1996. *Peace by Peaceful Means: Peace and Conflict, Development and Civilization*. Oslo and London: International Peace Research Institute, Oslo, and SAGE Publications.

George, Alexander L, and Andrew Bennett. 2005. *Case Studies and Theory Development in the Social Sciences. BCSIA Studies in International Security*. Cambridge, MA: MIT Press.

Gissel, Line Engbo. 2017. 'Legitimising the Juba Peace Agreement on Accountability and Reconciliation: The International Criminal Court as a Third-Party Actor?' *Journal of Eastern African Studies* 11 (2): 367–387. doi:10.1080/17531055.2017.1303249.

Goddard, Stacie E. 2012. 'Brokering Peace: Networks, Legitimacy, and the Northern Ireland Peace Process.' *International Studies Quarterly* 56: 501–515.

Graf, Roman. 2012. 'The International Criminal Court and Child Soldiers.' *Journal of International Criminal Justice* 10 (4): 945–969.

Griffiths, Aaron, and Catherine Barnes. 2008. 'Incentives and Sanctions in Peace Processes.' In *Powers of Persuasion: Incentives, Sanctions and Conditionality in Peacemaking, Accord 19*, edited by Aaron Griffiths and Catherine Barnes, 9–13. London: Conciliation Resources.

Hampson, Fen Osler. 1996. *Nurturing Peace: Why Peace Settlements Succeed or Fail*. Washington, DC: United States Institute of Peace Press.

Hartmann, Eva. 2011. 'The Difficult Relation between International Law and Politics: The Legal Turn from a Critical IPE Perspective.' *New Political Economy* 16 (5): 561.

Hartzell, Caroline, and Matthew Hoddie. 2003. 'Institutionalizing Peace: Power Sharing and Post-Civil War Conflict Management.' *American Journal of Political Science* 47 (2): 318–332.

Hay, Colin. 2007. *Why We Hate Politics*. Cambridge: Polity.

Hazan, Pierre. 2006. 'Measuring the Impact of Punishment and Forgiveness: A Framework for Evaluating Transitional Justice.' *International Review of the Red Cross* 88 (861): 19–47. doi:10.1017/S1816383106000038.

Helfer, Laurence R. 2002. 'Overlegalizing Human Rights: International Relations Theory and the Commonwealth Caribbean Backlash against Human Rights Regimes.' *Columbia Law Review* 102 (7): 1832–1911.

Hirschl, Ran. 2006. 'The New Constitutionalism and the Judicialization of Pure Politics Worldwide.' *Fordham Law Review* 75: 721–753.

Hirschl, Ran. 2008. 'The Judicialization of Mega-Politics and the Rise of Political Courts.' *Annual Review of Political Science* 11 (1): 93–118.

Howse, Robert, and Ruti Teitel. 2010. 'Beyond Compliance: Rethinking Why International Law Really Matters.' *Global Policy* 1 (2): 127–136.

Howse, Robert, and Ruti Teitel. 2011. 'Posner's Missing Concept of Law.' *Global Policy* 2 (1): 117. doi:10.1111/j.1758-5899.2010.00063.x.

Jenkins, Laura. 2011. 'The Difference Genealogy Makes: Strategies for Politicisation or How to Extend Capacities for Autonomy.' *Political Studies* 59 (1): 156. doi:10.1111/j.1467-9248.2010.00844.x.

Jung, Courtney, Ellen Lust-Okar, and Ian Shapiro. 2005. 'Problems and Prospects for Democratic Settlements: South Africa as a Model for the Middle East and Northern Ireland?' *Politics & Society* 33 (2): 277–326.

Jung, Courtney, and Ian Shapiro. 1995. 'South Africa's Negotiated Transition: Democracy, Opposition, and the New Constitutional Order.' *Politics & Society* 23 (3): 269–308.

Kambale, Pascal. 2012. 'The ICC and Lubanga: Missed Opportunities.' *African Futures*. http://forums.ssrc.org/african-futures/2012/03/16/african-futures-icc-missed-opportunities/.

Kastner, Philipp. 2012. 'Towards Internalized Legal Obligations to Address Justice and Accountability? A Novel Perspective on the Legal Framework of Peace Negotiations.' *Criminal Law Forum* 23 (1): 193. doi:10.1007/s10609-012-9174-4.

Keen, David. 2012. 'Peace as an Incentive for War.' In *Peacebuilding, Power, and Politics in Africa*, edited by Devon Curtis and Gwinyayi A Dzinesa, 31–46. Athens, OH: Ohio University Press.

Kelley, Judith. 2007. 'Who Keeps International Commitments and Why? The International Criminal Court and Bilateral Nonsurrender Agreements.' *American Political Science Review* 101 (3): 573. doi:10.1017/S0003055407070426.

Kelsall, Tim. 2009. *Culture under Cross-Examination: International Justice and the Special Court for Sierra Leone. Cambridge Studies in Law and Society*. Cambridge: Cambridge University Press.

Kerr, Rachel. 2000. 'International Judicial Intervention: The International Criminal Tribunal for the Former Yugoslavia.' *International Relations* 15 (2): 17–26. doi:10.1177/004711780001500202.

Khadiagala, Gilbert M. 2002. 'Implementing the Arusha Peace Agreement on Rwanda.' In *Ending Civil Wars: The Implementation of Peace Agreements*, edited by Stephen John Stedman, Donald S Rothchild, and Elizabeth M Cousens, 463–498. Boulder and London: Lynne Rienner Publishers, Inc.

Koskenniemi, Martti. 1989. *From Apology to Utopia: The Structure of International Legal Argument*. Helsinki: Lakimiesliiton Kustannus, Finnish Lawyers' Publ. Co.

Koskenniemi, Martti. 2011. 'The Mystery of Legal Obligation.' *International Theory* 3 (2): 319. doi:10.1017/S1752971911000066.

Kurki, Milja, and Hidemi Suganami. 2012. 'Towards the Politics of Causal Explanation: A Reply to the Critics of Causal Inquiries.' *International Theory* 4 (3): 400–429. doi:10.1017/S1752971912000127.

Lebow, Richard Ned. 2009. 'Constitutive Causality.' *Millennium – Journal of International Studies* 38 (2): 211. doi:10.1177/0305829809347536.

Lee, SungYong, Roger Mac Ginty, and Madhav Joshi. 2016. 'Social Peace vs. Security Peace.' *Global Governance* 22 (4): 491.

Mamdani, Mahmood. 2001. *When Victims Become Killers: Colonialism, Nativism, and the Genocide in Rwanda*. Princeton, NJ: Princeton University Press.

Martin, Harriet. 2007. *Power in Mediation: Does Size Matter?* Oslo: The Oslo Forum. www.osloforum.org/retreats/oslo-forum-07-annual-mediators-retreat.

Maxwell, Joseph A. 2004. 'Causal Explanation, Qualitative Research, and Scientific Inquiry in Education.' *Educational Researcher* 33 (2): 3. doi:10.3102/0013189X033002003.

Moravcsik, Andrew. 2000. 'The Origins of Human Rights Regimes: Democratic Delegation in Postwar Europe.' *International Organization* 54 (2): 217. doi:10.1162/002081800551163.

Nadarajah, Suthaharan, and Dhananjayan Sriskandarajah. 2005. 'Liberation Struggle or Terrorism? The Politics of Naming the LTTE.' *Third World Quarterly* 26 (1): 87–100.

Nouwen, Sarah M H. 2013. *Complementarity in the Line of Fire: The Catalysing Effect of the International Criminal Court in Sudan*. Cambridge: Cambridge University Press.

Oberschall, Anthony. 2007. *Conflict and Peace Building in Divided Societies: Responses to Ethnic Violence*. London and New York: Routledge.

Olásolo, Hector. 2003. 'The Prosecutor of the ICC before the Initiation of Investigations: A Quasi-Judicial or a Political Body?' *International Criminal Law Review* 3: 87–150.

Peskin, Victor. 2009a. 'Caution and Confrontation in the International Criminal Court's Pursuit of Accountability in Uganda and Sudan.' *Human Rights Quarterly* 31 (3): 655–691.

Peskin, Victor. 2009b. *International Justice in Rwanda and the Balkans: Virtual Trials and the Struggle for State Cooperation*. Cambridge: Cambridge University Press.

Ramcharan, Bertrand G. 2009. 'Peace Process.' In *Post-Conflict Peacebuilding: A Lexicon*, edited by Vincent Chetail, 228–244. New York: Oxford University Press.

Ramsbotham, Oliver, Tom Woodhouse, and Hugh Miall. 2011. *Contemporary Conflict Resolution: The Prevention, Management and Transformations of Deadly Conflict*. Oxford: Polity Press.

Reus-Smit, Christian. 2007. *The Politics of International Law. Cambridge Studies in International Relations*. Cambridge: Cambridge University Press.

Risse, Thomas, Stephen C. Ropp, and Kathryn Sikkink, ed. 2013 *The Persistent Power of Human Rights: From Commitment to Compliance*, Cambridge Studies in International Relations. Cambridge: Cambridge University Press.

Rodman, Kenneth A. 2014. 'Justice as a Dialogue between Law and Politics: Embedding the International Criminal Court within Conflict Management and Peacebuilding.' *Journal of International Criminal Justice* 12 (3). doi:10.1093/jicj/mqu027.

Scheffer, David J. 1996. 'International Judicial Intervention.' *Foreign Policy*, No. 102: 34–51.

Scheingold, Stuart A. 1974. *The Politics of Rights: Lawyers, Public Policy, and Political Change*. New Haven and London: Yale University Press.

Schiff, Benjamin N. 2008. *Building the International Criminal Court*. Cambridge: Cambridge University Press.

Schomerus, Mareike. 2012. 'Even Eating You Can Bite Your Tongue: Dynamics and Challenges of the Peace Talks with the Lord's Resistance Army.' PhD Thesis, London School of Economics and Political Science.

Sikkink, Kathryn. 2011. *The Justice Cascade: How Human Rights Prosecutions Are Changing World Politics*. New York: W. W. Norton & Company.

Simmons, Beth A. 2000. 'International Law and State Behavior: Commitment and Compliance in International Monetary Affairs.' *The American Political Science Review* 94 (4): 819.

Simmons, Beth A. 2013. 'From Ratification to Compliance: Quantitative Evidence on the Spiral Model.' In *The Persistent Power of Human Rights: From Commitment to*

Compliance, edited by Thomas Risse, Stephen C Ropp, and Kathryn Sikkink, 43–59. Cambridge: Cambridge University Press.

Sisk, Timothy D. 2010. 'Introduction: The SRSGs and the Management of Civil Wars.' *Global Governance* 16 (2): 237.

Skaar, Elin, Camila Gianella Malca, and Trine Eide. 2015. 'Towards a Framework for Impact Assessment.' In *After Violence: Transitional Justice, Peace, and Democracy*, edited by Elin Skaar, Camila Gianella Malca, and Trine Eide, 29–66. Abingdon: Routledge.

Srinivasan, Sharath. 2012. 'The Politics of Negotiating Peace in Sudan.' In *Peacebuilding, Power, and Politics in Africa*, edited by Devon Curtis and Gwinyayi A. Dzinesa, 195–211. Athens, OH: Ohio University Press.

Stedman, Stephen John. 1997. 'Spoiler Problems in Peace Processes.' *International Security* 22 (2): 5.

Stedman, Stephen John. 2002. 'Introduction.' In *Ending Civil Wars: The Implementation of Peace Agreements*, edited by Stephen John Stedman, Donald S Rothchild, and Elizabeth M Cousens, 1–40. Boulder and London: Lynne Rienner Publishers, Inc.

Stedman, Stephen John, Donald S Rothchild, and Elizabeth M Cousens. 2002. *Ending Civil Wars: The Implementation of Peace Agreements*. Boulder, CO: Lynne Rienner.

Teitel, Ruti G. 2000. *Transitional Justice*. New York: Oxford University Press.

Von Stein, Jana. 2005. 'Do Treaties Constrain or Screen? Selection Bias and Treaty Compliance.' *American Political Science Review* 99 (4): 611. doi:10.1017/S0003055405051919.

Wallensteen, Peter. 2012. *Understanding Conflict Resolution*. 3rd edn. London: SAGE Publications.

Walter, Barbara F. 2002. *Committing to Peace: Successful Settlements of Civil Wars*. Princeton, NJ: Princeton University Press.

White, Hayden. 1989. *The Content of the Form: Narrative Discourse and Historical Representation*. Baltimore: The Johns Hopkins University Press.

Wood, Elisabeth Jean. 2003. *Insurgent Collective Action and Civil War in El Salvador*. Cambridge: Cambridge University Press.

Zartman, I William. 1995a. *Elusive Peace: Negotiating an End to Civil Wars*. Washington, DC: Brookings Institution.

Zartman, I William. 1995b. 'Dynamics and Constraints in Negotiations in Internal Conflicts.' In *Elusive Peace: Negotiating an End to Civil Wars*, edited by I William Zartman, 3–29. Washington, DC: Brookings Institution.

3 ICC involvement in the Juba Peace Talks

The only way to stop Joseph Kony is by arresting him and surrendering him to the ICC.

ICC Prosecutor Louis Moreno-Ocampo, Seventeenth Diplomatic Briefing, The Hague, 4 November 2009

It is cheaper ... and easier to destroy the LRA through peaceful means than through military means.

Dr Riek Machar, Chief Mediator, 17 June 2008, quoted in Dak (2008)

The Juba Peace Talks attempted to settle the conflict between the government of Uganda and the LRA. It followed roughly the three-phase model of a peace process, but with an unusual implementation phase: the Final Peace Agreement was never signed by the LRA leader, Joseph Kony, yet the government proceeded to implement selected provisions of the Juba agreements. To underline the character of the trajectory of the process of ICC involvement and that of peacemaking, the chapter is structured chronologically and according to ICC stages and peace process phases, beginning with active ICC involvement in Stage 2.

ICC Stages 2 to 4

The ICC moved up the trajectory of involvement before the Juba Peace Talks commenced. As per the five-stage model of an ICC intervention, involvement began when Uganda ratified the Rome Statute in June 2002 (Stage 1). It moved up the trajectory a year later, when in Stage 2 (Preliminary Examination) the ICC Prosecutor invited Uganda to refer its situation to the ICC. The ICC began investigations in January 2004, entering Stage 3 (Investigation), and issued arrest warrants for five LRA leaders in July 2005 as part of Stage 4 (Indictment). Roughly six months later, the peace process began at its initial, prospective phase. This meant that the Juba Peace Talks took place in the context of high-level ICC involvement.

ICC Stage 2: Preliminary Examination (16 June 2003–28 January 2004)

The ICC's involvement in Uganda is commonly assumed to derive from the government's referral of the northern situation to the ICC. However, the Prosecutor, Louis Moreno-Ocampo, had already initiated a preliminary examination of the northern situation prior to the Ugandan referral. Soon after the ICC became functional in 2003, the Prosecutor began to receive information about crimes committed in Northern Uganda, the DRC and Colombia. As the two East African countries were not prosecuting these acts, the OTP (2006, 7) 'adopted the policy of inviting and welcoming voluntary referrals' by them. This policy involved the threat of a *proprio motu* investigation, so in fact it was not entirely voluntary (Schabas 2011, 166).

The government of Uganda referred the 'situation concerning the Lord's Resistance Army' to the ICC on 16 December 2003, roughly six months after the Prosecutor took office. The 27-page referral letter argued that it was 'befitting both from a *practical and moral* viewpoint' to entrust the investigation and prosecution of serious crimes to the ICC because Uganda's judicial system was unavailable due to its inability to obtain the accused (Government of Uganda 2003, para. 24, emphasis in original). The Prosecutor shared this sentiment, moving swiftly to the Investigation stage.

ICC Stage 3: Investigation (29 January 2004–5 May 2005)

On 29 January 2004, Uganda's President Museveni and the Prosecutor held a joint press briefing in London, announcing that the OTP (2004a) had 'determined' that there was a sufficient basis to start planning for the Court's first investigation.[1] The joint briefing signalled close relations between the OTP and the government and attracted criticism by the war-affected population, which saw the government as a conflict party (Allen 2006, 128; Apuuli 2007, 44). The LRA reacted to the new alliance between the government and the ICC, attacking Abia camp for internally displaced persons (IDP) in Lira district and killing 52 people.

The OTP judged LRA's crimes to be graver than those of the national army, the Uganda People's Defence Forces (UPDF), finding the LRA responsible for at least 2,200 killings and 3,200 abductions between July 2002 and June 2004 (Brubacher 2010, 269). It selected six incidents that were representative of LRA crimes and conducted over 50 missions to the field (OTP 2006, 15–16). In March and April 2005, the OTP invited local government leaders, MPs, and religious and traditional leaders from Northern Uganda to The Hague. Betty Bigombe, the government's peace envoy in the mid-1990s, had re-established contact with LRA leaders in late 2004 and was meeting Kony in early 2005, supported by the UN and several European donors. The meetings in The Hague led, according to the Prosecutor, to 'a greater understanding between the parties and an agreement to continue dialogue in pursuit of the common goal of ending violence' (OTP

2006, 17). The Ugandan contingent understood these meetings very differently, thinking that 'Ocampo agreed to give us some time' so Bigombe's peace initiative could be pursued.[2] Walter Ochora (quoted in Nolen 2005), the government representative on the trip, similarly found that 'we have a gentleman's agreement'. However, shortly afterwards, the Prosecutor submitted the request for arrest warrants.

ICC Stage 4: Indictment (6 May 2005–5 December 2016)

On 6 May 2005, the OTP submitted a sealed request for arrest warrants for five LRA leaders charged with war crimes and crimes against humanity: Kony, Vincent Otti, Okot Odhiambo, Dominic Ongwen and Raska Lukwiya. PTC II authorised these warrants two months later, keeping them under seal out of concern for the safety of victims and witnesses. The PTC unsealed the warrants on 13 October 2005 in response to a request by the Prosecutor, who felt that lifting the seal would garner international attention and ease the mobilisation for arrest efforts. When news of the arrest warrants reached Bigombe (quoted in Kakaire 2006), she abandoned her track-II process, explaining that it was 'now extremely difficult for me to talk meaningfully to the LRA leadership when they know they are being hunted down to be locked up behind bars in Europe.'

Within a week of the unsealing of the arrest warrants, the UPDF pursued the LRA in Southern Sudan. The Sudanese government had signed an agreement with the OTP to execute the arrest warrants. The rebels, however, began to move their camps to Garamba Forest in Haut Uele Province in north-eastern DRC. They also symbolically targeted international relief agencies, killing six staff in less than a month. Aid agencies halted their activities in the affected areas and appealed to the UN Security Council for protection.

Amnesty, peace and justice

The arrest warrants immediately altered the context of peacebuilding by making the prosecution of the LRA leaders a legal imperative. This development contradicted Uganda's Amnesty Act, which offered amnesty to 'any Ugandan who has at any time since the 26th day of January, 1986, engaged in or is engaged in war or armed rebellion against the government'.[3] The Amnesty Act had been inconsistent with Uganda's obligations to the Rome Statute since the latter was ratified in 2003, but the government had ignored this problem. In the eyes of the OTP, however, the amnesty law had to exclude the LRA indictees: they could not be subject to international prosecution while eligible for national amnesty. The Prosecutor therefore lobbied President Museveni to amend the Act, obtaining a promise that this would be done during the Preliminary Examination stage (OTP 2004a; see also Branch 2007, 179). Human rights NGOs followed up, wanting Uganda to 'revoke its unlawful national amnesty' (Vision Reporter 2005). The Amnesty Act was amended in May 2006, to the effect that the Minister of Internal Affairs, subject to parliamentary approval, could lapse the amnesty-granting Part II of the Act or declare a person ineligible. The new provision was invoked in 2012, after the end of the Juba Peace Talks, and was thus initially a 'tactical concession' to the ICC.

By late 2005, around 1.8 million people were internally displaced in Northern Uganda, living in camps without adequate government protection (Dolan 2009; Mwenda 2010). Camps in Acholi region had an even higher mortality rate than those in Darfur (Checchi 2006). Thousands of children and young people walked to urban areas every evening to sleep in relative safety. In this context, news of the indictments sparked a peace/justice debate. The justice discourse focused on an ideal future scenario, based on a deontological commitment to retributive justice or a consequentialist deterrence narrative. For instance, Laouries Okello (quoted in Sheikh 2005), a 15-year-old displaced girl, found that 'Kony and other rebel leaders who formed the group should be thrown into jail. He's done a bad thing.' Members of the peace discourse community questioned the practicality of enforcement and articulated the incentives narrative. For instance, William Oyet (quoted in Aduk 2005), a 30-year-old camp resident, said, 'I wonder who will arrest [Kony] especially because the government has been trying to do that for long now.' The debate lasted throughout the Juba Peace Talks and pitted international organisations against local NGOs, and human rights bodies against religious leaders.

Juba Peace Talks: Pre-Negotiation phase (30 November 2005–13 July 2006)

Representing the 'new world' of peace and justice, the Juba Peace Talks took place in the context of ICC involvement, confusion over the status of the amnesty law, and the peace/justice debate. The peace process began after the arrest warrants had been unsealed and thus happened in the context of high-level ICC involvement at Stage 4.

The Pre-Negotiation phase of the Juba process was preceded by dramatic changes in the LRA's political, military and strategic environment and in the government's interest in a peaceful South Sudan.[4] The political settlement between the Sudanese government and the Sudan People's Liberation Movement/Army (SPLM/A) in January 2005 created a new political situation that made the resolution of the LRA conflict imperative for the SPLM, an ally of the National Resistance Movement (NRM) government.[5] The Comprehensive Peace Agreement established a semi-autonomous government of Southern Sudan and envisaged a future referendum to determine whether the southern region should remain part of Sudan.

The conflict between the LRA and the Ugandan government threatened the political achievements of the 2005 Agreement, prompting Southern Sudan's president, Salva Kiir Mayardit, to give the LRA and UPDF the option to '[n]egotiate peace, leave our territory, or be chased from Sudanese territory by the SPLA' (Simonse *et al.* 2010, 229). Kiir's vice president, Riek Machar Teny Dhurgon, and SPLA Deputy Commander, Paulino Matiep Nhial, had led militias, which had at times been allied with the LRA. The past contact between Kony, Machar and Matiep was now exploited with the new objective of facilitating negotiations.

In late 2005, the Southern Sudan regional government made some 'credible contacts' with the LRA, while LRA leaders contacted different persons inside and outside Uganda with a view to future negotiations.[6] On 30 November, Otti (quoted in Mukasa 2005) told the BBC World Service, 'The chairman, General Joseph Kony, has authorized me to talk to you that we want peace talks with the government of Uganda.' By February 2006, the Southern Sudan government and the LRA signed a formal pre-negotiation agreement centring on three points: Southern Sudan would serve as mediator in the peace process, the LRA would stop initiating hostile activities inside Sudan, and the LRA would be expelled if they could not accept the two previous points (Atkinson 2010, 210). Southern Sudan also assured the LRA leaders that they would support the withdrawal of the ICC arrest warrants, while Sudanese officials told US diplomats that it supported peace talks with the LRA (US Embassy Khartoum 2006a). Atkinson (2010) reports that 'very few' LRA attacks were reported inside Uganda after February and March 2006.

Following the pre-negotiation agreement, Kony and Otti met with Machar, a delegation of Southern Sudanese MPs, mediators from Pax Christi (a Catholic NGO) and Dutch journalists near the DRC/Sudan border (Atkinson 2010, 212). Machar signalled goodwill by giving the LRA a monetary gift of US$20,000, while Kony showed goodwill by allowing the South Sudanese contingent to record video of his verbal commitment to enter peace talks.[7] Kony (quoted in *The Monitor* 2006) told Machar that:

> we, the LRA, want peace and we agree to what you are going to say to us. We don't want to fight, we don't want to exchange fire with SPLA, we want to talk to Museveni, but only that Museveni did not want to talk with us.... We want to talk. I agree to everything, I am a human being; I want my tribe to be ok also. I want you to communicate to me the next thing to do, but what I want you to know is that I want to talk.[8]

The video recording was presented to Museveni as evidence of Kony's willingness to talk peace, together with information about the pre-negotiation agreement.[9] Museveni agreed to enter the peace process. He was one of the guarantors of the Comprehensive Peace Agreement and had an interest in a stable Southern Sudan.[10] Perhaps he felt 'bound by the historically close ties between the SPLM and [the government of Uganda]' (US Embassy Khartoum 2006b). Following the commitment to negotiations, Museveni offered the LRA leadership a security guarantee, stating publicly that 'much as Kony and four of his cohorts had been indicted by the ICC, if he got serious about a peaceful settlement, the Government of Uganda would guarantee him safety' (Mukasa 2006). Shortly thereafter, Museveni declared that his government would grant Kony 'total amnesty' in spite of the ICC indictments (Vision Reporter 2006b). To Museveni, a Kony jailed in The Hague may become a martyr, 'a beacon of hope to the Acholis to continue their struggle against his government'.[11]

In mid-June, the LRA sent a peace delegation to Juba, which included Otti. The government responded by sending the former external security director, David Pulkol, who by then ran an NGO, the African Leadership Institute. This enabled the government to meet the LRA delegation without violating their commitments to the ICC and Interpol. Pulkol came as the president's emissary to advance a delegation that would establish contact with the LRA, but also told US diplomats of 'skepticism in Kampala' that the peace initiative 'would fly' (US Embassy Khartoum 2006b).[12] The commitment to peace talks with the LRA was therefore 'not open-ended'.

There was internal disagreement between hardliners and moderates within the government over how to deal with LRA, which sent mixed messages. The Security Minister, Amama Mbabazi, had stated, 'There is no amnesty for Kony and we cannot speak to Kony', while the Minister of State for Foreign Affairs, Henry Okello Oryem, warned, 'We cannot have a head-to-head meeting with the indicted LRA commanders. We would have to arrest them immediately' (IRIN 2006a). UPDF officials repeatedly highlighted that Kony had never before been serious about peace talks.

The government also felt uncertain about how to deal with the ICC if Uganda reached an arrangement with the LRA. Inasmuch as Museveni had offered a 'total amnesty' and Uganda had an amnesty law, Pulkol told the Americans that 'any agreement would not necessarily be binding on anyone involved', citing the case of Charles Taylor (US Embassy Khartoum 2006b). Mbabazi also travelled to The Hague to explain the government position to the ICC Prosecutor (OTP 2006).

International reactions to the security guarantee

As soon as Museveni offered a security guarantee, the ICC reacted by reminding him that the government had 'made a commitment' and was obliged to arrest the LRA indictees (BBC 2006). On 1 June 2006, seven months after the arrest warrants were unsealed but immediately after Museveni's amnesty offer, the Court requested Interpol to issue a 'Red Notice' for the LRA leaders. Mobilisation for the arrest of the LRA leaders was complemented by a campaign to delegitimise the peace process even before it was formally launched. This campaign claimed that Joseph Kony's stated willingness to enter a peace process was insincere, his real intentions being to 'buy time' to rebuild his army. The following extract illustrates the discourse:

> For 20 years, the LRA has abducted children from their homes and schools, forcing boys to kill and compelling girls to kill and to serve as sex slaves.... Kony recently attempted to negotiate a political deal. In the past, he has used negotiations to buy time and regroup. To do justice and re-establish security in the region, the justice network has to arrest the LRA commanders.
>
> (Moreno-Ocampo 2006)

Thus, in reaction to Museveni's security guarantee, the Prosecutor abandoned his earlier talk of 'bringing a justice component to justice and reconciliation' and instead adopted a more adversarial approach (Peskin 2009, 655–691).

In stark contrast to international peacebuilding in the 1990s, the ICC's initial position was immediately backed by the main donors to Uganda and Sudan, such as the EU, the US and the UK (Council of the European Union 2006; Nyakairu 2006). US diplomats leaned on Machar, trying to impress upon him 'the delicacy of dealing with the LRA' (US Embassy Khartoum 2006c). Human rights organisations argued that the peace talks endangered the 'credibility and legitimacy' of the ICC (Anderson 2006).

The mediators and LRA/M negotiators found the delegitimisation of Kony's interest in the peace talks deeply problematic.[13] Their job was not only to negotiate or mediate, but also to convince the government to believe in the process and to bring Kony to a point at which he was willing to abandon war. Kony's initial interest in talking peace did not necessarily mean an automatic commitment to the outcomes of the talks: he needed to be brought to that point.

Southern Sudan was disappointed by the international criticism. Kiir (Vision Reporter 2006a) claimed authority over the LRA issue because 'the people who they kill are southern Sudanese, the women they rape are southern Sudanese women and girls, and the boys they abduct are southern Sudanese'. He also appealed to pragmatism, asking, 'What is wrong with [peace talks] if that can bring them back to [be] law abiding citizens of Uganda?' Machar (quoted in *The New Vision* 2006) told Otti, 'We defied the whole world so you could have a chance to come and say your viewpoints.'

The chairperson of the Gulu District Council, Norbert Mao (quoted in *IRIN* 2006b), felt that Interpol and the ICC 'sabotaged the peace process' even before it had begun. He said they should 'hold on and give room to the negotiations and see how far this new dialogue can go. … The timing is very bad.' Traditional and religious leaders agreed in numerous statements and interviews. The LRA/M delegation arrived in Juba in June 2006, one month earlier than the government delegation.

Juba Peace Talks: Negotiation phase (14 July 2006–14 December 2008)

The Juba Peace Talks opened formally on 14 July 2006, marking the beginning of the Negotiation phase. The process was mediated by Machar and facilitated by Hizkias Assefa, a mediator and academic linked to Pax Christi. Three Ugandan lawyers and consultants from the Swiss foreign office, Pax Christi and the Community of Sant'Egidio (a church public lay association) assisted the mediation team. The talks were structured around an agenda with six items: cessation of hostilities; comprehensive solution to the conflict; accountability and reconciliation; ceasefire; demobilisation, disarmament and reintegration (DDR); and implementation modalities.

The peace delegations

The conflict parties' expectations for the Talks were represented by their delegations' composition. The government delegation consisted of 16 members, of which 13 had a security profile. It included a military commander formerly in charge of operations against the LRA (Schomerus and Ogwaro 2010, 11). Its counterpart had 15 members, of which two were from the LRA while the rest were sympathisers mainly from the Acholi diaspora.[14] The government delegation thus had a military bias, while the rebel delegation had no military insight to speak of (Baaré 2008). This proved an acute disadvantage in the negotiations on DDR, cessation of hostilities and a permanent ceasefire. Later the government replaced two top military delegates with an official from the Amnesty Commission and the UPDF spokesperson, signalling a more political approach.

The government delegation was led by the Minister for Internal Affairs, Dr Ruhakana Rugunda, who represented a more conciliatory approach to the LRA than Mbabazi and other long-standing ministers. It included Henry Okello Oryem, Minister of State for International Affairs and the son of former President Tito Okello, whom Museveni's army displaced in the 1986 military coup.[15] As a member of the government delegation, Okello Oryem symbolised the irrelevance of past grudges and the inclusivity of the NRM project. When the negotiations commenced, the LRA became the Lord's Resistance Army/Movement (LRA/M), taking a leaf out of the books of the NRA/M and SPLA/M. Kony appointed Martin Ojul as the delegation leader and Chrispus Ayena Odongo as its lawyer, but most of the delegation was selected by Ojul.[16] A civilian working in Nairobi, Ojul had not lived in Northern Uganda during the conflict.

In the opening remarks at the launch of the peace process, Rugunda emphasised the government's sincere desire to negotiate a just settlement and repeated the offer of amnesty for LRA members who would opt for peace. He expected to negotiate the surrender of the LRA, giving the rebels a 'soft landing'.[17] Meanwhile, the UPDF continued their pursuit of the LRA, killing Raska Lukwiya. The LRA/M delegation was incensed by the suggestion that they were negotiating a 'soft landing', as it undermined their political project.[18] Obonyo Olweny's 18-page opening speech launched a radical critique of the NRM government, the cause for Uganda's 'political haemorrhage' (LRA/M 2006). Thereafter he outlined the group's political agenda, which included: protection against 'state-backed' land grabbers; reparations; respect for cultural diversity; democracy and good governance; equal opportunities; respect for international law; a private-sector-driven economy; and a professional and motivated civil service. The programme listed IDP camps as the second-last issue after the bureaucracy, a prioritisation that suggests the delegation's psychological distance from the realities of life in Northern Uganda.

The opening statement was written by a delegation member, who had never been a rebel.[19] The delegation wrote all its position papers, usually after a process of brainstorming.[20] Its relative autonomy provided its members with a wide scope for shaping the talks and agreements, with some of them negotiating on behalf of the northern population rather than, narrowly, the LRA/M leadership. As a delegate explained with hindsight:

> I wanted to get the best out of the peace talks for my people. And one of the things I thought was very important was to bring about total cessation of hostilities.... If the war stopped, whatever happened to Kony was not so much my business as it was the business of government.[21]

Back in Uganda, Museveni's amnesty offer and defence of traditional accountability processes coexisted with a hardliner discourse articulated by the UPDF, some government ministers and, paradoxically, the president. According to an observer, 'Museveni was consistent about being inconsistent about the talks!'[22]

Asymmetries

The two peace delegations were unevenly matched in terms of their capacity to handle issues and speak for the two principals. The Talks aimed to compensate for this 'through appropriate technical assistance, particularly legal, for the LRA' (Hendrickson and Tumutegyereize 2012, 16). Machar worried about the rebel delegation's insufficient decision-making power, visiting Kony several times to persuade him to send more high-level commanders to the negotiations. However, citing the ICC arrest warrants, Kony and Otti refused to participate in person.

The arrest warrants affected the Talks in two structural senses, altering the LRA/M's bargaining power and legitimacy. In a relationship where military strength is the chief political resource, the ICC indictments made the LRA leaders more insecure and less powerful; as Kony remarked, the 'ICC is for the weak'.[23] To assert its strength or objection to the ICC process, the LRA carried out attacks on civilians and internationals when ICC involvement entered the Investigation and Indictment stages. Furthermore, the LRA leaders often referred to the arrest of Charles Taylor, Liberia's former president, as 'a scenario that they [were] keen to avoid' (Unger and Wierda 2009, 271). Taylor was indicted by the SCSL and arrested in exile in March 2006.

Being internationally wanted, the LRA/M leadership became enemies of the world (Nouwen and Werner 2011). Delegitimised, it sought an international audience. It contacted Western journalists in August 2005, agreeing to speak to them for the first time (Schomerus 2010a, 96). Until then, the LRA had sought Ugandan or regional audiences, running at some point a radio station. In his interview with Schomerus (2010b), Kony cast himself as a freedom fighter wanting to liberate the people of Uganda. He also perceived Museveni to have mobilised the ICC. Museveni (quoted in Wasike 2003) seemed to agree, having stated, 'I am preparing an international arrest warrant for these terrorists.... I am targeting Kony, Otti and a couple of other leaders.' The OTP's decision to not pursue any cases against state actors contributed to the conflict parties' asymmetric relationship, as it enabled the government to construct the LRA as the sole author of atrocity. The LRA/M delegation argued that 'the international community, and indeed the ICC' failed to 'comprehensively' address justice issues in a 'fair manner to both parties' (LRA/M 2006).

Initial approach by the international community

The international community was initially ambivalent about the Juba negotiations. In spite of having called for negotiations in 2003, the donors and international actors did not know whether to support them once they began three years later. According to Afako (2006, 1), legal advisor to the mediation team, the prospect of dialogue between Uganda and the LRA raised 'a chorus of protest from various international actors, especially human rights organisations and other States Parties to the Rome Statute'. Another mediator felt that the outside world 'would not even touch the LRA talks with a long, dry stick'.[24]

Within the UN, there was little support for the Peace Talks (Perrot 2010, 194). When negotiating the cessation of hostilities, the Office of Coordination of Humanitarian Affairs (OCHA) asked the mediators to remove any reference to the UN from the draft agreements (Baaré 2008, 32n). The Department of Political Affairs, the UN focal point for peace process support, only became involved later, when the Secretary-General appointed Joachim Chissano as a Special Envoy. Instead, OCHA was asked to coordinate the external funding for the process, establishing in October 2006 the Juba Initiative Fund. According to OCHA's head, Jan Egeland (2010, 20), 'Nobody else was able to organize meaningful international support to the Southern Sudanese peace effort, so we did it.' UN circles nick-named the Talks 'Egeland's rogue project'.

The international ambivalence stemmed from the ICC indictments, which sparked a peace/justice debate within UN bodies and Western foreign ministries. A meeting between OCHA and the Acting US Consul General in Juba illustrates the two global discourses, the US diplomat articulating the justice discourse:

> The OCHA reps believed the talks were a good opportunity for peace and wanted to see how they could provide help to ensure their success, focusing on humanitarian concerns....
>
> The [Acting Consul General] expressed fears that this may just be a stalling tactic to allow the weakened LRA to regroup, as had happened in past negotiations, and said that the United States did not support granting impunity for those who had committed atrocities.
>
> The [OCHA] reps explained that, although LRA leader Joseph Kony had been erratic during the talks, they believed this attempt at peace was genuine and that the people of Northern Uganda had decided to support the talks because the needs of a million and a half internally displaced persons (IDPs) should outweigh the need to detain and prosecute five people.
>
> The [Acting Consul General] cautioned that exchanging justice for peace often led to getting neither; the OCHA representatives said that the people of Northern Uganda were ready for peace and should be allowed to seek justice in their own way, through a traditional reconciliation process known

> as 'mato oput.'[25] ... While acknowledging that the ICC indictments had helped push the LRA into talks, they said the ICC was now a major hindrance. Because the ICC prevented top LRA leaders from attending the talks in Juba, they said that the next round of talks may take place in the bush.
>
> The [Acting Consul General] explained that the United States remained focused on the well-being of the people of Uganda, providing humanitarian aid, and ensuring that atrocities would not be committed with impunity. Lending international legitimacy to a process that could not be legitimate was dangerous, so while the [US government] was following the talks, there were no plans to get involved.
>
> (US Embassy Khartoum 2006d, para. 2–4)

Switzerland was an exception to the international approach, providing mediation support from the beginning. Although Switzerland was party to the Rome Statute, it was not a member of the EU and therefore was not obliged to follow the latter's rules on terrorist-designated groups. Switzerland agreed to act as an informal 'ambassador' to the ICC, explaining the peace process to the Prosecutor. However, when confronted with the peace/justice debate, Switzerland decided to 'not engage on issues to do with accountability and justice' (Hottinger 2010, 15).

Agenda Item 1: Cessation of hostilities

Overcoming the bad atmosphere following Olweny's opening speech, the negotiators agreed to a few 'ground rules', while the mediators organised workshops on ceasefire modalities, the conditions and needs of the local population, and the ICC. While the second workshop was designed to 'ground' the diasporic LRA/M delegation, the third workshop concerned the possibilities and constraints of the Rome Statute in relation to the LRA conflict and fed into the negotiations on accountability and reconciliation. First, however, the parties addressed the ongoing violence.

Negotiations on Item 1 of the agenda began on the basis of the delegations' position papers on the cessation of hostilities. The two position papers illustrated the security orientation of the government delegation and the grievance-orientated perspective of the LRA/M delegation. The latter sought to repoliticise the ethnic composition of the UPDF, demanding the 'total disbandment' of the national army because it is 'ethnic, partisan and pledges its loyalty to President Yoweri Museveni personally' (*IRIN* 2006c). It advocated an internationally supervised recruitment process that would seek a regional balance and integration of ex-rebels. The government's position paper demanded that 'the LRA cease all forms of hostilities, dissolve itself and hand over all arms and ammunitions in its possession together with their inventory and assemble in agreed locations' (quoted in *The Sudan Tribune* 2006). It also repeated the offer of an amnesty for the LRA leaders. Given the LRA/M delegation's lack of military experience, there were two separate negotiations: one between the mediators and the government delegation (Baaré 2008, 28) and another between the LRA/M delegation and their high command.

The negotiation teams signed the Agreement on Cessation of Hostilities on 26 August 2006, committing to 'cease all hostile military action' and to let the rebels assemble at two particular geographical points: east of the Nile at Owiny-ki-Bul in Sudan's Eastern Equatoria State or west of the Nile at Ri-Kwangba in Sudan's Western Equatoria State (Government of Uganda and LRA/M 2006). The government promised the LRA safe passage within Uganda, while the LRA would assemble within three weeks of the declaration of cessation of hostilities. The SPLA agreed to monitor and protect the LRA at the assembly areas, leading a Cessation of Hostilities Monitoring Team, which included a representative from each conflict party and two military officers appointed by the AU. AU involvement constituted a security guarantee, but the personnel only arrived between 21 April and 5 June 2007 (AU Peace and Security Council 2009, 2).

The cessation of hostilities commenced on 29 August 2006.[26] LRA groups came out of hiding and began to make their way to the assembly points. By mid-September 2006, there were nearly 400 LRA members approaching Owiny-ki-Bul, and fighters had already started to assemble in Ri-Kwangba. The LRA never assembled as agreed, but stayed close enough to the assembly points for the Talks to continue (Baaré 2008). Both parties violated the Cessation of Hostilities Agreement, but violations by the UPDF were 'seemingly both more frequent and more serious' (Atkinson 2010, 215), a fact that escaped international attention. In an effort to boost the talks, the Sudanese parliament called for the non-renewal of the 2002 Sudan–Uganda agreement, which allowed the UPDF to operate inside Sudan (*The Sudan Tribune* 2006). To external observers, the relative cessation of hostilities created a momentum in favour of the Talks. In December 2006, the UN supported the Talks by appointing Joachim Chissano, the former Mozambican president, as the UN Secretary-General's Special Envoy for LRA-Affected Areas.

Agenda Item 2: Comprehensive solutions to the conflict

The LRA/M left the Talks in early 2007, citing dissatisfaction with the SPLM, but was eventually persuaded to continue. A new round of the Talks began on 26 April 2007, and found a more supportive international community. Fourteen countries contributed to the Juba Initiative Fund, while Canada and Denmark supported the Cessation of Hostilities Monitoring Team. In negotiating Item 2 of the agenda, it became apparent that the Pre-Negotiation phase had never included a discussion of the terms of the negotiations and therefore the conflict parties had very different expectations for this agenda item. The government thought it was 'charged with reaching peace, not rewriting the Ugandan Constitution or drafting a history of the conflict' (Rugunda, quoted in US Embassy Khartoum 2007). In contrast, the LRA/M 'sought to use the talks to raise issues on the root causes of the conflict', including the marginalisation of Northern Uganda and the atrocities committed during Museveni's consolidation of power in Northern

Uganda.[27] As a participant explained, 'The Acholi had very legitimate grievances against the government of President Yoweri Museveni.... So maybe the opportunity is now there for us to deal with it.'[28]

The LRA/M (2007) wanted the discussions to address solutions to the economic, social and political problems in Eastern and Northern Uganda, insisting that the Juba Peace Talks were 'the only peaceful political forum to agree on how to solve the problems identified under item 2'. For the government, the LRA/M did not have the credibility to speak for Northern Uganda, having inflicted so much suffering on its population. However, the LRA/M won the argument.

The Agreement on Comprehensive Solutions, signed 2 May 2007, understood the conflict in the context of regional marginalisation and committed the parties to a number of structural remedies. The Agreement recognised 'the regional disparities and imbalances in terms of socio-economic and infrastructural development of the country as a result of history and the conflict' (Government of Uganda and LRA/M 2007a). It outlined a diverse range of actions to be taken to make Uganda a fairer and more equal society and remedy the effects of war, such as affirmative action, land access and compensation for loss of land and livestock, political rights, the integration of insurgent forces into the UPDF, the return of IDPs, and the use of constructive and unifying language. The government had secured donor funding for the Northern Uganda Peace, Recovery and Development Plan (PRDP) prior to the Juba Peace Talks and it therefore agreed to a list of measures it could fulfil under this Plan. A government negotiator explains:

> Our entire structure of the agreement was based on what we knew we could achieve as a government. So, we didn't give any concessions in reality … [Since PRDP] had elements of what was these people's objectives to fight, of dissatisfaction against [the] government, it was a question of taking that language of theirs into what would be the PRDP projects.[29]

Agenda Item 3: Accountability and reconciliation

Following the agreement on comprehensive solutions, the negotiations quickly moved on to Item 3 of the agenda on accountability and reconciliation. When the Juba Peace Talks began in July 2006, the two negotiation teams had agreed on the concept of 'alternative justice', but still had to clarify its meaning. The government had proposed the reintegration of LRA members responsible for atrocities following amnesty and the traditional Acholi ceremony of *mato oput*. It signalled the importance of security for the LRA leadership, but did not address state-authored crimes. The initial LRA position emphasised 'the need for various actors (not least the government) to accept responsibility for causing the conflict' and proposed traditional justice rituals, compensation and the establishment of a truth and reconciliation commission (Otim and Wierda 2008, 23).

When the negotiations on Item 3 began in May 2007, the most important issue was the ICC indictments, a 'very touchy issue', which was at times thought to 'break' the negotiations.[30] Accountability issues, being inextricably linked to the personal fates of key persons, could determine whether the peace process as a whole obtained the required commitment from the conflict principals. Had the LRA leaders subscribed to the underlying premise of international justice – that those most responsible for serious international crimes must be prosecuted – there would not have been a dilemma between peace and justice. However, Kony and Otti had repeatedly called for the withdrawal of the arrest warrants and Olweny warned that the 'LRA has already become a system', and if the ICC indictees were arrested '[t]he war can only become more intensive' (LRA/M 2006). To the LRA, criminal justice processes constituted an alternative to a political solution. The government used the ICC indictments as a 'bargaining chip' by hedging future actions to obtain a UN Security Council deferral on the demobilisation and disarmament of the LRA (Afako 2010). The conflict parties thus shared the view that a negotiated peace was incompatible with criminal justice.

Faced with the arrest warrants, the LRA's refusal of the criminal justice process, and international involvement in the Talks, peace process participants worked creatively with the issue of accountability. Negotiators, mediators and observers from traditional and religious constituencies took part in a workshop on legal issues relating to Item 3 of the agenda: A Discussion around Local, National and International Justice Systems.[31] Following this workshop, participants agreed on a set of principles to guide the negotiations, including that 'a national legal and institutional framework provides a sufficient basis for ensuring accountability and reconciliation in Uganda with respect to crimes and violations committed during the conflict' (quoted in US Embassy Kampala 2007). Any solution would thus entail a justice mechanism taking place in Uganda.

The Proposed Solution

The solution – formalised in the Agreement on Accountability and Reconciliation (signed 29 June 2007) and an Annexure to the Agreement (signed 19 February 2008) – was an elaborately defined alternative justice process that would 'resolve the conflict while promoting reconciliation' (Government of Uganda and LRA/M 2007b). For this justice mechanism to create the conditions for peace, it had to accommodate both Kony's self-interest and the idea of international justice. It did not ignore ICC involvement at the Indictment stage, but worked creatively with the parameters of the Rome Statute. The Agreement's preamble thus recalled the Statute's principle of complementarity. Hottinger (2010, 15), the Swiss mediation advisor, explained:

> Following long nights of discussions I was comfortable that a solution could be found through the creation of some form of special court that would operate within Uganda. This concept was vague in the beginning. But we did have a clear idea of alternatives that could deliver some form of justice without prejudicing the ICC.

The mediators realised quickly that the LRA leadership could not be amnestied as it knew too much about the international environment to trust a promise of amnesty.[32] Furthermore, the indictments and the peace process enjoyed widespread national, regional and international attention, reflected in the presence of regional and international observers in the negotiation room. The mediators felt that 'at that level of mobilisation, you couldn't go for the Mozambican solution' – a political settlement that rehabilitated and transformed the insurgent army into a political party.[33] Given the 'new world' of peace and justice, only strong countries would be able to defend a Mozambican solution; to the mediators, 'a full blown amnesty' might not be respected, 'but only end up putting the government under pressure'.[34] After all, major powers had leaned on Nigeria to extradite Taylor in 2006.

The proposed justice mechanism reinterpreted international justice, while still offering a formal and judicial process. Given the LRA's resistance to the ICC, the drafters had to 'accommodate other things than prosecutions followed by long-term imprisonment as the model. You had to introduce other elements of accountability.'[35] The justice mechanism had five features: national proceedings, a restorative notion of accountability, an alternative penalty and sentencing regime, a focus on individual responsibility and a forward-looking victim approach.

National proceedings

National proceedings meant that nobody was going to The Hague. Instead there would be 'national legal arrangements, consisting of formal and non-formal institutions and measures for ensuring justice and reconciliation with respect to the conflict' (Government of Uganda and LRA/M 2007b). The Annexure established a truth commission and a special high court division. The former would inquire into, analyse and publicise the history and nature of the conflict, encourage truth-telling and investigate disappearances, while the latter would recognise traditional and community processes in the formal proceedings. To ensure that these processes would be Uganda-based, the government committed to undertake 'any necessary representation or legal proceedings nationally or internationally' and address 'conscientiously the question of the ICC arrest warrants' (Government of Uganda and LRA/M 2007b). These provisions directed the government to obtain a Security Council request for deferral of prosecutions and to challenge the admissibility of the case before the ICC.[36]

According to one of the Ugandan lawyers in the mediation team, the starting point for the discussions on accountability was the return of Ugandan jurisdiction over the case. His understanding was that Uganda had regained jurisdiction because the LRA/M came to the negotiation table.[37] According to Christopher Gashirabake of the government delegation,

> We agreed with ICC that it would intervene when Uganda has proved it has ignored to prosecute the rebel leaders and have [*sic*] no institutions to try

them. But we have credible judges and the courts are in place. So the ICC will not come in.

(Kazooba and agencies 2007)

Restorative accountability

The justice process was an alternative accountability process without conventional criminal procedures and punishment. The Agreement committed the parties to promote traditional justice mechanisms 'as a central part of the framework for accountability and reconciliation' and stated that 'any meaningful accountability proceedings should … promote reconciliation and encourage individuals to take personal responsibility for their conduct' (Government of Uganda and LRA/M 2007b). The framework was to provide for the 'adoption and recognition of complementary alternative justice mechanisms', which 'shall include traditional justice processes, alternative sentences, reparations, and any other formal institutions or mechanisms'.

Reconciliation was seen as the interpretive context of accountability, justice being both restorative and judicial.[38] Throughout the two agreements, therefore, accountability is semantically paired with reconciliation: the terms 'accountability' and 'reconciliation' appear 27 and 28 times, respectively, in the Agreement, and six and nine times, respectively, in the Annexure. The documents do not mention 'punishment'. In order to insulate the ordinary criminal justice system from the negotiated justice, the alternative justice process was to take place in a special division.

Alternative sentencing

The third feature was a regime of 'alternative penalties and sanctions which shall apply, and replace existing penalties' even with respect to serious crimes (Government of Uganda and LRA/M 2007b). It was orally agreed that a 'law would be passed to introduce alternative sentences', which were to reflect the gravity of the crimes, promote individual and collective reconciliation, rehabilitate offenders, take into account their admissions or other cooperation, and require them to give reparations (Civil Society Organisations for Peace in Northern Uganda 2009, 7). The focus was on reconciliation rather than punishment: provided one cooperated and showed remorse, penalties could be substantially reduced.[39] The alternative sentencing process sought to do two things: it sought to make the accountability process acceptable to the LRA high command and maintain the judicial nature of the justice process.

The sentences and penalties would be linked to a programme of rehabilitation. Offenders would undergo a programme of psycho-social counselling to restore them as human beings, and social workers, family counsellors and medical staff would be attached to the special division of the high court. These rehabilitative aspects did not make it into the formal agreements; the fact that they were a part of a sentencing policy was deemed too deviant from the established view and it was agreed that they should be introduced later.[40]

Individual responsibility

The policy emphasised the individual nature of justice. Individuals, not groups, were going to be charged, given the opportunity to respond, and rehabilitated. The traditional rituals of *ailuc*, *culo kwor*, *kayo cuk*, *mato oput*, and *tonu ci koka* were defined as taking place 'after full accountability' and were to have 'necessary modifications' (Government of Uganda and LRA/M 2007b). Individual perpetrators could not hide behind groups, but after taking individual responsibility for their actions they could be symbolically and materially reconciled with, say, clans or ethnicities. Children were, however, exempted from the justice proceedings as a group, but could, where appropriate, participate in reconciliation processes.

The first individual to go through this process was going to be Otti. He was accessible and understood the different concepts and plans involved in the alternative accountability process. There was a verbal agreement for him to come back to Uganda, be subjected to the process and send back word to Kony and the other leaders that he was OK – he had not been tortured, killed or sent to The Hague.[41] Otti was, however, killed by Kony in October 2007 (Atkinson 2010, 219; Brubacher 2010, 276), a development that revealed the extent to which the peace process relied on Otti.

Forward-looking victimhood

Finally, victims were conceptualised in a forward-looking perspective. Their suffering would be 'honour[ed]' and alleviated by 'promoting lasting peace with justice' (Government of Uganda and LRA/M 2007b), the chief means being the demobilisation of the LRA. Their dignity would not be restored by the imprisonment of their tormentors, but rather through the latter's admissions of guilt and truth-telling, combined with reparations. Accountability meant 'proceedings seeking compensation to the victim rather than just punishment to the offender' (Civil Society Organisations for Peace in Northern Uganda 2009, 7). It was the view of the mediators that there would be 'no shady deals, but you say we are not putting this person in prison because they [prisons] have no answers to victims'.[42] Thus, perpetrators should be rehabilitated not because of political expediency, but because the restoration of thousands of ex-LRA soldiers would be better for all Northern Ugandans, including the many victims. This view explains the Agreement's unusual sentence that the 'Parties agree that it is essential … to promote and facilitate [the victims'] right to contribute to society'.

Through the five features that made up a national, individual and alternative accountability system, the justice policy sought to create an overlap that offered all serious perpetrators, including the ICC indictees, rehabilitation and the possibility of being symbolically cleansed. The negotiators and mediators were aware of the need to 'sell' their proposal to the international community. The implementation of the envisaged justice mechanism depended on external actors: the Security Council needed to invoke its authority under Rome Statute Article

16 to request a deferral of prosecution for 12 months, subject to renewal.[43] Thereafter, having begun the alternative justice process, and in response to a formal admissibility challenge by the government, the PTC would return jurisdiction to Uganda. Both steps were legal within the framework of the Rome Statute. The deferral would buy Uganda time to establish the special court division, so as to be able to lodge a genuine admissibility challenge. The government delegation would only approach the Security Council once the LRA had demobilised.

International reception of the justice agreement

The Agreement on Accountability and Reconciliation prompted the OTP, PTC and Registry to convene a status conference to determine admissibility of the LRA case, which they confirmed (ICC 2007). Subsequently, the PTC sought information from the government about the nature of the special court, the role of traditional justice mechanisms and Uganda's cooperation with the Court (ICC 2008a; 2008b). Until Kony's April 2008 failure to sign the Final Peace Agreement, the government's explanations were loyal to the Juba agreements, but afterwards it expressed a commitment to arrest the LRA leaders and urged the Court to facilitate the permission of the DRC to that end (Uganda 2008a; 2008b).

The justice policy agreed in Juba provided the Prosecutor and other ICC officials with an opportunity to continue the earlier campaign to effect the indictees' marginalisation, arrest and ICC prosecution. For instance, the OTP (2007, 3) advised diplomats that the LRA leadership had regained credibility, strength and financial means as a result of the peace process. It asked them to 'contribute to their re-marginalization and to use all public occasions to recall that those 4 individuals are responsible for massive crimes'.

The ICC, and in particular the OTP, tried to influence actors with sway over the talks. It conducted outreach activities in the affected areas to reach local civil society activists (Roach 2013, 264). It published opinion pieces and gave interviews to Ugandan newspapers to reach individuals and institutions involved in the Juba process. Donors to the Talks were asked to cut their support to the Juba Initiative Fund, with non-engagement framed as a question of cooperation with the Court: 'Ultimately, the decision to uphold the law will be the decision of States Parties. If States Parties do not actively support the Court, in this area as in others, then they are actively undermining it' (Moreno-Ocampo 2009, 12).

Western embassies tended to differ from their line ministries in their approach to the Juba Peace Talks and the question of justice, with ministries embodying the justice discourse and in-country staff sympathising with the peace discourse (Ginifer 2006, 22; Perrot 2010, 198). Field staff were wary of expressing public support for the accountability agreement, but did not criticise it, taking refuge instead in the idea that it was 'an African solution to an African problem'.[44] The US embassy in Kampala prepared a public statement of support for the Agreement and joined the donor corps in January 2008 along with the EU. The embassies of the Netherlands, Norway, Sweden and the US funded the government's national consultation on the Agreement on Accountability and Reconciliation.

In the capital cities of Western members of the international community, however, the accountability agreements attracted criticism: international criminal judges condemned Uganda, and human rights NGOs called upon Uganda to abandon its commitments to the Agreement and Annexure. Amnesty International (2008a, 19; 2008b, 1) advocated the revocation of amnesties granted to more than 20,000 former insurgents and abductees and warned the Security Council that a deferral of prosecutions could 'undermine the effectiveness of the ICC and any deterrent effect it has by allowing any leader of armed opposition groups or of national armed forces … to blackmail the Security Council'.

Agenda Items 4, 5 and 6: Ceasefire, DDR and implementation

The negotiations on a permanent ceasefire (Item 4) took place after the national consultation process and built on the earlier Cessation of Hostilities Agreement. In the period between the Agreement on Accountability and Reconciliation and these negotiations, Kony had killed Otti and replaced Ojul with David Matsanga, a UK-based Ugandan, as the head of the delegation. Signed on 23 February 2008, the Agreement on a Permanent Ceasefire committed the parties to a permanent ceasefire, the assembly of LRA forces at Ri-Kwangba and a Ceasefire Monitoring Team that was to include representatives from the conflict parties, the SPLA, four African observer countries (DRC, Kenya, Tanzania and South Africa), and the UN (Government of Uganda and LRA/M 2008). Six days later, on 29 February 2008, the parties signed both Item 5 of the agenda, the Agreement on Disarmament, Demobilisation and Reintegration, and Item 6, the Agreement on Implementation and Monitoring Mechanisms. The former committed the LRA to demobilisation and the government to integrating the DDR provisions into the PRDP for Northern Uganda.

The negotiations on the last three agenda items had been observed by representatives from the four African observer countries, the EU, the US, Norway and Canada. Negotiators felt that 'sometimes in the presence of all these people we could not move things'.[45] They thus created an unofficial track of negotiations:

> Now, you see, the international community was there; they were sponsoring these things. International observers sitting there; we had the government of Kenya there, alright? Now, whereas on the face of it there were some things we were making public, at night we were having separate meetings to see how the process could move.… So, we had meetings at night with [Kony's] people, outside the framework of the peace talks. That's why sometimes it [the peace process] moved on.[46]

The Final Peace Agreement

The Final Peace Agreement was preambular in nature and incorporated all the other agreements into one document.[47] While some peace processes work towards a framework agreement with detailed provisions covering many issues, others create consensus issue by issue in a set of agreements that are ultimately ratified by a comprehensive final agreement (Bell 2006, 378). The Juba Peace Talks took the latter approach, tying the implementation of the six agreements to the signing of the Final Peace Agreement by Kony and Museveni. This event was planned for 10 April 2008, but Kony refused to appear. He had ceased communication with his peace team and the Special Envoy, but maintained contact with a group of traditional leaders, who tried to persuade him to sign the Agreement. He told them in May that he was 'annoyed' with his delegation because he had not received uniforms, ropes and butternut oil, all of which indicated to them that he was remobilising (Iya 2010, 180). In September 2007, Kony communicated several times with the Acholi Paramount Chief, Rwot Acana II, articulating a wish to get peace back on the table and explaining a failure to understand the ICC arrest warrants. A new signing date and the final deadline were set for 29 and 30 November 2008.

On 28 and 29 November 2008, the LRA/M delegation and a group of northern elders, MPs and religious leaders met the LRA leadership in Ri-Kwangba in a last attempt to persuade Kony to sign the Final Peace Agreement. In this meeting, Kony's concerns centred on the negotiated justice policy. He told them that he could not accept the Agreement on Accountability and Reconciliation since it was negotiated by Ojul whom he no longer trusted. He had understood from Chissano that Uganda would pursue a Security Council deferral request after the Accountability and Reconciliation Agreement had been signed, complaining that the lack of this action 'was a sign of bad faith' (US Embassy Kampala 2008). He said he knew the war was soon returning and asked the group to tell the government to refrain from attacking.[48] He asked for more time, another week. The Acholi leaders went straight to Juba, where they met with Machar, Chissano and the government delegation. At that point, the government and Chissano, however, had lost patience with the process, while Machar wanted to delay military action against the LRA (US Embassy Kampala 2008). Two weeks later, on 14 December 2008, Uganda's US-supported Operation Lightning Thunder reignited the war and marked the end of the Negotiation phase.

Participants' reflections on the nature of ICC involvement

The participants of the talks found the ICC activities very problematic. The following quotes illustrate the sentiments of two mediators: an Acholi observer and a government official. Contrary to the claims of the justice discourse, none of them found ICC involvement helpful.

> They [the ICC] made so many statements, during the peace process.... That's why I keep saying, these guys were determined to kill the peace talks. [To the ICC:] 'Why don't you observe, for now just observe, what is going on?'[49]

> They were undermining the process. They were waging a propaganda campaign. [Interviewer: In which way?] By saying 'Oh, Kony is rearming.'[50]

> After all, the primary responsibility to deal with the question [of accountability] actually lies within the states, and unless the state is actually unable and unwilling.... So, we should recognize this kind of efforts, and this is what I was sharing with other people: 'Look, international community, Uganda is trying to make a break-through; let's not criticise, let's support it. Let's support what is happening in Uganda.... Let's support it, you know?' To me even when the country addresses the question of impunity, the message sings to me much louder when trials are being conducted nationally.[51]

> I think the ICC should have really given peace a chance. I think peace would have been more important than anything. And to go to the definition of justice, to me justice is done when two conflicting people go before somebody they accept and whatever that person decides, they find acceptable to them.[52]

Juba Peace Talks: Implementation phase (15 December 2008–11 July 2011)

Although the Juba process did not achieve a political settlement, a fragile peace settled on Northern Uganda. The war was 'exported' to the DRC, Central African Republic (CAR) and Southern Sudan (Allen *et al.* 2010), the LRA killing more than 1,000 and displacing over 200,000 Congolese civilians in retaliation for Operation Lightning Thunder. In Northern Uganda, up to 75 per cent of the displaced had returned to their previous homes by December 2008 (Marino 2008, 1). However, an LRA at large provided a sense of insecurity, a common sentiment being 'We have peace but we do not have security' (International Alert 2013, 17).

In spite of the failure of the peace process, the Ugandan government decided to implement selected provisions of the Juba agreements, in particular the PRDP and the establishment of a special division of the high court, both of which were heavily donor funded. The Implementation phase reflected a contradictory mix of accommodation and war, which had characterised the Ugandan approach to the LRA since the beginning of the insurgency.

The PRDP, launched in October 2007, was explicitly linked to the Juba Peace Talks and allocated part of its funding to the implementation of aspects of the peace agreements on comprehensive solutions and DDR. The Plan aimed, among other things, to disarm and reintegrate former insurgents, de-mine areas, provide policing, re-establish the judiciary, disarm local defence units and resettle IDPs. With a view to the justice policy, it also sought to 'explore' traditional reconciliation initiatives.

The International Crimes Division of the High Court (ICD) was established in July 2008 formally as the fulfilment of government obligations to the Agreement on Accountability and Reconciliation (Mukiibi 2014). Contrary to the requirement for constitutional incorporation of the Special Tribunal of Kenya, Uganda's

ICD was set up administratively and without parliamentary endorsement. Its creation suited factions in the security establishment who had never approved of the amnesty law, such as Museveni, Mbabazi and other hardliners. There was therefore nothing alternative, traditional or conciliatory about the ICD. Instead it was an ordinary criminal court providing retributive justice.

The judiciary saw the ICD as 'derived from the Complementarity provision of the Rome Statute' and potentially becoming a regional criminal court, the 'Hague in Africa' (Ogoola quoted in Nouwen 2013, 181). Although it represented Uganda's willingness and ability to prosecute ICC crimes, the ICD received a frosty welcome from the Court (Dolan 2008, 3).[53] Accusing Uganda of creating forum-shopping opportunities for the LRA, the Prosecutor insisted that the ICD prosecute other LRA rebels (ICC 2009, 6). The head of the ICD confirmed this focus on non-indictees, but emphasised that cases are identified by the Director of Public Prosecutions.[54] Consistent with the hardliner approach within the government, the ICD's first case was against Thomas Kwoyelo, an LRA commander captured in 2009.

The Juba process represents the 'new world' of peace and justice. Its mediators navigated without a map, formulating a path to political settlement that combined their interpretation of the complementarity provision of the Rome Statute with the idea of a national alternative accountability process. By the time the Negotiation phase ended, the LRA leadership had not felt able to commit to the settlement, citing difficulties with understanding the envisaged justice process. Dominic Ongwen, ICC indictee and then second-in-command, stated that senior LRA commanders would kill Kony if he signed the Final Peace Agreement without 'clearly defined packages and positions outlining the future' (US Embassy Kampala 2008). This intra-LRA situation begs the question of how much ICC involvement affected the outcome of the Talks, understood both interactively and constitutively, as opposed to other factors. The next chapter chases this question, building an understanding of why the Juba Peace Talks failed and analysing the impact of ICC involvement on the peace process and its outcome.

Notes

1 The OTP (2004b, para. 1) dates the beginning of investigation to 28 July 2004 in order to argue that the decision to investigate was based on a 'thorough analysis of available information'.
2 Interview with member of the mediation team, Kampala, April 2011.
3 Amnesty (Amendment) Act, 2000.
4 The first two paragraphs draw mainly on Afako (2009) and Atkinson (2010).
5 Interview with member of mediation team, April 2011.
6 Interview with member of the LRA/M delegation, Kampala, March 2011.
7 Interview with close observer, June 2010; interview with member of the mediation team, 19 April 2011.
8 Commas have been inserted in the first and the last sections of the quote.
9 Interview with close observer, June 2010. See also Simonse *et al.* (2010).
10 Interview with close observer, May 2010; interview with member of the mediation team, February 2013.

11 Interview with member of the government delegation, May 2011.
12 Pulkol had too much confidential information to have come on his own initiative; his explanation that he was sent by Museveni therefore seems genuine.
13 Interview with members of the mediation team, April 2011 and February 2013.
14 Apart from the two LRA insurgents, the LRA peace team consisted of Martin Ojul (chairman), Obonyo Olweny, Chrispus Ayena Odongo, Rock Okidi, Peter Ongom, Otim Okullo, Justin Labeja, Joshua Otukene, Yusuf Okongo Adek, Wilson Owiny, Rei Achama, Dennis Okirot and Sunday Achaya.
15 The delegation also included the head of the Chieftaincy of Military Intelligence, Col. Leopold Kyanda; the Director of the External Security Organisation, Angalefo Maku' Iga; the Director of the Internal Security Organisation, Mr Makumbi; Col. Otema Awany; the Principal State Attorney, Mr Gakirabake; and Mr Kyomukama, a government lawyer.
16 Interviews with members of the LRA/M delegation, March 2011.
17 Interviews with participant observer, June 2010 and with member of the mediation team, February 2013.
18 Interview with LRA/M negotiator, March 2011.
19 Individual interviews with two members of the LRA/M delegation, March 2011.
20 Interviews with members of the LRA/M delegation, March 2011; interview with member of mediation team, April 2011.
21 Interview with member of the LRA delegation, March 2011.
22 Interview with close observer of the talks, March 2011.
23 Interview with member of the mediation team, 31 May 2010.
24 Interview with member of mediation team, April 2011. A staff member of one of the donors to the Juba Initiative Fund similarly stated that most countries at this point were pessimistic about talking to the LRA; interview in April 2011.
25 *Mato oput* is a traditional Acholi justice ritual that involves the admission of guilt and symbolic healing. During the *mato oput* ceremony, both perpetrator and victim are required to drink a local brew, *kwete*, mixed with a bitter-tasting *mato* root. By consuming the 'bitterness of vengeance', the afflicted parties are moved beyond hatred, distrust and hostilities. See Roach (2013).
26 The Cessation of Hostilities Agreement was renewed in six addendums and further supported by the Extension of the Cessation of Hostilities Agreement and an agreed Declaration on LRA Crossing River Nile.
27 Presentation, Wilton Park conference, September 2010.
28 Interview with Juba participant, April 2011.
29 Interview with government negotiator, May 2011.
30 Interview with observer participant, June 2010.
31 Interview with observer participant, June 2010.
32 Interview with member of the mediation team, April 2011; interview with member of the LRA/M delegation, March 2011.
33 Interview with member of the mediation team, January 2013.
34 Interview with member of the mediation team, January 2013.
35 Interview with member of mediation team, February 2013.
36 Interviews with member of the LRA/M delegation (March 2011), member of the government delegation (May 2011), and member of the mediation team (February 2013).
37 Interview with member of the mediation team, April 2011.
38 Interviews with observer participant, June 2010, and member of the mediation team, February 2013.
39 Interview with member of the mediation team, February 2013.
40 Interview with member of the mediation team, February 2013.
41 Interview with member of the mediation team, February 2013.
42 Interview with member of the mediation team, February 2013.
43 Interview with member of the government delegation (May 2011), member of the

LRA/M delegation (March 2011), and member of the mediation team (February 2013).

44 Interview with donor representative, Kampala, April 2011.

45 Interview with member of the government negotiation team, May 2011.

46 Interview with member of the government negotiation team, May 2011.

47 The Final Peace Agreement was preceded by an agreed Implementation Schedule for the Final Peace, signed on 23 March 2008.

48 Interview with Acholi leader, June 2010.

49 Interview with member of the mediation team, April 2011.

50 Interview with member of the mediation team, February 2013.

51 Interview with observer participant, June 2010.

52 Interview with government official, who had spoken to Kony many times over the years, April 2011.

53 Interview with donor representative, Kampala, April 2011.

54 Interview with Justice Kiiza, head of the Special Division of the High Court, Kampala, 3 June 2010. See also Nouwen (2013, 179–187).

References

Aduk, Flora. 2005. 'Hoping for a Brighter Day.' *The Daily Monitor*. http://allafrica.com/stories/200511080615.html.

Afako, Barney. 2006. 'Not a Crime to Talk: Legal Aspects of Dialogue with the Lord's Resistance Army.' Paper on file with the author. doi:www.jurisafrica.org.

Afako, Barney. 2009, 16 April. 'No Quick Fix for the LRA.' *Guardian*.

Afako, Barney. 2010. 'Negotiating in the Shadow of Justice.' In *Protracted Conflict, Elusive Peace: Initiatives to End the Violence in Northern Uganda. Accord*, edited by Elizabeth Drew, Update to: 21–23. London: Conciliation Resources.

Allen, Tim. 2006. *Trial Justice: The International Criminal Court and the Lord's Resistance Army. African Arguments*. London: Zed.

Allen, Tim, Frederick Laker, Holly Porter, and Mareike Schomerus. 2010. 'Postscript: A Kind of Peace and an Exported War.' In *The Lord's Resistance Army: Myth and Reality*, edited by Tim Allen and Koen Vlassenroot, 279–288. London and New York: Zed Books Ltd.

Amnesty International. 2008a. *Letter to Security Council*. www.amnesty.org/en/library/asset/AFR59/003/2008/en/052ed470-1125-11dd-a414-a101e24af105/afr590032008eng.pdf.

Amnesty International. 2008b. *Uganda: Agreement and Annex on Accountability and Comprehensive Solutions Fall Short of a Comprehensive Plan to End Impunity. AFR 59/001/2008*. London: Amnesty International.

Anderson, Janet. 2006. 'World Court Faces Biggest Challenge.' Institute for War and Peace Reporting, *Africa Report* No. 67, June 17. https://iwpr.net/global-voices/world-court-faces-biggest-challenge.

Apuuli, Kasaija Phillip. 2007. 'Taking Stock of the First Arrest Warrants of the International Criminal Court.' *African Centre for the Constructive Resolution of Disputes (ACCORD)* 7 (1): 43–62.

Atkinson, Ronald R. 2010. '"The Realists in Juba"? An Analysis of the Juba Peace Talks.' In *The Lord's Resistance Army: Myth and Reality*, edited by Tim Allen and Koen Vlassenroot, 205–222. London and New York: Zed Books Ltd.

AU Peace and Security Council. 2009. *Report of the Chairperson of the Commission on the AU Observation Mission for Northern Uganda and Conflict Affected Areas, Peace and Security Council, 189th Meeting, 21 May 2009, Addis Ababa*. Addis Ababa: African Union.

Baaré, Anton. 2008. 'Negotiating Security Issues in the Juba Process.' In *Negotiating Disarmament: Reflections on Guns, Fighters and Armed Violence in Peace Processes*, edited by Cate Buchanan, 2: 20–32. Geneva: Centre for Humanitarian Dialogue.

BBC. 2006, 18 May. 'Uganda "Must Arrest" Rebel Leader.' *BBC*.

Bell, Christine. 2006. 'Peace Agreements: Their Nature and Legal Status.' *The American Journal of International Law* 100 (2): 373–412.

Branch, Adam. 2007. 'Uganda's Civil War and the Politics of ICC Intervention.' *Ethics & International Affairs* 21 (2): 179.

Brubacher, Matthew. 2010. 'The ICC Investigation of the Lord's Resistance Army: An Insider's View.' In *The Lord's Resistance Army: Myth and Reality*, edited by Tim Allen and Koen Vlassenroot, 262–277. London and New York: Zed Books Ltd.

Checchi, Francesco. 2006. 'Humanitarian Interventions in Northern Uganda: Based on What Evidence?' *Humanitarian Exchange* 36: 7–11.

Civil Society Organisations for Peace in Northern Uganda. 2009. *The Juba Peace Initiative (JPI) July 2006–March 2008: Analysis of the Validity and Applicability of the Juba Agreements in the Absence of a Signature on the Final Agreement*. CSOPNU Briefing Paper March 2009. Copy on file with the author.

Council of the European Union. 2006. *Council Conclusions on Uganda*, Brussels, 15 May. www.eu2006.at/en/News/Council_Conclusions/1505Uganda.pdf.

Dak, James Gatdet. 2008, 19 June. 'UN Security Council to Discuss Uganda Peace Process.' *Sudan Tribune*.

Dolan, Chris. 2008. *Imposed Justice and the Need for Sustainable Peace in Uganda. Presentation to the Beyond Juba/AMANI Forum Training in Transitional Justice for Parliamentarians*. Refugee Law Project, Makerere University, Uganda. www.refugeelawproject.org/seminars/imposingjustice.pdf.

Dolan, Chris. 2009. *Social Torture: The Case of Northern Uganda, 1986–2006. Human Rights in Context*. New York and Oxford: Berghahn Books.

Egeland, Jan. 2010. 'Interview: Jan Egeland. The United Nations and Juba.' In *Initiatives to End the Violence in Northern Uganda: 2002–2009 and the Juba process*, edited by Elizabeth Drew, 19–20. London: Conciliation Resources.

Ginifer, Jeremy. 2006. *Internal Report of DfID's Engagement with the Conflict in Northern Uganda*. London: Department for International Development. www.oecd.org/countries/uganda/36503954.pdf.

Government of Uganda. 2003. *Referral of the Situation Concerning the Lord's Resistance Army*. Kampala: Government of Uganda.

Government of Uganda and LRA/M. 2006, 26 August. *Agreement on Cessation of Hostilities between the Government of Uganda and the Lord's Resistance Army/Movement*. https://peacemaker.un.org/uganda-cessation-hostilities-LRAM2006.

Government of Uganda, and LRA/M. 2007a, 2 May. *Agreement on Comprehensive Solutions*. https://peacemaker.un.org/uganda-comprehensive-solutions2007.

Government of Uganda and LRA/M. 2007b, 29 June. *Agreement on Accountability and Reconciliation*. https://peacemaker.un.org/uganda-accountability-reconciliation2007.

Government of Uganda, and LRA/M. 2008, 23 February. *Agreement on a Permanent Ceasefire*. https://peacemaker.un.org/uganda-permanent-ceasefire2008.

Hendrickson, Dylan, and Kennedy Tumutegyereize. 2012. *Dealing with Complexity in Peace Negotiations: Reflections on the Lord's Resistance Army and the Juba Peace Talks*. London: Conciliation Resources.

Hottinger, Julian. 2010. 'Interview: Julian Hottinger. Perspectives of a Mediator.' In *Initiatives to End the Violence in Northern Uganda: 2002–2009 and the Juba process*, edited by Elizabeth Drew, Update to: 15. London: Conciliation Resources.

International Alert. 2013. *Monitoring the Impact of the Peace, Recovery and Development Plan on Peace and Conflict in Acholi and Lango, 2011–2012*. International Alert.

International Criminal Court. 2007. *Transcript. Status Conference, 11 December 2007 (ICC-02/04–01/15-T-3-ENG ET WT 11–12–2007 1/57 SZ PT)*. The Hague: International Criminal Court.

International Criminal Court. 2008a. *Request for Information from the Republic of Uganda on the Status of Execution of the Warrants of Arrest. Public Document.* The Hague: International Criminal Court.

International Criminal Court. 2008b. *Request for Further Information from the Republic of Uganda on the Status of Execution of the Warrants of Arrest. Public Document.* The Hague: International Criminal Court.

International Criminal Court. 2009. *Fifteenth Diplomatic Briefing of the International Criminal Court. Compilation of Statements*. Hague: The International Criminal Court.

IRIN. 2006a, 12 June. 'Prospects for Peace Talks between Gov't and LRA Uncertain.' *IRIN*.

IRIN. 2006b, 2 June. 'Give Peace a Chance, Northern Leaders Tell ICC.' *IRIN*.

IRIN. 2006c, 18 July. 'Juba Talks to Focus on Cessation of Hostilities.' *IRIN*.

Iya, Ronald. 2010. 'Encountering Kony: A Madi Perspective.' In *The Lord's Resistance Army: Myth and Reality*, edited by Tim Allen and Koen Vlassenroot, 177–184. London and New York: Zed Books Ltd.

Kakaire, Apollo. 2006, 15 April. 'Ugandan Mediator Critical of ICC Indictments.' *Institute for War and Peace Reporting*.

Kazooba, Charles, and agencies. 2007. 'LRA Threatens War over Museveni, Kabila Pact.' *The New Times*. www.newtimes.co.rw/news/index.php?i=1286&a=897.

LRA/M. 2006. 'Opening Speech', 14 June. Reprinted in *The New Vision*, Kampala, 15 July. Copy on file with author.

LRA/M. 2007. *A Synopsis on Uganda Peace Talks*. Vol. 8 February. http://groups.yahoo.com/neo/groups/AfricansPolitics/conversations/topics/965.

Marino, Jonathan. 2008. *Is the PRDP Politics as Usual? Update on the Implementation of Uganda's Peace, Recovery and Development Plan*. Kampala: Beyond Juba Project. www.beyondjuba.org/BJP1/briefing_papers/PRDP_Briefing_Note.pdf.

Moreno-Ocampo, Luis. 2006, 19 June. 'A Global Web of Justice Is Up and Running, the International Criminal Court.' *International Herald Tribune*.

Moreno-Ocampo, Luis. 2009. 'Building a Future on Peace and Justice: The International Criminal Court.' In *Building a Future on Peace and Justice: Studies on Transitional Justice, Peace and Development*, edited by Kai Ambos, Judith Large, and Marieke Wierda, 9–13. Berlin and Heidelberg: Springer-Verlag.

Mukasa, Henry. 2005, November 30. 'Otti Wants Talks.' *The New Vision*.

Mukasa, Henry. 2006, May 16. 'Museveni Gives Joseph Kony Final Peace Offer.' *The New Vision*.

Mukiibi, Moses. 2014. *Key-Note Address by Hon. Justice Moses Mukiibi, head of the International Crimes Division of the High Court of Uganda at Parliamentary Conference to Give Full Effect to the Principle of Complementarity in Uganda and the Democratic Republic of Congo*. New York: Parliamentarians for Global Action.

Mwenda, Andrew. 2010. 'Uganda's Politics of Foreign Aid and Violent Conflict: The Political Uses of the LRA Rebellion.' In *The Lord's Resistance Army: Myth and*

Reality, edited by Tim Allen and Koen Vlassenroot, 45–58. London and New York: Zed Books Ltd.

Nolen, Stephanie. 2005, May 7. 'Peace First, Justice Later?' *The Globe and Mail.*

Nouwen, Sarah M H. 2013. *Complementarity in the Line of Fire: The Catalysing Effect of the International Criminal Court in Sudan.* Cambridge: Cambridge University Press.

Nouwen, Sarah M H, and Wouter G Werner. 2011. 'Doing Justice to the Political: The International Criminal Court in Uganda and Sudan.' *The European Journal of International Law* 21 (4). Oxford University Press: 941–965. doi:http://dx.doi.org/10.1093/ejil/chq064.

Nyakairu, Frank. 2006, July 2006. 'Museveni Amnesty to Kony Illegal – International Criminal Court.' *The Monitor.*

Office of the Prosecutor. 2004a. *President of Uganda Refers Situation Concerning the Lord's Resistance Army (LRA) to the ICC.* Press Release. The Hague: International Criminal Court.

Office of the Prosecutor. 2004b. *Prosecutor of the International Criminal Court Opens an Investigation into Northern Uganda.* Press Release. Doc. ICC-OTP-20. The Hague: International Criminal Court.

Office of the Prosecutor. 2006. *Report on the Activities Performed during the First Three Years (June 2003–June 2006).* The Hague: International Criminal Court.

Office of the Prosecutor. 2007. *Statement by Mr. Luis Moreno-Ocampo, Prosecutor of the International Criminal Court, Eleventh Diplomatic Briefing of the International Criminal Court. The Hague 10 October 2007.* The Hague: International Criminal Court.

Otim, Michael, and Marieke Wierda. 2008. 'Justice at Juba: International Obligations and Local Demands in Northern Uganda.' In *Courting Conflict? Justice, Peace and the ICC in Africa*, edited by Nicholas Waddell and Phil Clark, 21–28. London: Royal African Society.

Perrot, Sandrine. 2010. 'Northern Uganda: A "Forgotten Conflict" Again? The Impact of the Internationalization of the Resolution Process.' In *The Lord's Resistance Army: Myth and Reality*, edited by Tim Allen and Koen Vlassenroot, 204–288. London and New York: Zed Books Ltd.

Peskin, Victor. 2009. 'Caution and Confrontation in the International Criminal Court's Pursuit of Accountability in Uganda and Sudan.' *Human Rights Quarterly* 31 (3): 655–691.

Roach, Steven C. 2013. 'Multilayered Justice in Northern Uganda: ICC Intervention and Local Procedures of Accountability.' *International Criminal Law Review* 13 (1): 249–268.

Schabas, William A. 2011. *An Introduction to the International Criminal Court.* 4th edn. Cambridge: Cambridge University Press.

Schomerus, Mareike. 2010a. 'Chasing the Kony Story.' In *The Lord's Resistance Army: Myth and Reality*, edited by Tim Allen and Koen Vlassenroot, 93–112. London and New York: Zed Books Ltd.

Schomerus, Mareike. 2010b. '"A Terrorist Is Not a Person Like Me"; An Interview with Joseph Kony.' In *The Lord's Resistance Army: Myth and Reality*, edited by Tim Allen and Koen Vlassenroot, 113–131. London and New York: Zed Books Ltd.

Schomerus, Mareike, and Betty Acan Ogwaro. 2010. 'Searching for Solutions in Juba: An Overview.' In *Initiatives to End the Violence in Northern Uganda: 2002–2009 and the Juba process*, edited by Elizabeth Drew. Vol. 11 Update to. London: Conciliation Resources.

Sheikh, Fawzia. 2005, May 26. 'A Road to Hell, Paved with Good Intentions?' *Inter Press Service.*

Simonse, Simon, Willemijn Verkoren, and Gerd Junne. 2010. 'NGO Involvement in the Juba Peace Talks: The Role and Dilemmas of IKV Pax Christi.' In *The Lord's Resistance Army: Myth and Reality*, edited by Tim Allen and Koen Vlassenroot, 223–241. London and New York: Zed Books Ltd.

The Monitor. 2006, 25 May. 'I Am Not a Terrorist, I Am a Freedom Fighter, Says Kony.' *The Monitor*.

The New Vision. 2006, July 12. 'Kony, Otti Skip Talks.' *The New Vision*.

The Sudan Tribune. 2006. 'MPs Demand Ugandan Army Withdrawal from South Sudan.' *The Sudan Tribune*. www.sudantribune.com/spip.php?article18849.

Uganda, Republic of. 2008a. *[Reply to] Request for Information from the Republic of Uganda on the Statute of the Execution of the Warrants of Arrest*, 27 March. Doc. ADM/70/269.

Uganda, Republic of. 2008b. *[Reply to] Request for Further Information from the Republic of Uganda on the Status of Execution of the Warrants of Arrest*, 9 July. Doc. ADM/70/269.

Unger, Thomas, and Marieke Wierda. 2009. 'Pursuing Justice in Ongoing Conflict: A Discussion of Current Practice.' In *Building a Future on Peace and Justice: Studies on Transitional Justice, Peace and Development*, edited by Kai Ambos, Judith Large, and Marieke Wierda, 263–302. Berlin and Heidelberg: Springer-Verlag.

US Embassy Kampala. 2007. *Northern Uganda Notes (June 4–16 2007)*. Vol. 07Kampala1. wikileaks.org.

US Embassy Kampala. 2008. *Northern Uganda: Kony Living in A Fool's Paradise (08KAMPALA1579)*. wikileaks.org.

US Embassy Khartoum. 2006a. *NCP and SPLM Hold Three-Day Official Meeting*. Vol. 06Khartoum. wikileaks.org.

US Embassy Khartoum. 2006b. *LRA Negotiators in Town; Ugandans Yet to Come*. wikileaks.org.

US Embassy Khartoum. 2006c. *GOSS Contacts with the Lord's Resistance Army (LRA)*. wikileaks.org.

US Embassy Khartoum. 2006d. *LRA Talks: UN Begins Technical Assistance*. wikileaks.org.

US Embassy Khartoum. 2007. *Sudan/Uganda/DRC: Peace Talks Resume in Juba*. wikileaks.org.

Vision Reporter. 2005, October 22. 'Ban Amnesty Law.' *The New Vision*.

Vision Reporter. 2006a, May 31. 'Kony Talks Set for Juba.' *The New Vision*.

Vision Reporter. 2006b, June 5. 'Museveni Gives Kony Amnesty.' *The New Vision*.

Wasike, Alfred. 2003. 'Museveni Backs IGG on Wealth Disclosure.' *The New Vision*. www.newvision.co.ug/new_vision/news/1254409/museveni-backs-igg-wealth-disclosure.

4 Narratives, justice and the return to war

Our mandate is judicial. Neither the OTP nor the ICC are parties to the talks.
Luis Moreno-Ocampo, ICC Prosecutor, Eighth Diplomatic Briefing, The Hague, 26 October 2006

They [ICC officials] made so many statements during the peace process. That's why I keep saying, these guys were determined to kill the peace process.
Member of the mediation team, interviewed April 2011

In line with the book's theoretical model, ICC involvement in Uganda followed the first four involvement stages of Membership, Preliminary Examination, Investigation, and Indictment. Of these, Stages 2–4 (from Preliminary Examination to Indictment) were an active form of involvement. The peace process followed the Pre-Negotiation, Negotiation, and Implementation phases, although the government's unilateral and selective implementation of the Juba agreements took place in the context of a return to war. The two processes of ICC involvement and peacemaking interacted in numerous ways, representing the UN Secretary-General's 'new world' of peace and justice.

This world revealed a peacemaking landscape with new features, such as the Rome Statute, ICC arrest warrants, advocacy by the ICC Prosecutor and international insistence on criminal accountability for LRA atrocities. Fearing that the international road maps would lead to nowhere, negotiators and mediators sought to walk a new path through the contested terrain. These efforts ended in December 2008, when the Ugandan army launched Operation Lightning Thunder against the LRA. Measured against the goal of agreeing a political settlement that demobilises the LRA and brings 'negative' peace, the Juba process became a dead end. Having traced the steps of this path in the previous chapter, this chapter provides a deeper understanding of Juba's judicialised peacemaking. It analyses how judicialisation by the ICC affected the Talks and explains why the Talks failed.

Scholarly claims about the nature and effects of the interaction between the Ugandan peace and justice processes tend to be general or abstract, and mainly focused on the Indictment phase. The arrest warrants have been described as a 'stumbling block' to peace (Atkinson 2010, 212) and a 'sticking point' in the talks (Apuuli 2008, 803; Olupot 2010). However, without showing how and why this happened, such claims fail to persuade the proponents of international justice who dismiss them as 'cynical' political realism that seek peace 'by appeasing the powerful' (Akhavan 2009, 625). Moving closer to the identification of mechanisms, some scholars propose interactive effects such as attracting the LRA to the negotiations, preventing the rebel leaders' direct participation in the negotiations, and removing their incentives for a post-conflict life. Others advance constitutive claims, arguing that ICC involvement 'completely changed the space for peace initiatives in Northern Uganda' (Simonse *et al.* 2010, 227–228). And some argue that the ICC 'played a role in ending the war exactly because it drew attention to a situation that the international community had disregarded' (Akhavan 2009, 645).

Such 'thin' mechanism-based arguments about the Juba Peace Talks suffer from a lack of clarity about how the mechanisms work or a failure to demonstrate them empirically: how exactly would international attention ensure a political settlement, and how did representation through a delegation prevent it? What did a closed political space entail and in what ways did it affect the Talks? The Kenya Dialogue achieved a settlement although the two conflict principals did not participate directly, so it is clearly possible. It is also clearly possible to be lavished with international attention without agreeing a solution, as the Middle East conflict demonstrates. Thus, explanations for the effects of ICC involvement need to rely on empirical 'depth', that is, based on actions that are analysed as meaningful to its actors.

The chapter has two parts. The first part analyses the ways in which ICC involvement affected the peace process, identifying five interactive and constitutive effects. The second part proposes an explanation of why the peace process failed, arguing that moderates were defeated by extremists within each conflict party. These immediate causes, however, cannot be understood independently of the nature of the ICC's judicialisation as the high level of ICC involvement dealt Juba's moderates a bad hand: conflict parties had agency to fail the peace process, but no authority to take decisions that could create the necessary turning point. The chapter concludes by examining alternative explanations.

Part 1 How ICC involvement affected the peace process

This part of the chapter identifies and analyses five interactive and constitutive effects of ICC involvement on the peace process in Juba. Some effects were associated with the beginning of active ICC involvement, while others emerged once indictments had been issued. Most effects interacted with the Pre-Negotiation and Negotiation phases. The extent to which these different effects impacted on the peace process outcome is discussed in the second part of the chapter. The effects of ICC involvement were: 1) the militarisation of the conflict since the government referral; 2) the delegation of discursive authority in Stage 2 (Preliminary Examination), which in Stage 4 (Indictment) enabled the Prosecutor to launch a campaign against the Talks and constructed the sense that the ICC 'acquitted' the UPDF; 3) the creation of a sticking point, given the LRA leaders' approach to the arrest warrants; 4) the depoliticisation and decontestation of justice; and 5) the delegation of politico-legal authority in the Indictment stage.

Militarisation of the conflict

Since December 2003, the government and the Court had been engaged in a relationship of mutual constitution between claimant and court (see Lund and Sikor 2009). By self-referring, the government sought legitimisation by the ICC of its military pursuit of the LRA (Branch 2011; Freeland 2015; Nouwen 2012). The referral decision had taken place in the context of 'immense' popular, civil society, donor and UN pressure to settle the conflict peacefully and politically (Refugee Law Project 2004, 2; see also Mpagi 2003; US Embassy UN 2006b, para. 2), but ICC involvement enabled the UPDF's continuing counter-insurgency. The OTP provided legitimation of the military solution when taking ICC involvement to the Investigation stage. At the same time, involvement in Uganda constituted the ICC as a legitimate authority: politico-legal institutions need claimants in order to translate their power into authority.

At the Indictment stage, the arrest warrants made the military pursuit of the LRA seem appropriate. Once the warrants were issued, the Prosecutor called repeatedly on regional and non-regional governments to arrest the indictees. He thereby sought to militarise the conflict internationally in order to prosecute its crimes. The approach of the OTP and government hardliners thus converged: the LRA's continued existence was understood as a military problem.

The shared military approach, the one-sided prosecution and the narrative of LRA culpability enabled the OTP and the government to develop rapport. As a result, the Prosecutor ignored or underestimated the government's role as a conflict party (Branch 2017) and relied on government actors to inform him of progress at the negotiation table: he opened 'channels of communication' about the Juba Peace Talks and promised to 'stay apprised of developments in these negotiations' (OTP 2006, 17). The sourcing of information from one conflict party may have influenced the Prosecutor in his understanding of the LRA, including of Kony's intentions in the negotiations.

The government and the OTP continued their collaboration on an internationalised military approach in the Implementation phase. For instance, in July 2009, the Prosecutor met with the president, the respective Security and Defence Ministers, the Attorney-General, and Okello Oryem, who was Minister of State for Foreign Affairs and one of the Juba negotiators, to discuss 'the need for enhanced international support for arrest efforts' (ICC 2009, para. 12).

Delegation of discursive authority

Stage 2 involvement transferred discursive authority over the LRA problem from the Ugandan state to the ICC: before the government's ICC referral, the discourse about the LRA belonged primarily to the government and the UPDF. The government had consistently denied that the LRA had any political objectives (Branch 2005; Finnström 2008; Schomerus 2007), a narrative that excluded the rebels from the public sphere. In government and army discourse, LRA rebels were portrayed as terrorists, bandits and 'hyenas', wild creatures that symbolise vitality, power, danger, death and sorcery (Finnström 2008, 114). This narrative was validated by the inclusion of the LRA on the US and EU terrorist lists in 2001 and 2002, respectively.

The OTP entered this discursive space when it launched a preliminary examination in mid-2003. It initially sought to adopt a low public profile 'in an effort to address concerns expressed by local leaders and demonstrate respect for on-going peace talks' (OTP 2006, 3). Signalling a relatively open approach, the Prosecutor expressed awareness of 'local initiatives' to find 'negotiated solutions' to the LRA war and wanted to 'ensure that international justice plays a proper role in these efforts' (OTP 2004, 5). In April 2005, he declared that '[as] soon as there is a solution to end the violence and if the prosecution is not serving the interest of justice, then my duty is to stop investigation and prosecution' (quoted in *The New Vision* 2005). He added that although immunity is not possible, the 'main interest of the victims now is their life'.

Museveni's security guarantee in the Pre-Negotiation phase changed the OTP's approach to Ugandan peacemaking. The scenario of Uganda 'ensur[ing] Kony's security' came into normative conflict with the core idea of international justice, the duty to prosecute. If Kony and the other LRA leaders enjoyed an amnestied return to civilian life, it would imply impunity, a 'blackmailing' of humanity by terrorists, and law subjugated by power politics. The Prosecutor's response to Museveni's security guarantee illuminates the fact that discursive authority had been transferred from the national to the international level.

The narrative of Kony's real intentions

The OTP responded to its normative conflict by engaging in what mediators describe as a 'propaganda campaign'.[1] The campaign sought to render the peace process meaningless by providing a narrative about Joseph Kony's real intentions: the LRA leader used the Talks to gain a space to regroup and rearm his rebels and therefore was not sincerely interested in peace. By implication, the Talks became futile. The narrative would appear at least 28 times in 2006, and seven times in 2007.[2] Through its frequent articulation, it created a discursive environment within which only naïve persons could believe that the Talks could lead to a political settlement.

The narrative originated in government and UPDF discourse. It appeared for the first time in June 2002 in an editorial in the government-controlled publication *The New Vision*, in the context of the counter-insurgency Operation Iron Fist and Rome Statute ratification. The editorial stated:

> Negotiation with Kony and the LRA failed in 1995. Kony only used the opportunity to regroup, recruit and rearm. Since then, when the LRA is

> under military pressure, it retreats to the Sudan. When the heat is off, they come back. Now there is a chance to finish Kony for good.
>
> (Vision Reporter 2002)

The narrative served the purpose of legitimising the hardliner government strategy of pursuing the LRA militarily: if Kony was insincere, negotiations were futile and coercive means the only remaining option. In June, July and August 2006 the narrative was articulated nine times by the Prosecutor and 11 times by the Government, the UPDF and *The New Vision* editors. These months covered the decision by the government's moderate wing to enter negotiations and the difficult beginning following the LRA/M opening statement. In late 2007, the LRA refuted the claim twice in the local media.

Evidence disproving that Kony was using the Juba Peace Talks to mobilise for a war does not, by itself, prove that he wanted peace. But it highlights the possibility that the LRA was a serious participant in the peace process. Atkinson (2009, 16) argues that the claim that Kony used the Talks to regroup and rearm is 'almost surely inaccurate'. Information from former abductees and the LRA shows, he argues, that the rebels were training 'virtually no new abductees' as fighters and had not been receiving arms and supplies from their patron, the Sudanese government. If the LRA leaders were using the Talks to prepare for war, it is strange that they declared a unilateral ceasefire in August 2006 to 'express the LRA's seriousness' and moved their troops to the assembly points following the Cessation of Hostilities Agreement. Furthermore, the LRA only left their camp in Garamba National Park after they were attacked during Operation Lightning Thunder in December 2008. The group had received many high-profile visitors there during the course of the peace process and surely knew that its location must be known to the government.

The regrouping and rearming narrative delegitimised the peace process. As a Court representative and outsider to the conflict, the Prosecutor was associated with impartiality and objectivity. His narratives were thus believable as truths. Moreover, he had the ear of the donors, telling them:

> It is confirmed that Kony used the Juba peace talks to gain time and support, to rearm and attack again. We have collected information indicating that at the end of 2007, Joseph Kony issued orders to abduct 1,000 persons to expand the ranks of the LRA.
>
> (ICC 2008, para. 6)

The Prosecutor's advocacy affected the international community's willingness to morally and financially support the peace process. The AU, UN and donors (bar Switzerland) gave 'Egeland's rogue project' a hostile reception: the UN did not want to provide mediation support and wanted to be left out of the Cessation of Hostilities Agreement; only OCHA offered to manage the Juba Initiative Fund. The AU supported the process diplomatically only after receiving a request to that end by Chissano. Throughout the process, the AU Peace and Security

Council failed to equip its officials with a mandate, while its military personnel on the Cessation of Hostilities Monitoring Team arrived as late as April 2007. The US consulate in Juba continued to flag the narrative of Kony's intentions to State Department policy-makers.

The narrative of LRA culpability

The delegation of discursive authority over the conflict also had implications for how the ICC's strategy of prosecution was interpreted in Uganda. The OTP decided to implicate only one conflict actor in the binary northern conflict because it interpreted UPDF crimes to be of lesser gravity, given the temporal jurisdiction of the Rome Statute: the ICC has jurisdiction over crimes committed after 1 July 2002. In what is an interactive effect of ICC involvement, Branch (2011, 189) and Okello (2007) argue that the ICC intervention granted the UPDF impunity for its violence in Northern Uganda. The UPDF committed atrocities without being held accountable for them. However, this interactive granting of impunity accompanied a productive dimension with more widespread effects: the Prosecutor's decision to only indict LRA actors created a discourse of culpability that implicated the LRA and acquitted the UPDF.

The indictment decisions in the Uganda involvement process supported and legitimised the narrative that the LRA was the sole author of atrocity in Northern Uganda. This story of culpability preceded ICC involvement and was not created by the Prosecutor. Like the narrative about Kony's intentions, it was a government creation. For instance, during the Investigation stage, the Attorney-General, Mbabazi, stated that the UPDF was not guilty of crimes and would not be tried by the ICC (Branch 2011, 189). Such claims served to legitimise the policy of forced displacement in 'protected villages': the government was protecting the population from LRA massacres by moving them into displacement camps. The reality was, however, that the camp-based population had a higher mortality rate than did IDPs in comparable camps in Darfur at the height of that conflict (Checchi 2006).

By prosecuting the LRA's violence and not prosecuting state violence, the ICC decontested the government narrative: the claim at the centre of this narrative went from being war propaganda by one conflict party to being a legal, objective and internationally recognised fact. As *The New Vision* cover page put it: 'ICC Clears UPDF in the North' (Mugisa and Nsambu 2008). The establishment of the ICD to 'try the perpetrators of war crimes and crimes against humanity including commanders of the LRA and other rebel groups'[3] and its first case against Thomas Kwoyelo represented and further consolidated the discourse of LRA culpability. While the negotiators intended the ICD to try 'individuals who are alleged to have committed serious crimes during the conflict' from both sides in the conflict (Government of Uganda and LRA/M 2008), it became identified with rebel culpability during the Implementation phase.

The discourse of culpability was contested by ordinary people in Northern Uganda as well as the LRA. War-affected communities publicly called for the investigation of UPDF crimes (Lawino 2009) and continuously pointed to government crimes when interviewed by anthropologists, journalists and survey researchers. At the opening ceremony, Olweny complained that 'the international community, and indeed the ICC, has already passed a verdict of guilty' on the LRA (LRA/M 2006). Another LRA/M negotiator lamented the injustice created by the ICC's temporal jurisdiction:

> If you make a cut-off period at 2002 and you're talking about the same people who are involved – some killed earlier, some killed later – it means you are going to leave [untouched] those who killed earlier, some under more gruesome circumstances than those killed later.[4]

The inclusion of the south-west Ugandan Ankole justice mechanism of *Okukaraba* in the negotiated justice policy reflects contestation of the OTP's culpability narrative by Juba participants. Banyankole communities were not directly affected by the LRA conflict, but are represented in the army leadership: President Museveni, most Army Commanders since 1986, and 43.5 per cent of top UPDF commanders are Banyankole (Lindemann 2011). The inclusion of *Okukaraba* in the justice policy therefore acknowledges the UPDF's violence.

The creation of sticking points

The arrest warrants became sticking points in the Negotiation phase because of the way they were understood by the LRA leaders. Conceived as political, the arrest warrants could be bargained and withdrawn. Kony and Otti therefore made their withdrawal a precondition for entering the peace talks and later highlighted this demand in meetings with Machar, Chissano, the African observer officials and Egeland. They also cited the indictments as the main reason for not participating in person in the Talks.

Stemming from his political reading, Kony saw the arrest warrants as a political tool used by Museveni (Schomerus 2010, 127). The misconception about the indictments' authorship was partly created by the president, who had repeatedly claimed that he was issuing international arrest warrants for the LRA leaders (see, e.g. Wasike and Osike 2003). For the government, referral of the LRA situation to the ICC was clearly a weapon used against the LRA: it would restrict Sudanese support for the LRA, make Kony 'untouchable', and spark his international arrest (Parliament of the Republic of Uganda 2004a, 2005). Kony and Otti thus interpreted the government correctly, but misread the ICC. The fact that the OTP prosecuted LRA crimes, but not UPDF equivalents, contributed to the LRA's sense that the indictments were a government conspiracy. Both Kony and his delegation were informed by a feeling of unfairness stemming from the one-sided prosecution.[5]

The LRA leadership's attempt to politicise the arrest warrants was meaningful: Kony and Otti had observed how post-colonial politics had always taken precedence over law and, furthermore, were unlikely to have internalised the norms associated with the rapidly emerging field of international justice. In Uganda's wars, politics had always taken primacy over law. Insurgent armies had, as recently as 2002, been able to negotiate their lawlessness: the Uganda People's Army (UPA), Uganda People's Democratic Army (UPDA), West Nile Bank Front and Uganda National Rescue Force II and other groups had initially been outlawed, then militarily opposed and lastly politically rehabilitated. Comparable internal conflicts in Mozambique, Angola, Liberia, Sierra Leone and Sudan had seen the same trajectory.

Kony frequently referred to the arrest and transfer of Charles Taylor (Schomerus 2012, 291; Unger and Wierda 2009), but did not understand the practical implications of international criminal law. During the Pre-Negotiation phase, the LRA wanted the talks to take place in Kenya, Italy or South Africa, all of which are ICC states parties that have an obligation to arrest the Court's wanted persons. In November 2006, Barney Afako, a legal advisor to the peace process, briefed Kony on the implications of the indictments and the possibilities that existed within the Rome Statute (US Embassy Khartoum 2006). At the end of the meeting, Kony had indicated that he wanted to reflect on what he had heard and continue the discussion in a follow-up meeting.

The LRA leaders' political approach to the arrest warrants meant that they could not be relied on to share the view that their atrocities demanded a criminal justice response. Had they understood the indictments as legal and non-negotiable, there could have been a zone of possible agreement within which to find a justice solution. In the absence of this understanding, the LRA's approach to the arrest warrants made these a sticking point in the Negotiation phase.

Depoliticisation and decontestation of justice

Independently of the LRA leadership's approach to the arrest warrants, their fixed and international nature had the constitutive effect of depoliticising the agenda Item 3 negotiations on accountability and reconciliation. As the warrants could not be negotiated and thus were immune to national politics, they transferred the issue of justice to the realm of necessity and fate. One member of the mediation team explained the loss of agency:

> You see, the issue is, would the statement we were going to make, make the warrants go away? For as long as the warrants were there, it doesn't matter what you said. Because for Kony, he was looking at the warrants.[6]

The non-negotiable nature of the indictments came together with the primacy of international law over domestic law to narrow the options for a negotiated policy on accountability and reconciliation. A policy that lay outside the parameters of international justice was out of the question because it would be unable to replace the indictments. Thus, involvement at the Indictment stage created a situation whereby the possibilities of the Rome Statute framed the negotiations on the sticking point: the imperative of criminal punishment, the notion of complementarity, the possibility of a Security Council deferral and the option to challenge admissibility became the framework within which the parties negotiated justice. Representing one particular kind of justice – international criminal accountability – the arrest warrants sought to decontest the nature of justice by rendering other kinds of justice insufficient for triggering inadmissibility.

Negotiators and mediators sought to repoliticise the issue of justice while seeking to legitimise their justice output. They agreed on an alternative notion of accountability that was both restorative and retributive: it should facilitate the reintegration of the LRA and be sufficiently non-retributive to be acceptable to the LRA leaders. At the same time, it needed enough retributive features to enable the Security Council to justify an Article 16 deferral and convince the PTC to return the case to Uganda.

Knowing that their solution was controversial, Juba participants sought to obtain its national and international legitimation. As a member of the mediation team explains, 'We couldn't come away from Juba with an agreement that would be shot to pieces by everyone, with an international outcry about the [policy] package.'[7] To enable this legitimisation, Juba participants worked within a 'shorthand description of complementarity' as a test of the willingness and ability of the overall justice system of the state in question (Nouwen 2013, 120–121). They also embarked on the national consultation process, sequenced the disclosure of the controversial aspects of their policy and adopted a 'multivocal legitimation strategy' (Goddard 2012) that spoke to the LRA leadership, the ICC and the international community. Through linguistic deception, the agreements sought to appear prosecutorial but in fact built a different alternative justice process.

Normalising transitional justice

During the Implementation phase, the justice policy became subject to a process of normalisation (Gissel 2017). The carefully worded multivocal accountability and reconciliation agreements said too little to be easily understood and therefore needed a great deal of interpretation in order to be realised. In the process of implementation, therefore, the Annexure's special division became the conventional and retributive ICD. Moreover, Part II of the Amnesty Law (2000) was lapsed to enable Uganda to meet its duty to prosecute. Juba's negotiated alternative justice became ordinary justice.

The normalisation process was a result of the legalisation, internationalisation and professionalisation of the Ugandan field of transitional justice. UN agencies, bilateral donors and international human rights organisations became involved in establishing and running the ICD. This included international rule-of-law advisors, capacity-building workshops and study trips to Bosnia, Sierra Leone and The Hague (Asiimwe 2012; Danida 2011; Human Rights Watch 2012). The ICD became understood as an instrument of Rome Statute complementarity, rather than the institutionalisation of a unique Ugandan path to transitional justice.

Delegation of politico-legal authority

Juba's alternative justice policy relied on an Article 16 deferral by the Security Council and thereafter a successful admissibility challenge before the PTC. This dependence on international agency was necessary because national actors, including the government, had insufficient politico-legal authority to remove the indictments and thus overcome the sticking point of the negotiations. The Rome Statute vests this authority in the Prosecutor and the Security Council, as specific clauses provide these actors with agency to make discretionary decisions to defer prosecution out of concern for peace negotiations (Greenawalt 2007; Rodman 2009; Schabas 2008). Had the Prosecutor invoked Article 53(2)(c) to terminate his case against the LRA leaders 'in the interests of justice' or had the Security Council agreed to use its Article 16 authority to defer the Indictment stage to protect 'international peace and security', agency to settle the conflict would have been returned to the conflict parties: government moderates could have traded the LRA's demobilisation for 'clearly defined packages and positions outlining the future' for rebel leaders, as per Ongwen's implicit demands. The next two sub-sections trace the non-exercise of this politico-legal authority, analysing first the Prosecutor's interpretation of the interests of justice and then investigating the deliberations in the Security Council. As we shall see, both actors deemed their formal authority irrelevant to the Ugandan situation.

Discretionary Prosecutor authority

In the Indictment stage, the Prosecutor could legitimately have used his discretionary powers under Article 53(2)(c) to roll back his process, had he wanted to. The OTP policy on the interests of justice contributes to an understanding of why the Prosecutor did not use his discretionary powers to remove the central sticking point of the Juba negotiations. Coterminous with the Juba Peace Talks, the OTP was exploring the meaning of the Statute provision for cancelling investigations or prosecutions in the interests of justice, a process that culminated in a September 2007 policy paper.

The Rome Statute is silent on the particular meaning of the interests of justice, but Article 53(1)(c) and (2)(c) provides the Prosecutor with discretionary powers to refrain from an investigation or prosecution 'in the interests of justice'. It reflects concerns during the negotiations on the Statute that the ICC would hamper transitions to peace and democracy. Unable to agree on the concept of the interests of justice, delegates at the Rome Conference 'settled on a language that opened the door to [alternative justice] processes but provided no guidance as to the circumstances under which alternatives to prosecution might be accepted' (Greenawalt 2009, para. 133). Article 53 reflected 'creative ambiguity' to potentially allow the Prosecutor and judges to recognise an amnesty exception to ICC jurisdiction (Scharf 1999, 522; see also Schabas 2012), hence the OTP need for policy direction.

The OTP policy does not establish specific criteria for the interests of justice, and defines the concept mainly by what it is not. It sees the exercise of political discretion under Article 53 (1)(c) and (2)(c) as 'exceptional' and direct considerations of the interests of justice towards the objects and purposes of the Rome Statute, understood as the prevention of international crimes through 'ending impunity' (ICC 2007, para. 1). Importantly, it defines the interests of justice as different from the interests of peace. The policy thereby constitutes issues of peace as irrelevant to any consideration of the interests of justice. Schabas (2008, 749), who attended the Rome Conference, comments:

> There is certainly no evidence in the drafting history of the ICC Statute that a distinction between 'interests of justice' and 'interests of peace' was intended. To be sure, there were those at the Rome Conference who would have preferred language limiting the 'interests of justice' concept by excluding the 'interests of peace', but their views are not reflected in the ICC Statute because there was no consensus on the issue.

With its 2007 policy, the OTP reinterpreted the concept of the interests of justice, developing a restrictive understanding that reflected the positions of Western states and certain NGOs. To that end, human rights organisations such as Amnesty International, Fédération Internationale de Ligues des Droits de l'Homme and Human Rights Watch had been invited to submit their interpretations of the concept to the official policy process at the OTP.

It is likely that the policy process was influenced by the Prosecutor's reading of the Juba Peace Talks, as they are mentioned several times. To the OTP, the Juba process 'demonstrates well the exceptional nature of the provision on the interests of justice as well as the differences between this concept and the interests of peace' (ICC 2007, para. 4). With this Ugandan pretext, the policy states that 'other forms of justice decided at the local level' need to be integrated into the ICC justice process and thus cannot constitute an alternative to ICC justice. Furthermore, the OTP will work constructively with and respect the mandates of peacemakers, but will nevertheless pursue its own judicial mandate independently. These interpretations of justice, peace and peacemaking brought the Prosecutor's policy into alignment with his Uganda involvement: his position on the Juba Peace Talks justified the policy, while the policy legitimised his position on the Talks.

Between the 1998 Rome discussions and the OTP policy paper, the provision for the interests of justice was transformed, separated from issues of peace. This change was cemented at the 2010 Rome Statute Review Conference, where the Prosecutor's seven-page speech, 'The Importance of Justice in Securing Peace', made no mention of the Statute's interests of justice provision (ICC 2010). The connection between peace and justice was now understood as wholly dependent on the Security Council:

> States made a conscious decision in Rome to create a justice system that could stop or prevent violence rather than an ad hoc creation acting *a*

> *posteriori*. They also connected peace and justice, providing for interaction of the Court with the UN Security Council.
>
> (ICC 2010, para. 4)

UN Security Council authority

The Security Council was aware of the ICC dilemma from the beginning of the Juba Peace Talks (US Embassy UN 2006a), but the issue of requesting an Article 16 deferral of the LRA cases never reached its formal agenda. The dilemma was first discussed by the Council when it decided to make a statement in support of the Juba Peace Talks in the latter half of 2006. In preparing the statement, it became 'unclear what position the Council will take on the justice and reconciliation dilemma and the related issue of arrest warrants' (Security Council Report 2006, para. 3). There were 'strong views' among members on the implications of the peace process for accountability; some members were in favour of a sequencing solution, while others had 'already indicated that a solution that undermines justice and the ICC is unacceptable' (Security Council Report 2006, para. 4). Articulating the deterrence narrative of the justice discourse, these Council members were 'aware of the dangers to the Court's credibility and to perhaps long-term stability in Northern Uganda, if, in practice, what prevails is impunity' (Security Council Report 2006, para. 4). Appropriated by the Council members, the discourses of the peace/justice debate thus framed their understanding of the Juba dilemma and shaped their agency.

As a reflection of the Council's lack of agreement, the presidential statement of support to the Juba Peace Talks, published on 16 November 2006, included a general commitment to justice that omitted explicit mention of the ICC:

> The Security Council ... invites UN Member States to support efforts to bring an end to this conflict so that peace and security can be restored to the region and the rule of law re-established, and to ensure that those responsible for serious violations of human rights and international humanitarian law are brought to justice.
>
> (UN Security Council 2006, para. 4)

On 22 March 2007, the Council again issued a presidential statement, this time to get the LRA/M delegation back to the negotiation table (UN Security Council 2007). It again called for justice without mentioning the ICC process. The following year, in the context of Operation Lightning Thunder and Kony's failure to take the deal, the Security Council mentioned the ICC arrest warrants for the first time. It recalled the warrants and invoked the deterrence narrative of the justice discourse: justice and the rule of law is 'indispensable' to lasting peace as 'ending impunity is essential for a society recovering from conflict to come to terms with past abuses' (UN Security Council 2008, para. 6).

Coterminous with the Juba Peace Talks, and particularly in 2008, Council members seriously considered the use of their Article 16 authority in relation to the situation in Darfur. This fact indicates that less importance was attached to the LRA situation. Leaked diplomatic reports by US officials in Khartoum, London, New York, Paris and The Hague show that key Council members at different times contemplated using their Article 16 discretion to incentivise the Sudanese government to solve the Darfur crisis. Members who opposed triggering Article 16 saw the instrument as a political act of very last resort.

In September 2006, the British government developed an informal list of incentives for the Sudanese regime to do 'the right thing on Darfur', including giving assurances that two Sudanese ministers indicted by the ICC 'will not be arrested and put on trial' (US Embassy London 2006). According to US officials, this idea was 'controversial within Whitehall, but it is possible per Article 16 of the Rome Statute'. However, the Security Council split in two over the issue after the ICC indicted President al Bashir and the AU requested the Security Council to defer his prosecution. The US Embassy at the UN (2009) made an 'informal breakdown regarding an Article 16 resolution' that had seven Council members in favour (Burkina Faso, China, Libya, Russia, Turkey, Uganda and Vietnam) and eight against (Austria, Costa Rica, Croatia, France, Japan, Mexico, the UK and the US).

In late 2008 and early 2009, Security Council meetings included heated exchanges over the issue in relation to the situation in Darfur. The AU, the Organization of Islamic Countries, the Arab League and the Non-Aligned Movement supported an Article 16 deferral, but the permanent Council members of France, the UK and the US were against it. Libya (quoted in US Embassy UN 2009) asked, 'If the Security Council will not act on Article 16 now, with two-thirds of the international community requesting it, then when?' By implication, this debate on Sudan suggests that a request to defer the ICC's LRA cases never entered the formal agenda because the LRA conflict was considered a relatively small problem. Had the issue been formally discussed, there would have been insufficient support for a deferral request.

The Juba Peace Talks failed to meet an unarticulated threshold for serious Security Council consideration of the use of its Article 16 authority to remove its sticking point, while being deemed outside the scope of the provision for ICC withdrawal in the interests of justice. These judgements depoliticised the indictments at the international level as it moved them to the realm of fate. These institutional parameters were set in a wider discursive context that emphasised the futility of talks with Kony; as we saw, the internationalisation of this claim became possible when discursive authority was transferred from the government to the ICC. Peace process failure should be understood within this context of internationalised political, legal and discursive authority.

Part 2 Why the Juba process failed

Two immediate factors ended the Juba peace negotiations and returned the war: the LRA leadership did not commit to the Final Peace Agreement on 30 November 2008 and two weeks later the government reignited the war with Operation

Lightning Thunder. The respective decisions to stay away from the signing ceremony and to launch a major counter-insurgency operation represent the intra-party power balance and the relationship between the conflict parties. The story of the failure of the Juba Peace Talks is one of defeat of moderates by extremists within each conflict party. However, the high level of international judicialisation had dealt Juba's moderates a bad hand: conflict parties had agency to fail the peace process, but no authority to take decisions that could create a turning point.

The two immediate causes of peace process failure cannot be understood independently of the nature of Juba's judicialised peace process, as analysed in the first part of this chapter. The following sections make sense of the immediate causes within the framework of hardliner–moderate relations, after which they connect these relations to first the role of time and then to the effects of ICC involvement on the peace process as analysed above. The chapter concludes by examining alternative explanations.

Conflict parties' internal relations: Hardliners and moderates

Intra-party relations may be as important for the conclusion and implementation of a political solution as relations between conflict parties. Oberschall (2007, 33) theorises that rivalry between moderates and hardliners may result in 'six adversaries waging three simultaneous conflicts: the two conflicts between rejectionists and moderates within each adversary are added to the main conflict between the two adversaries'. While such inter-linked conflicts may not all be violent, they highlight the importance of the ability of pro-settlement factions to overpower those with interests or identities vested in the continuation of war. As Jung *et al.* (2005, 286) ask, 'Can the reformers and moderates agree on a settlement and successfully face down the hardliners and radicals on their flanks?' These actor labels should be associated with positions rather than personalities, as individuals may move between them.

In late 2008, Kony may have belonged to the moderate or hardliner factions within the LRA. The LRA leader refused to appear at the planned events to sign the Final Peace Agreement and had abandoned contact with his delegation for most of the year. Yet he was within reach and does not appear to have exited the Talks: he responded to the political pressure created by the high-level stakeholders' conference in November 2008 and summoned a contingent of northern traditional and religious leaders to his camp. There he told them his reasons for not signing, launching a 'diatribe' (US Embassy Kampala 2008), and warned the government not to reignite the war.

Observers who met Kony several times link his commitment failure to the question of accountability, the sticking point of the negotiations (Iya 2010; Otim and Wierda 2008; but see Schomerus 2012).[8] Kony had told the elders and religious leaders that he needed more information on the Agreement on Accountability and Reconciliation, in effect requesting more time. According to US intelligence, Kony told the Acholi Paramount Chief, Rwot Acana, 'I have internal problems. Some people in the group need to feel part of the process. If something comes through from the Government of Uganda, there has to be something in it for them' (US Embassy Kampala 2008, para. 6). At the meeting, Dominic Ongwen unwittingly corroborated this explanation, stating that Kony would be killed if he signed the Agreement 'as it is, without clearly defined packages and positions outlining the future' of the senior commanders (US Embassy Kampala 2008, para. 6).

LRA hardliners could not commit to peace because they lacked a clear compensation package and did not trust or understand how the negotiated justice policy would deliver them from the ICC. The LRA leadership was within political reach, but could not accept the conditions for committing to demobilisation: the possibility of Security Council deferral of prosecution, which had not yet been requested by the government, an unclear national justice process, which hinged on the Security Council deferral, and the incorporation of willing LRA fighters into the UPDF. The government decision to tie its international deferral request to the prior signing of the Final Peace Agreement by Kony weakened LRA moderates vis-à-vis hardliners. The precondition suggests that the government wanted to leave the peace process or underestimated contestation within the LRA leadership.

The decision to launch Operation Lightning Thunder relates to the internal government contest between hardliners and moderates. Hardliners had continuously advocated the military elimination of the LRA, to which end they had furthered the narrative of Kony's 'real intentions'. They had re-written the history of earlier political settlements to describe these as military victories. As Amama Mbabazi told parliament in 2004, 'For 18 years we have defeated all of these people and I will list them again. We defeated Obote back in Busia and we brought back their leaders; we defeated UPA in Teso; we defeated UPDA the North – *(Interruption)*' (Parliament of the Republic of Uganda 2004b, 15). In fact, the insurgencies by UPA and UPDA had been settled politically; MPs knew this, hence their '*Interruption*' of Mbabazi's statement.

When the traditional and religious leaders in late November 2008 relayed Kony's request for more time and his warning against the resumption of war, a frustrated Rugunda responded that Kony was 'living in a fool's paradise' (US Embassy Kampala 2008). Using a phrase that describes happiness derived from not knowing or accepting how bad a situation really is, Rugunda's remark implied that Kony was ignorant or in denial about who or what he was up against. It suggested that time and continued negotiations were not for the government delegation to give; there was no government willingness to draw on.

'When talks fail, those who advocated them risk looking naïve, unwise, or worse – accomplices, albeit unwitting, of a terrorist group that thrives on public attention and official recognition' (Quinney and Coyne 2011, 20). This may even result in a 'backlash from both domestic constituencies and international actors'. Signifying the end of the Negotiation phase, and perhaps to avoid a backlash, Rugunda left the country the day before Operation Lightning Thunder. Stepping down as Internal Affairs Minister, he became Uganda's Permanent Representative to the UN in New York. The Juba Peace Talks were clearly a thing of the past. To see how temporal aspects of the Juba Peace Talks played a role in inter and intra-party relationships, the next section examines the role of time.

The role of time

Time was a crucial aspect of the Juba Peace Talks. Most importantly, the resolution of the sticking point was dependent on the international granting of time. In order to create the conditions for a return of jurisdiction over the ICC cases to Uganda, a precondition for implementation of the justice policy, the government needed time to establish the special high court division. Thereafter, the conflict parties needed time to begin to carry out the alternative justice process, in order to subsequently launch a successful admissibility challenge. A Security Council request for deferral of prosecution was to make this time available to the conflict parties.

Temporal expectations and pressure by conflict parties and third-party actors played a role in the decisions to end the Negotiation phase. Initially, the government thought it could negotiate a 'soft landing' for the LRA in a matter of weeks, and Museveni set 12 September 2006 as the deadline for LRA disarmament. Both the government and Southern Sudan's President Kiir stressed that the process was 'not open-ended'. Already in early 2007, less than a year into the Negotiation phase, Chissano signalled to the US that the Talks could 'not go on forever' (US Embassy Khartoum 2007, para. 14). For its part, the US State Department stressed repeatedly that the US government 'will not support an open-ended peace process' (US Senate Committee on Foreign Relations 2007, para. 6). Donors wanted to conclude negotiations by January 2008 and set 30 November 2008 as the final deadline for signing the Final Peace Agreement.

In contrast to the marked government and international focus on the length of the Negotiation phase, the LRA leadership was in no hurry to conclude a deal. In fact, the government's temporal pressure suggested to the LRA a lack of genuine commitment to peace talks by its adversary. As Otti (quoted in Schomerus 2012, 103) said in an interview on Radio Mega FM on 13 September 2006:

> I am telling you clearly listeners, peace talks have no date. If he [Museveni] says that talks are expiring, I don't know what he is saying. It may be expiring on their side but not on our side because we are still continuing talking peace.

More than two years later, Kony requested more time to consider the Agreement on Accountability and Reconciliation. Even if he had wanted to sign the Final Peace Agreement, and this is a subject of dispute, Kony needed time to win over the hardliners within the LRA leadership.

Operation Lightning Thunder in December 2008 signified the loss of patience by the government and thereby the victory of government hardliners over moderates. Following Kony's non-appearance at the first signing event in April 2008, the Acting Attorney-General asked the ICC Registry to put pressure on the DRC, a state party, to grant Ugandan troops access to Garamba National Park (Uganda 2008). During 2007, Museveni had met with US State Department officials to discuss US military assistance to capture Kony, preparing 'Plan B', an alternative to negotiations (Hendrickson and Tumutegyereize 2012, 27). The dual strategy was consistent with the State Department's approach of providing both military and diplomatic pressure on the LRA (US Senate Committee on Foreign Relations 2007).

Third-party actors and donors also lost patience with the peace process. After the final signing deadline, Chissano agreed to reignite the war, arguing that 'force was now needed to comply [Kony] to sign' (US Embassy UN 2008). While president of Mozambique, Chissano held talks with insurgent RENAMO that had taken longer than did the LRA negotiations, so his impatience was arguably unwarranted; perhaps he felt more was at stake in 1994 or considered RENAMO more serious than the LRA. Over the course of the Negotiation phase, peace process donors (Canada, Denmark, the EU, Ireland, the Netherlands, Norway, Sweden, the UK and the US) swung from being hostile to supportive to giving up on the Talks. Their confidence in the LRA/M negotiators may have been hampered by the latter's focus on monetary facilitation, while their belief in 'an African solution to an African problem' turned out to be short-lived. Feeling that they had taken great moral risks in becoming involved, donors did not see a return on their investment and created a pressure for a quick settlement (Hendrickson and Tumutegyereize 2012, 11, 26).

The temporal horizons of the external actors were at odds with those of leaders from the affected communities. At the Investigation stage, northern leaders had requested the Prosecutor to give the Bigombe initiative 'some time' by holding off the issuance of indictments. When this request was ignored, they criticised the ICC intervention for having 'bad timing'. Among their displaced constituents, some agreed, while others wished for a 'swift' ICC process that could end the insurgency (Ochowun and Onyalla 2005). Northern leaders and parliamentarians also disagreed with the decision to reignite the war and end the Negotiation phase, calling on Uganda, the DRC and Sudan to halt Operation Lightning Thunder and the parties to return to negotiations.[9]

The role of ICC judicialisation in the peace process outcome

The decisions to return to war and fail the Juba Peace Talks relate to the effects of ICC involvement on the peace process. ICC involvement did not determine the outcome of the peace process, but it created the conditions of possibility for the failure to agree a political settlement. Organised in relation to stages of ICC involvement, this argument has five components. First, in the Preliminary Examination stage, the OTP-solicited state referral of the LRA conflict to the ICC at first legitimised the military approach to the conflict. Subsequently, Indictment-stage involvement necessitated this approach. Militarisation of the conflict benefitted the respective hardliner factions against the moderates: it strengthened and legitimised government hardliners' belief in a military victory and helped build international support for yet another counter-insurgency operation by the UPDF. The earlier donor critique of the UPDF's civilian casualties was transformed into scepticism about talks and support for a military pursuit. For instance, in 2003 Dutch officials (quoted in Mpagi 2003) had argued that 'the military option has failed', but in July 2006, a month into the Negotiation phase and participating in a high-level meeting at the UN Secretariat, they 'expressed doubts' that 'positive outcomes' could stem from the Juba Peace Talks and supported 'ICC arrests' by UN peacekeepers in the region (US Embassy UN 2006a). More generally, in 2006 US and European diplomats argued that the only solution to the war was to eliminate Kony (Finnström 2008, 112).

Second, from the Preliminary Examination onwards, delegation of discursive authority made the discursive environment contingent on the Prosecutor's interpretations and positions and this played into the hands of government hardliners. His internationalised narratives about the LRA's 'real' intentions weakened the position of government moderates: it was difficult to prove that Kony was not regrouping and rearming. In fact, the LRA had to regroup as per the Cessation of Hostilities Agreement, which stipulated the assembly of LRA fighters. Given the low-intensity pursuit of the LRA by UPDF forces during the Negotiation phase (Atkinson 2010; Schomerus 2012), it would have been dangerous for the LRA leadership to disclose the size of their armaments.

As analysed above, discursive action to delegitimise the Talks had an impact on the extent to which donors and the UN wanted to be involved. Rather than creating an unambiguous international pressure in support of government moderates, discourse and decision-making by donors and the UN was mostly closer to the hardliner position. Having called for negotiations in 2003, their reluctance to support the Juba Peace Talks could derive either from the LRA's terrorist designation or the ICC indictments. The latter is the most likely explanation, because international organisations and Western states supported several talks with terrorist-labelled groups during 2005 and 2006. The EU, Japan, Norway and the US supported peace talks between the Liberation Tigers of Tamil Eelam and the Sri Lankan government, while Norway, Spain and Switzerland supported talks between Ejército de Liberación National and the government of Colombia. Canada, Germany, Ireland, Norway, Sweden and the UK had supported Bigombe's initiative to talk to the LRA in 2004–2005, during the ICC's Preliminary Examination and Investigation stages.

Third, in the Indictment stage, the arrest warrants and the Prosecutor's narrative of sole LRA culpability strengthened the hardliner position within the government as it framed the LRA's violence as criminal and thus apolitical and the government's military response as therefore appropriate. It 'acquitted' the UPDF and delegitimised the suggestion that some of the LRA's grievances may be legitimate and warranting a political process. Furthermore, the one-sided prosecution legitimised the LRA hardliner position that Museveni and his NRM government can never be trusted and uses the international environment against the LRA. In late 2007, Otti (quoted in Schomerus 2012, 170) may have reflected on the dynamics within the LRA leadership as he told community members in Nabanga, 'Sometimes it is hard for us because we don't know if we can trust. But to get to peace also means to learn to trust.'

Fourth, the depoliticisation of the issue of accountability prevented resolution of the sticking point by moderates at the national level, as conflict parties did not have authority to roll back the prosecution of LRA leaders. President Museveni did offer them a security guarantee, but his words were not politically and legally authoritative, as they did not affect the ICC. Internationally, possibilities for creating a turning point were misunderstood, ignored or undermined by those with the required politico-legal authority: the Prosecutor and the Security Council. Last, and in a related point, the unsuccessful efforts by negotiators and mediators to define an alternative justice notion were constrained by the decontestation of justice associated with the Indictment stage. Had they been able to present an internationally endorsed alternative justice notion – and had this notion caused an interests-of-justice-based withdrawal of prosecution – moderates within both conflict parties would have been strengthened vis-à-vis hardliners.

Counter-factually, in the absence of judicialisation by the ICC and given the roots of the conflict, a likely sticking point in the Negotiation phase would have been the issue of governance. The history of previous political settlements in Uganda does not suggest that justice issues would have been a government priority. This issue would never have generated a power-sharing solution, but the government would have been in a position to have made a number of apparent concessions derived from the already planned and donor-pledged Peace, Recovery and Development Programme for Northern Uganda. This programme addresses a number of northern grievances, including many mentioned by the LRA/M delegation. If an agreement on governance was combined with unambiguous international support for a settlement, a security guarantee policed by international forces and international condemnation of the military approach, moderates on both sides of the conflict may have been able to defeat their intra-party adversaries.

Alternative explanations

There are three dominant alternative explanations for the failure of the Juba Talks to achieve a political settlement. The most prevalent alternative explanation circulates in the international justice community and beyond.[10] It argues that Kony was never seriously interested in peace, the Talks being a 'still birth' (Owino Dollo, quoted in Kersten 2012, 73). This explanation addresses Kony's failure to commit to the Final Peace Agreement, but can only be made if one disregards evidence to the contrary as well as Kony's own explanation for not signing. While this disregard seems reasonable in the face of Kony's obviously untrue statements – that the LRA has not abducted children or attacked civilians – it overlooks his consistent identification of what he sees as the chief obstacle: the ICC arrest warrants. Evidence for Kony's genuine participation is his mediation request to Pax Christi, his delegation's early arrival in Juba, his unilateral ceasefire, his forces' move to the agreed assembly points, the fact that the

UPDF's well-documented presence near these assembly points and its attack on LRA soldiers forced the LRA to scatter again, the non-training of new abductees, and his willingness to become exposed and vulnerable through the many meetings with peace emissaries and international media.

A second explanation centres on the quality of the LRA/M delegation. It argues that its internal split and delegates' inferior capacity to handle the complexity of the negotiations, tendency to advance personal interests and agendas, and inability to communicate adequately with the LRA leadership prevented the achievement of a political solution.[11] Right from the beginning of the Negotiation phase, Machar tried to get high-level LRA participation because he worried about the delegation's ability to represent the LRA leadership. While the nature of the LRA/M delegation undoubtedly complicated matters, they were not the only actors with access to the LRA leadership. Had the LRA leaders wanted to commit to the final agreement in 2008, they had many other channels of communication to utilise, not least a telephone line to Museveni. For instance, in November 2008, Kony called Chissano. While the LRA/M delegation focused insufficiently on the security of the LRA leaders, even the best LRA/M peace delegation could not have compelled the relevant international actors to mitigate or alleviate the indictees' problem of international justice.

A third alternative explanation relates to how the LRA experienced the Juba Peace Talks. Schomerus (2012, 19) argues that 'the crucial element that led to the non-signing of the final agreement' was the dynamics between the conflict parties and how these dynamics were experienced by the LRA/M. The government and the LRA were unable or unwilling to leave behind the 'power patterns' of the conflict and forge a new relationship (Schomerus 2012, 19). Thus, the Negotiation phase took place in the context of low-intensity war between the UPDF and LRA, and the role of the SPLA and SPLM was at times unclear to the LRA. The Juba Peace Talks confirmed the conflict parties' narratives and even entrenched the conflict. According to Schomerus (2012, 18), explanations that point to the ICC arrest warrants are 'easy and lazy' because they overlook how the Talks were experienced by the LRA. However, as this book shows, arguments that take seriously the ICC's judicialisation are not necessarily incompatible with the focus on perceptions, narratives and experiences. In fact, it is entirely possible that the LRA/M delegates and their principals in the bush experienced the Talks as a cementation of conflict dynamics because the effects of judicialisation created a bias towards militarisation, sole LRA culpability and hardliner discourse. To obtain a deeper sense of such effects, it is useful to analyse and compare with a second case. This is the purpose of the next three chapters.

Notes

1 Interview with member of the mediation team, February 2013.

2 The claim was traced in an English-language LexisNexis search for the terms 'LRA AND regroup' with no date limit. The search included 'major world publications', which according to LexisNexis includes 'the world's major newspapers, magazines and trade publications which are relied upon for the accuracy and integrity of their

reporting'. The search identified 165 records, 43 of which included statements about the LRA or Kony regrouping in relation to a peace process.

3 From the official website of the ICD, www.judiciary.go.ug/data/smenu/18/International%20Crimes%20Division.html (accessed 6 April 2017).

4 Interview with member of the LRA/M delegation, April 2011.

5 Interview with member of the LRA/M delegation, April 2011. See also Schomerus (2012, 291).

6 Interview with member of the mediation team, April 2011.

7 Interview with member of the mediation team, London, UK, February 2013.

8 Interview with observer participant, June 2010.

9 'Conflict Timeline' from www.arlpi.org/women-empowerment/contact-us/s/conflict-timeline?tmpl=%2Fsystem%2Fapp%2Ftemplates%2Fprint%2F&showPrintDialog=1 [accessed 25 April 2017].

10 Participant observation, Rome Statute Review Conference, Kampala, May-June 2010.

11 Interview with donor to the Talks, April 2011.

References

Akhavan, Payam. 2009. 'Are International Criminal Tribunals a Disincentive to Peace?: Reconciling Judicial Romanticism with Political Realism.' *Human Rights Quarterly* 31 (3): 624. doi:10.1353/hrq.0.0096.

Apuuli, Kasaija Phillip. 2008. 'The ICC's Possible Deferral of the LRA Case to Uganda.' *Journal of International Criminal Justice* 6: 801–813.

Asiimwe, Tadeo. 2012. 'Effecting Complementarity: Challenges and Opportunities: A Case Study of the International Crimes Division of Uganda.' Paper Presented at a Regional Forum on International and Transitional Justice, Avocats Sans Frontières-Uganda Mission, Entebbe, Uganda, 30 July 2012.

Atkinson, Ronald R. 2009. *From Uganda to the Congo and Beyond: Pursuing the Lord's Resistance Army*. New York: International Peace Institute.

Atkinson, Ronald R. 2010. '"The Realists in Juba"? An Analysis of the Juba Peace Talks.' In *The Lord's Resistance Army: Myth and Reality*, edited by Tim Allen and Koen Vlassenroot, 205–222. London and New York: Zed Books Ltd.

Branch, Adam. 2005. 'Neither Peace nor Justice: Political Violence and the Peasantry in Northern Uganda, 1986–1998.' *African Studies Quarterly* 8 (2): 1–31. doi:10.1111/j.1747-7093.2007.00069.x.

Branch, Adam. 2011. *Displacing Human Rights: War and Intervention in Northern Uganda*. New York: Oxford University Press.

Branch, Adam. 2017. 'Dominic Ongwen on Trial: The ICC's African Dilemmas.' *International Journal of Transitional Justice* 11 (1): 30–49.

Checchi, Francesco. 2006. 'Humanitarian Interventions in Northern Uganda: Based on What Evidence?' *Humanitarian Exchange* 36: 7–11.

Danida. 2011. *Governance for Development: Five Years Support to Democracy, Human Rights, Justice, and Peace in Uganda*. Kampala: Danida's Human Rights and Good Governance Office, Uganda.

Finnström, Sverker. 2008. *Living with Bad Surroundings*. Durham and London: Duke University Press.

Freeland, Valerie. 2015. 'Rebranding the State: Uganda's Strategic Use of the International Criminal Court.' *Development and Change* 46 (2): 293–319.

Gissel, Line Engbo. 2017. 'Contemporary Transitional Justice: Normalising a Politics of Exception.' *Global Society* 31 (3): 353–369. doi:10.1080/13600826.2016.1255933.

Goddard, Stacie E. 2012. 'Brokering Peace: Networks, Legitimacy, and the Northern Ireland Peace Process.' *International Studies Quarterly* 56: 501–515.

Government of Uganda, and LRA/M. 2008, 19 February. *Annexure to the Agreement on Accountability and Reconciliation*. https://peacemaker.un.org/uganda-annex-accountability2008.

Greenawalt, Alexander K A. 2007. 'Justice without Politics? Prosecutorial Discretion and the International Criminal Court.' *New York University Journal of International Law and Politics* 39 (3): 583.

Greenawalt, Alexander K A. 2009. 'Complementarity in Crisis: Uganda, Alternative Justice, and the International Criminal Court.' *Virginia Journal of International Law* 50 (1): 107.

Hendrickson, Dylan, and Kennedy Tumutegyereize. 2012. *Dealing with Complexity in Peace Negotiations: Reflections on the Lord's Resistance Army and the Juba Peace Talks*. London: Conciliation Resources.

Human Rights Watch. 2012. *Justice for Serious Crimes before National Courts: Uganda's International Crimes Division*. New York: Human Rights Watch.

International Criminal Court. 2007. *Policy Paper on the Interests of Justice*. The Hague: International Criminal Court.

International Criminal Court. 2008. *Fourteenth Diplomatic Briefing of the International Criminal Court. Compilation of Statements*. The Hague: International Criminal Court.

International Criminal Court. 2009. *Report of the International Criminal Court to the UN General Assembly, 64th Session*. New York: UN.

International Criminal Court. 2010. *The Importance of Justice in Securing Peace*. Review Conference of the Rome Statute. The Hague: International Criminal Court.

Iya, Ronald. 2010. 'Encountering Kony: A Madi Perspective.' In *The Lord's Resistance Army: Myth and Reality*, edited by Tim Allen and Koen Vlassenroot, 177–184. London and New York: Zed Books Ltd.

Jung, Courtney, Ellen Lust-Okar, and Ian Shapiro. 2005. 'Problems and Prospects for Democratic Settlements: South Africa as a Model for the Middle East and Northern Ireland?' *Politics & Society* 33 (2): 277–326.

Kersten, Mark. 2012. 'Peace from Juba: Peace Talks between the LRA and the Government of Uganda (2006–2008).' In *Beyond Kony 2012: Atrocity, Awareness, & Activism in the Internet Age*, edited by Amanda Taub. Leanpub.com.

Lawino, Sam. 2009, June 24. 'War Crimes Court Should Try UPDF.' *The Daily Monitor*.

Lindemann, Stefan. 2011. 'Just Another Change of Guard? Broad-Based Politics and Civil War in Museveni's Uganda.' *African Affairs* 110 (440): 387–416. doi:http://dx.doi.org/10.1093/afraf/adr023.

LRA/M. 2006. 'Opening Speech', June 14. Reprinted in *The New Vision*, Kampala, 15 July. Copy on file with author.

Lund, Christian, and Thomas Sikor. 2009. 'Access and Property.' *Development and Change* 40 (1): 1. doi:10.1111/j.1467-7660.2009.01503.x.

Mpagi, Mwanguhya Charles. 2003, October 25. 'Museveni, Dutch Minister Disagree over Kony War.' *The Daily Monitor*.

Mugisa, Anne, and Hillary Nsambu. 2008, August 30. 'ICC Clears UPDF in the North.' *The New Vision*.

Nouwen, Sarah M H. 2012. 'The International Criminal Court: A Peacebuilder in Africa?' In *Peacebuilding, Power, and Politics in Africa*, edited by Devon Curtis and Gwinyayi A Dzinesa, 171–192. Athens, OH: Ohio University Press.

Nouwen, Sarah M H. 2013. *Complementarity in the Line of Fire: The Catalysing Effect of the International Criminal Court in Sudan*. Cambridge: Cambridge University Press.

Oberschall, Anthony. 2007. *Conflict and Peace Building in Divided Societies: Responses to Ethnic Violence*. London and New York: Routledge.

Ochowun, Chris, and Harriette Onyalla. 2005, December 12. 'Mixed Feelings about ICC Warrants.' *Institute for War and Peace Reporting*.

Office of the Prosecutor. 2004. *Statement of the Prosecutor Luis Moreno-Ocampo to the Diplomatic Corps, The Hague, Netherlands, 12 February 2004*. The Hague: International Criminal Court.

Office of the Prosecutor. 2006. *Report on the Activities Performed during the First Three Years (June 2003–June 2006)*. The Hague: International Criminal Court.

Okello, Moses Chrispus. 2007. 'The False Polarisation of Peace and Justice.' Paper prepared for 'Workshop 2, Justice in Situations of Ongoing Conflict', Building a Future on Peace and Justice, Nuremberg, 25–27 June 2007.

Olupot, Milton. 2010, 27 May. 'ICC Failed the Kony Talks, Says Oulanyah.' *The New Vision*.

Otim, Michael, and Marieke Wierda. 2008. 'Justice at Juba: International Obligations and Local Demands in Northern Uganda.' In *Courting Conflict? Justice, Peace and the ICC in Africa*, edited by Nicholas Waddell and Phil Clark, 21–28. London: Royal African Society.

Parliament of the Republic of Uganda. 2004a. 'Tuesday 24 February 2004.' *Hansard*. Kampala: Parliament of the Republic of Uganda

Parliament of the Republic of Uganda. 2004b. 'Wednesday 25 February 2004.' *Hansard*. Kampala: Parliament of the Republic of Uganda

Parliament of the Republic of Uganda. 2005. 'Tuesday 7 June 2005.' *Hansard*. Kampala: Parliament of the Republic of Uganda

Quinney, Nigel, and A Heather Coyne. 2011. *Talking to Groups That Use Terror*. Washington, DC: United States Institute of Peace.

Refugee Law Project. 2004. *Position Paper on the Announcement of Formal Investigations of the Lord's Resistance Army by the Chief Prosecutor of the International Criminal Court and Its Implications on the Search for Peaceful Solutions to the War in Northern Uganda*. Kampala: Refugee Law Project.

Rodman, K A. 2009. 'Is Peace in the Interests of Justice? The Case for Broad Prosecutorial Discretion at the International Criminal Court.' *Leiden Journal of International Law* 22 (1): 99. doi:10.1017/S0922156508005657.

Schabas, William A. 2008. 'Prosecutorial Discretion v. Judicial Activism at the International Criminal Court.' *Journal of International Criminal Justice* 6: 731–761. doi:http://dx.doi.org/10.1093/jicj/mqn045.

Schabas, William A. 2012. *Unimaginable Atrocities: Justice, Politics and Rights at the War Crimes Tribunals*. Oxford: Oxford University Press.

Scharf, Michael P. 1999. 'The Amnesty Exception to the Jurisdiction of the International Criminal Court.' *Cornell International Law Journal* 32: 507–527.

Schomerus, Mareike. 2007. 'The Lord's Resistance Army in Sudan: A History and Overview.' *Small Arms Survey* Vol. 8. Geneva: Graduate Institute of International Studies.

Schomerus, Mareike. 2010. '"A Terrorist Is Not a Person Like Me"; An Interview with Joseph Kony.' In *The Lord's Resistance Army: Myth and Reality*, edited by Tim Allen and Koen Vlassenroot, 113–131. London and New York: Zed Books Ltd.

Schomerus, Mareike. 2012. 'Even Eating You Can Bite Your Tongue: Dynamics and Challenges of the Peace Talks with the Lord's Resistance Army.' PhD Thesis, London School of Economics and Political Science.

Security Council Report. 2006. *Update Report No. 2: Uganda (14 November 2006)*. New York: Security Council Report.

Simonse, Simon, Willemijn Verkoren, and Gerd Junne. 2010. 'NGO Involvement in the Juba Peace Talks: The Role and Dilemmas of IKV Pax Christi.' In *The Lord's Resistance Army: Myth and Reality*, edited by Tim Allen and Koen Vlassenroot, 223–241. London and New York: Zed Books Ltd.

The New Vision. 2005, April 18. 'Court Rules out Kony Immunity.' *The New Vision*.

Uganda, Republic of. 2008. *"[Reply to] Request for Further Information from the Republic of Uganda on the Status of Execution of the Warrants of Arrest."* Doc. ADM/70/269.

UN Security Council. 2006. *Statement by the President of the Security Council*. UN Doc. S/PRST/2006/45. New York: United Nations.

UN Security Council. 2007. *Statement by the President of the Security Council*. UN Doc. S/PRST/2007/6. New York: United Nations.

UN Security Council. 2008. *Statement by the President of the Security Council*. UN Doc. S/PRST/2008/4. New York: United Nations.

Unger, Thomas, and Marieke Wierda. 2009. 'Pursuing Justice in Ongoing Conflict: A Discussion of Current Practice.' In *Building a Future on Peace and Justice: Studies on Transitional Justice, Peace and Development*, edited by Kai Ambos, Judith Large, and Marieke Wierda, 263–302. Berlin and Heidelberg: Springer-Verlag.

US Embassy Kampala. 2008. *Northern Uganda: Kony Living in a Fool's Paradise*. 08KAMPALA1579. wikileaks.org.

US Embassy Khartoum. 2006. *Lawyer Briefs LRA's Kony on ICC*. 06Khartoum2701. wikileaks.org.

US Embassy Khartoum. 2007. *Sudan/Uganda/DRC: Peace Talks Resume in Juba*. 07KHARTOUM671. wikileaks.org.

US Embassy London. 2006. *Sudan: FCO Thoughts on Incentives and Disincentives for Bashir*. 06LONDON7036. wikileaks.org.

US Embassy UN. 2006a. *Gambari, Kalomoh, Guehenno, Egeland Attend Core Group Meeting on Northern Uganda*. 06USUNNEWYORK1404A. wikileaks.org.

US Embassy UN. 2006b. *UN on LRA: 'Symptom of Problem That Only Uganda Can Resolve'*. 06USUNNEWYORK912A. wikileaks.org.

US Embassy UN. 2008. *Chissano to UN: Kony Won't Go to ICC; to US: Try Him in Uganda*. 08USUNNEWYORK1203. wikileaks.org.

US Embassy UN. 2009. *UNMIS Consultations and the ICC*. 09USUNNEWYORK98. wikileaks.org.

US Senate Committee on Foreign Relations. 2007. *Testimony of Jendayi E. Frazer, Assistant Secretary, Bureau of African Affairs, Before the US Senate Committee on Foreign Relations Subcommittee on African Affairs 'Exploring the US Role in Consolidating Peace and Democracy in the Great Lakes Region'*. Washington, DC. www.foreign.senate.gov/imo/media/doc/FrazerTestimony071024a.pdf

Vision Reporter. 2002, 10 June. 'Time to Finish Kony', editorial. *The New Vision*.

Wasike, Alfred, and Felix Osike. 2003, September 18. 'Gen. Museveni Warns Sudan.' *The New Vision*.

5 ICC involvement in the Kenya National Dialogue and Reconciliation

The AU Panel for Kenya chaired by former Secretary-General Kofi Annan has made the ICC part of a comprehensive solution for Kenya.

ICC Prosecutor Louis Moreno-Ocampo, speech to Qatar Law Forum, Doha, 30 May 2009

This chapter investigates the interplay between ICC involvement in Kenya and the country's peace process that ended the post-election violence in 2008, the Kenya National Dialogue and Reconciliation. Structured like Chapter 3, it provides a chronological account of the case study's three phases of peacemaking and three stages of ICC involvement in Kenya, from the first attempts to persuade the conflict parties to enter a dialogue, to the signing of a power-sharing agreement, implementation of the justice policy and efforts to navigate a high level of ICC involvement. It traces the actors, actions and ideas that converged to create, but also destabilise, the conditions of possibility for the political settlement in Kenya: conflict parties, mediators, external actors, parliament, the ICC Prosecutor and the ICC's PTC.

The peace process responded to a crisis of spontaneous and organised violence and revenge attacks carried out by ordinary people, ethnic militias and security forces in reaction to the Electoral Commission's official announcement that Mwai Kibaki had won the presidential elections on 27 December 2007.[1] The violence began on 30 December 2007 and took the form of murder, maiming, rape, forced circumcision, arson, evictions, looting and threats of violence (Republic of Kenya 2008g). Over the next two months, more than 1,300 people were killed and up to 600,000 were internally displaced. The underlying conflict stemmed from land-related grievances and perceptions of indigeneity and foreignness going back to colonial and early post-colonial patronage politics.

The peace process aimed to 'achieve a sustainable peace, stability and justice in Kenya through the rule of law and respect for human rights' (Republic of Kenya 2008f). It followed roughly the linear three-phase model discussed in Chapter 2 (see Figure 2.3). Pre-Negotiation discussions began almost immediately as the conflict escalated to the violent stage, and the Negotiation phase commenced less than four weeks later. At this point, the process was named the

Kenya National Dialogue and Reconciliation. The trajectory of ICC involvement followed the Preliminary Examination, Investigation and Indictment stages. The Trial stage took place after the 2013 elections and therefore lies outside the case study. Active ICC involvement in Kenya took place during the Negotiation and Implementation phases. The Preliminary Examination stage, which marked the beginning of a low level of active involvement, began during the Negotiation phase.

Kenya Dialogue: Pre-Negotiation phase (30 December 2007–28 January 2008)

African and Western states swung rapidly into action as soon as the violence erupted. During the first two weeks of January 2008, several high-profile visitors extended their election observation visit or flew in to convince the parties on the need for dialogue: the head of the Commonwealth Observer Group, the former Sierra Leonean president, Ahmed Tejan Kabbah; South Africa's Archbishop, Desmond Tutu; four former heads of state from Botwana, Mozambique, Tanzania and Zambia, representing the African Forum network to prevent conflict; and the US Assistant Secretary of State for African Affairs, Jendayi Frazer (Africa Forum 2008; Lindenmayer and Kaye 2009). These initiatives were in vain. Mwai Kibaki's PNU denied the country's crisis of governance and maintained that any recourse had to go through the courts, while Raila Odinga's ODM refused to engage in dialogue (Lindenmayer and Kaye 2009, 5). In spite of the scale, spread and spiralling of violence, the conditions for entering into dialogue were absent. By the end of the first week of January 2008, violence had displaced around 250,000 people and caused over 300 deaths. In an attack reminiscent of Rwanda's 1994 genocide, perpetrators locked and set on fire the Kiambaa church in which 30 members of the Kikuyu community had taken refuge. This incident would later be investigated by the ICC.

The Chairperson of the African Union, Ghana's president, John Kufuor, was the first dignitary to obtain the conflict parties' commitment to enter into dialogue. His visit was at initially dismissed by government officials, who approached him as an official state visitor 'coming for a cup of tea' rather than as a crisis manager (Juma 2008).[2] Once the principals agreed to negotiate, Kufuor invited Kofi Annan, Benjamin Mkapa and Graça Machel to constitute the mediation team, the AU Panel of Eminent African Personalities. Mkapa was former president of Tanzania and a member of the Africa Forum, while Machel had overseen the 2005–2006 country review of Kenya under the African Peer Review Mechanism. Kufour's mediation plan, however, was temporarily undermined by Uganda's Museveni, who arrived with his own peace plan and was welcomed by the PNU government as a means to resist internationalisation (US Embassy Kampala 2008; Lindenmayer and Kaye 2009, 6). Kibaki delayed meeting with Annan and tried to use Museveni 'as a go-between' between the Panel and the government.[3]

The many high-profile visitors created opportunities for 'forum shopping', whereby conflict principals play mediators against each other in order to undermine negotiations or get favourable terms of engagement. Towards the end of the Pre-Negotiation phase, Annan therefore worked to ensure that his Panel was recognised as the sole mediator.[4] The other external actors stepped aside and the international community, including the UN Secretary-General and Security Council, issued statements of support for the Panel (Africa Forum 2008; The Elders 2008; UN News Centre 2008).

The conflict parties

Kibaki, the government and the PNU lacked legitimacy because of widespread suspicions of electoral fraud by the PNU and the Electoral Commission. Amplifying these suspicions, he was sworn in as president during the night and in the context of a media ban. During the Pre-Negotiation phase, however, the PNU discourse centred on four claims. First, the PNU won the presidency legitimately and any challenge to this would have to go through the courts. Second, political leaders who incite their followers to use violence – a reference to the ODM calls for mass action – are illegitimate. Third, there was no governance crisis to speak of and the government was taking steps to calm the country. Last, any dialogue with the opposition must be premised on the latter's recognition of the legitimacy of the president.

To remedy the president's legitimacy problem, the government sought to use the high-profile Pre-Negotiation visits as a source of legitimacy. Within a few hours of Kufuor's arrival, Kibaki controversially appointed the vice president and 16 other ministers, a move that signalled a president in control and created a central-eastern alliance (the new vice president was Kalonzo Musyoka, head of the party ODM-Kenya, who hailed from eastern Kenya) against Odinga and William Ruto's western alliance. Government press releases portray a president in convergence with his powerful visitors: Kibaki and Tutu jointly 'called for an end to the … violence', Kibaki and Frazer 'agreed' on the need to ensure peace, while Kibaki and Kufuor 'underscored' the need for peace and harmony and 'reiterated that dialogue is the only way forward' (Government of Kenya 2008a; 2008b). The crisis meeting with members of the Africa Forum was described as a 'courtesy call' to the president (Government of Kenya 2008a).

As the crisis unfolded, the PNU discourse became increasingly harder to maintain: the violence continued, ODM called for mass action and the international community paid a lot of attention to the situation. The elections of the Speaker and Deputy Speaker of parliament changed the game. This first act of parliament was protracted and bitter and went on until 2 a.m.; in the third round of voting, the ODM won both roles.[5] To international observers, the incumbent's loss of control over parliament illustrated a 'paralysis of governance' (interview with member of the mediation team, May 2011). During previous episodes of election-related violence, the government had maintained control of the political process.

The ODM's discourse centred on its claim that Kibaki had 'stolen' the presidential elections, while in fact Odinga had won the right to be president. ODM members therefore felt they could not enter into dialogue with Kibaki in the role as the president. Thinking that international involvement could create a level playing field, the party had a very clear preference for UN-led mediation. Seeking to secure as many concessions as possible before committing to negotiations, the ODM premised participation in peace talks on Kibaki's resignation as president, the formation of a transitional government, a rerun of the presidential elections and an agreement to undertake comprehensive legal and constitutional reforms, particularly with regard to the land issue (Lindenmayer and Kaye 2009, 8).

The ODM had one major tool to increase its leverage in the Pre-Negotiation phase: the organisation and control over mass protests by its many supporters. Mass action highlighted Odinga's widespread popularity and support, and fitted the narrative that he won the presidential elections. The ODM mass protests from early January heightened the tension and caused further violence and displacement. Odinga called for mass action several times, and threatened the same throughout the Pre-Negotiation and Negotiation phases to increase the ODM's power at the negotiation table. He also called off protests on a number of occasions, using this as a concession to Frazer and Annan.

Kenya Dialogue: Negotiation phase (29 January 2008–23 May 2008)

The Dialogue was formally launched on 29 January 2008. The negotiations were conducted under the formal auspices of the AU, but received logistical, technical and administrative support from the UN Department of Political Affairs (DPA), the UN Office in Nairobi and the Centre for Humanitarian Dialogue (HD), an international Geneva-based mediation NGO. The UN Development Programme managed the donor funds and the personnel contracts for the mediation team. The mediation secretariat for this process of 'hybrid mediation' was composed of staff from the AU, the DPA and the HD. Annan wanted to internationalise the peace process so as to boost the authority of the AU intervention (HD 2009).

Whether the PNU wanted it or not, the peace process was thoroughly internationalised, to the extent that the DPA drafted the annotated agenda that structured the peace process.[6] Experts from the DPA and the HD prepared and presented the documentation for the negotiations on how to deal with the disputed presidential elections.[7] The ODM wanted the negotiations to be named an 'international mediation effort', while the PNU wished to downplay the external involvement with the term 'national dialogue' (Juma 2009, 411). Annan went along with PNU's proposal to keep them on board and to signal national ownership.

In his role as the chief mediator, Annan combined the region and the international community in one person: he was Ghanaian and deployed by the AU, while also being the former UN Secretary-General and trusted by the West. As a member of his team put it, he was 'the African leadership that the rest of the world could get behind, because the rest of the world also thinks of Annan as theirs'.[8] Key actors in the international community, not least the US, supported him throughout the peace process (HD 2009). This support functioned as unified international pressure on the conflict parties to move in the direction of the mediators.

Negotiation structure

The two peace delegations were comparably small, their sizes encouraged by Annan who preferred two small, committed teams (Office of the Panel of Eminent African Personalities 2014, 27). The PNU delegation consisted of Martha Karua, Minister for Justice and Constitutional Affairs and leader of the PNU team; Sam Ongeri, Minister of Education; Moses Wetang'ula, Minister of Foreign Affairs; and Mutula Kilonzo from ODM-Kenya. The ODM delegation consisted of team leader Musalia Mudavadi, James Orengo, William Ruto and Sally Kosgei. Each team also had a liaison officer. The Kenyan principals themselves were not part of the negotiation teams.

In spite of relating to each other as government and opposition party, incumbent and electorally aggrieved, the two delegations were symmetrical in power and capacity:

> Half of them were lawyers; all of them had been ministers or were ministers. The level of debate and capacity to engage on both sides was extraordinarily high. And, of course, on both sides they also had technical teams that they were working with outside the room that were equally some of the great minds in Kenya.[9]

There was no need for capacity-building. The negotiators understood the issues and 'knew what was at stake'.[10] While the PNU controlled the government, ODM commanded enough protesters to destabilise the country.

While the PNU insisted on funding the Dialogue to keep it national, the UN Development Programme offered to manage a trust fund for international contributions. Donors to the Dialogue and the Juba Peace Talks overlapped greatly, but this time they were willing 'to fund the mediation quickly and generously' (Office of the Panel of Eminent African Personalities 2014, 33; see also Kanyinga and Walker 2013, 10).

The negotiations were structured by a four-item agenda: immediate action to stop the violence and restore fundamental human rights and liberties; immediate measures to address the humanitarian crisis, and promote reconciliation, healing and restoration; discussions on how to overcome the political crisis; and long-term issues and solutions. The agenda was designed to de-escalate the crisis. It saw as most urgent the need to stop the ongoing post-election violence, curbing the generation of fresh grievances and assisting the displaced populations, and left for later the problem of the disputed elections and the discussions on how to transform Kenya into a more just and equitable society. The long-term solutions in the last agenda item aimed to normalise social relations, paving the way for reconciliation.

The annotated agenda framed the negotiations and the way issues, problems and solutions were conceived. It operated with three different meanings of justice: social justice issues referred to the underlying grievances, procedural justice related to electoral practices and criminal justice was associated with the ongoing violence. The agenda provided a narrative of the underlying causes of conflict: '[p]overty, the inequitable distribution of resources and perceptions of historical injustices and exclusion on the part of segments of the Kenyan society' (Republic of Kenya 2008e). To solve the conflict by removing or transforming its causes, Item 4 of the agenda proposed a list of possible remedies in constitutional, legal, institutional and land reform; the tackling of poverty, inequality and unemployment; the consolidation of national cohesion and unity; and transparency, accountability and non-impunity.

Agenda Items 1 and 2: Stopping the violence and addressing the humanitarian crisis

The negotiations 'sailed through' the first two agenda items and resulted in agreements signed on 1 and 4 February 2008, respectively. The first agreement announced a number of steps to be taken by various institutions and actors in order to end the violence: refraining from retaliation attacks and hate speech, demobilising the militias, ensuring peaceful public assemblies and, on the part of the police force, ceasing the use of live bullets on unarmed civilians, enforcing law and order, securing the major transit routes, carrying out their duties without regard to ethnicity and political affiliation, and investigating instances of police brutality. In addition, a number of steps did not have an explicit recipient, but fell within the remit of the police and the public prosecutor, such as assisting IDPs to return to their homes and farms and uphold their rights to reside anywhere, and prosecuting all criminal activities.

The second agreement was concluded after only a weekend, and listed many measures to be taken to address the humanitarian and IDP crisis and promote reconciliation, healing and restoration. Again, most of these steps did not designate a specific implementing actor. The agreement also established the Truth, Justice and Reconciliation Commission (TJRC), which was detailed in later negotiations.

In spite of the rapid agreement on the first two agenda items, the atmosphere in the negotiations room was 'poisonous' (Lindenmayer and Kaye 2009). The PNU discourse now focused less on asserting the legitimacy of the elections and Kibaki's legitimacy as president and more on assigning responsibility for the violence to the ODM, alleging that the political incitement of supporters by Odinga, Ruto and other ODM politicians caused the violence. To the ODM, on the other hand, the level of political violence indicated that it could only have been organised by a government: by the first week of February, more than 600 people had been killed.

Agenda Item 3: How to resolve the political crisis

The negotiations of Item 3 of the agenda commenced in the second week of February 2008. These negotiations turned out to be the most difficult and protracted. In spite of the ongoing violence, rapid agreement on the previous two agenda items and public support for the peace process, the parties were unable to look towards possible solutions (Lindenmayer and Kaye 2009). ODM negotiators maintained that the election victory and the presidency belonged to them and that entering negotiations with PNU as the government had been a major concession. The PNU team insisted that Kibaki had won the elections legitimately. The right to govern was the major sticking point of the negotiations and the mutual accusations did not create a zone of possible agreement.

In response to this stalemate, the Panel divided the negotiations into two parts: a backward-looking part concerned with the contentious elections and a forward-looking part focusing on the future governance set-up. The parties first addressed the retrospective part. ODM negotiators insisted that they had raised the alarm six months prior to the elections over what they perceived to be flawed registration practices and the questionable re-composition of the Electoral Commission in favour of the incumbent. PNU delegates maintained that the accusations of electoral fraud by the EU Commission and the Commonwealth Observer Mission were without foundation, given that their observers only had visited 3 per cent of polling stations and had found only minor discrepancies. Each party brought in elections experts and lawyers, who presented 'equally convincing or unconvincing' arguments about why ODM or PNU had won the elections.[11] These presentations were for the benefit of the mediation team rather than the adversary, but afterwards the mediators still did not know who had won the elections. To them, therefore, the only feasible option was a unity government: 'We actually don't know who was the winner, so power-sharing was the only solution.'[12]

Given the conflict parties' disagreement about the nature of the elections, the mediation Panel sought to transform the issue. They turned the political issue of what was desirable into a technical issue of what was feasible and possible, asking the negotiation teams to examine four options for how to deal with the disputed elections: a re-count of the votes, a re-tally of the tallying sheets, a rerun of the presidential elections, and a judicial process. The mediators invited two technical experts from the DPA's Electoral Division to brief the parties on the details of the four options. The DPA's Craig Jennes (quoted in UN Department of Political Affairs 2008, 5) has explained that he provided the 'technical opinions that supported [Annan's] best political instincts', explaining that 'only a power-sharing agreement could resolve the crisis and that a re-count of the vote or rerun of the election – options the two sides were still debating – would be a recipe for disaster and confrontation and more violence'. Negotiators considered the four options. A re-count would require the opening of all the ballot boxes and the scrutiny of more than 11 million voting sheets, a process that would take some time. A re-tally of the results sheets from 27,500 polling stations and the 210 constituencies would take less time than a re-count, but, in both cases, the process would not necessarily guarantee a fairer result if ballot boxes had been stuffed or tally sheets had been manipulated. At this point, some ballot boxes had been destroyed by angry protesters. A rerun of the presidential elections implied that the election was flawed, which is why the parties disagreed about this policy. They did, however, agree on the need to reform the Electoral Commission and update the voter register (Republic of Kenya 2008b). The possibility of a judicial process was also ruled out, formally with reference to the expiry of the legal time limit but informally because the ODM lacked confidence in the judiciary.

Following the examination and rejection of the four options, the parties agreed that the best solution would be to establish an independent commission to review the 2007 elections and make recommendations for future electoral reform (Republic of Kenya 2008b). The Independent Review Committee (IREC) was Annan's preferred option from the beginning of the peace process (HC 2009, 10). He found it non-divisive and forward-looking at this point in the conflict. Importantly, it would move the truth about the elections to a point in the future where the country was more stable and less likely to generate violent responses (Elklit 2011). With the decision on the IREC, Annan also closed the issue of the elections results, insisting that the time for questioning Kibaki's legitimacy was over. This interpretation enabled Kibaki to retain his authority as president and shaped the nature of Kenya's power-sharing.

Negotiating a power-sharing deal

The negotiations on the forward-looking part of Item 3 of the agenda were the hardest, being 'tense and bitter' (Kanyinga and Walker 2013, 11). The idea of power-sharing had been floated early on. The ODM now proposed the introduction of the posts of a prime minister with executive powers and two deputy prime ministers. The executive powers were designed to make the role independent of the 'President's whim' (Lindenmayer and Kaye 2009, 18), a position derived from the 2002 elections when Kibaki had reneged on an earlier promise to share power with Odinga. The PNU rejected the proposal, insisting that these new posts would spell the end of Kenya's multi-party system. Having all along defined itself as the sovereign, constitutional and legitimate government, the PNU felt it could not allow a solution that did not conform to existing laws.

PNU negotiators succeeded in defining the issue of power-sharing as chiefly a constitutional issue, framed by the possibilities of Kenya's Constitution. According to their thinking, a shared executive would need to be subject to a referendum; at the same time, this kind of popular participation was perceived as impossible due to the violence across the country. According to them, the introduction of a prime minister could only be accommodated within Article 16 of the Constitution, which empowered the president to appoint ministers. For the ODM, however, Article 16 left too much room for presidential manoeuvre. Government changes, therefore, would need to be anchored in constitutional changes.

To end the stalemate, the Panel created two interventions. First, it invited the German Minister of State, Gernot Erler, to share his experience of coalition government. He described how to negotiate a coalition contract, build trust and manage crises, later noting that the parties 'were especially interested in the apportionment of ministries' (Spiegel Online 2008). The PNU government was not convinced about the transferability of the German case and detailed the many differences between the two systems (Lindenmayer and Kaye 2009, 16).

The second intervention was to again turn the contentious issue into a technical problem. Power-sharing became a question that chiefly concerned legal specialists. Annan drew on Hans Correll, his former legal counsel at the UN, to constitute the Legal Working Group on Governance comprising lawyers from both conflict parties. The Working Group came up with the Draft National Accord and Reconciliation Act 2008 on power-sharing, which built on ODM's proposition to create a prime minister and two deputy prime ministers. However, after further stalling, disagreements and a sense of loss of momentum by the mediators, the Panel decided to suspend the talks in order to directly engage the conflict principals (Khadiagala 2009, 21; Rashid 2008b).

Two days later, on 28 February 2008, in a closed-door meeting with Annan, Mkapa and Tanzania's president, Jakaya Kikwete, Kibaki and Odinga agreed to share power and perused the Draft Act. This agreement was formalised in Acting Together for Kenya, the power-sharing agreement, which was subsequently codified in act of parliament, the National Accord and Reconciliation Act. The parties formed a government of national unity (GNU), which reflected their relative parliamentary strength and took into account the 'principle of portfolio balance', the allocation of relatively powerful ministries to both main parties. It also established a prime minister with authority to coordinate and supervise the government, two deputy prime ministers, one from each member of the GNU, and the cabinet inclusion of these new roles. The prime minister and deputy prime ministers could only be removed by a vote of no confidence in parliament or the dissolution of the GNU; they were therefore independent of presidential 'whims'. The sticking point had been overcome.

Commenting on the power-sharing deal, Odinga (quoted in BBC 2008) described the coalition as sharing power on an equal basis: 'We recognise Mr Kibaki as president and he recognises that there were some flaws in the elections.' Kibaki (quoted in Wachira 2008) announced, 'Kenya has room for all if we enhance peace and tolerance.' Crowds, particularly in ODM constituencies, celebrated the deal – amidst being tear-gassed by the police (Nation Team 2008).

External involvement

The negotiations on Item 3 of the agenda were influenced by the involvement of powerful external actors, including visits by the UN Secretary-General, top AU representatives and the US Secretary of State. This involvement mainly took a coercive form. The UN Security Council, the EU and the US Congressional Subcommittee on Africa threatened to intervene if the parties were unable to agree on a solution to the political crisis (Office of the Panel of Eminent African Personalities 2014, para. 31). Canada, the EU, Switzerland, the UK and the US suggested using targeted sanctions and travel bans against those who obstructed the talks, while Australia warned of limiting contact with Kibaki's cabinet (Frazer 2008; Office of the Panel of Eminent African Personalities 2014, para. 32). The US Secretary of State (Rice 2008) threatened rejectionists with 'a wide range of possible actions' imposed by a unified international community:

> We will draw our own conclusions about who is responsible for lack of progress and take necessary steps. We will also exert leadership with the United Nations, the African Union, the European Union, and others to ensure that the political solution the Kenyan people deserve is achieved.

Neighbouring and regional countries, who depended on the Kenyan ports for a range of imported goods, also made their views known to the government.[13]

The international community early on relayed its preference for a power-sharing solution to Kenya's problem. The US State Department hinted at 'possible further sanctions' against those who obstruct a 'power sharing agreement' (Frazer 2008) and Rice (quoted in Magella 2008) dictated, 'There needs to be a coalition; they need to share power and share responsibility.' The PNU government felt cornered and asserted its sovereignty. Moses Wetang'ula (quoted in Rashid 2008a), warned that 'we encourage our friends to support us, to encourage us but not to make the mistake of putting a gun to anybody's head and say "either/or" because that cannot work'. Eventually, however, the PNU agreed to share power.

ICC Stage 2: Preliminary Examination (5 February 2008–30 March 2010)

As we saw in Chapter 2, once a country ratifies the Rome Statute the Prosecutor has authority to open an investigation on his own initiative (*proprio motu*). Less than four weeks after the violence erupted, on 23 January 2008, the ICC officially stated that it was 'closely observing' the post-election violence (Hirondelle News Agency 2008). In stating this, the ICC responded to the ODM's announcement earlier that day that it was filing a complaint at the ICC over 'crimes against humanity and state-sponsored terrorism' (Nzioka 2008). The party alleged that Kibaki, his cabinet, the Roads Minister, the Police Commissioner, and commanders of the paramilitary General Service Unit were responsible for the killing of ODM protesters in Nyanza, Western and Coast provinces. Earlier in January, MPs from the PNU threatened to report ODM leaders to the ICC over ethnic cleansing and genocide. In the context of animosity and violence, the conflict parties were engaged in 'the politics of naming' (Mamdani 2010).

Naming violence becomes a site of struggle because of the legal implications of certain names. Genocide, Mamdani (2010, 53) argues, 'goes with an international responsibility to intervene' militarily to stop it. Similarly, in the Membership stage, the Rome Statute imposes a duty upon states and the ICC to prosecute alleged war crimes, crimes against humanity and genocide. Both the PNU and the ODM mobilised the discursive power of atrocity crimes in their political struggle. They legitimised their claims against the other side by calling on the ICC, the authoritative world body mandated to oversee the punishment of these crimes. By responding to these complaints, the ICC made itself relevant to the Kenyan situation. It claimed legitimacy from the Kenyan complaints.

ICC involvement progressed from the monitoring role of the Membership stage to the Preliminary Examination stage shortly after it respond to the ODM 'complaint'. On 5 February 2008, the OTP (2008) stated that it 'considers carefully all information relating to alleged crimes within its jurisdiction committed on the territory of States Parties or by nationals of States Parties, regardless of the individuals or group alleged to have committed the crime'. The statement launched a preliminary investigation, indicating that Kenya's violence potentially fell within the jurisdiction of the ICC (Alai and Mue 2010, 1; ICC 2009b, 14). It also sought to deter the perpetrators of violence by reminding them of Kenya's membership. Through these perlocutionary actions, the statement built the Court's relevance and legitimacy.

The OTP statement was issued just as the peace process was about to begin work on Item 3 of the agenda, the sticking point. From interviews with mediators and one PNU negotiator, it appears that the participants took little notice of the ICC statement, although it was reported in Kenyan newspapers. To the members of the mediation team, the statement 'did not register' since the ICC 'wasn't doing anything real'.[14] In fact, at the time, ICC issues 'weren't really being discussed'.[15] Instead, the mediators were 'consumed by the national politics of it all: would a grand coalition work, would the president allow a prime minister, would it be embedded in the constitution?'[16] According to Mutula Kilonzo of the PNU delegation, the ICC statement 'never stuck in our minds'.[17] At the time, the ICC 'never featured in our thinking, at all'.[18] The negotiations on Item 3 of the agenda were thus unaffected by the ICC's monitoring and involvement at the Preliminary Examination stage. Emic accounts and academic analyses of the process of reaching the power-sharing deal confirm this interpretation (Kanyinga 2011; Kanyinga and Walker 2013; Khadiagala 2009; Lindenmayer and Kaye 2009; Preston McGhie and Wamai 2011).

Outside the negotiation room, justice proponents easily saw a link between the post-election violence and the Court's work. The Law Society of Kenya and the Kenya National Commission of Human Rights began to gather evidence to submit to the ICC (*East African Standard* 2008a; 2008b). Kenyans for Peace with Truth and Justice, a coalition of NGOs formed in response to the crisis, advocated accountability for the state's role in the violence and for the flawed vote count and election results (Kanyinga 2011, 94). This group enjoyed access to Annan's Panel and called for justice in media statements and opinion pieces. By means of funding from international justice NGOs, it was able to lobby the AU Peace and Security Committee, EU Commission, UN Secretariat and the US Senate and Congress (Kanyinga 2011, 99). Later, it visited the ICC Prosecutor, urging him to investigate Kenya's post-election violence.

The preliminary examination by the ICC lasted just over two years, covering most of the Negotiation phase (agenda Items 3 and 4) and almost half of the Implementation phase. After analysing Item 4, negotiations and the implementation of the justice policies, the chapter returns to the discussion of ICC involvement during the Preliminary Examination stage.

Agenda Item 4: Long-term issues and solutions

The establishment of the GNU had halted the large-scale violence and acts of displacement. However, as the government did not undertake a systematic disarmament, grassroot organisers of violence hid the weapons they had stockpiled during January and February 2008. For the negotiators, the remaining issue concerned the reforms that would address the underlying causes of conflict and prevent a recurrence of atrocity. These negotiations were mediated by Annan's designated successor as chief mediator, Nigeria's Foreign Minister, Oluyemi Adeniji.

The agenda Item 3 agreements had outlined a broad reform agenda, including land, constitutional, electoral, parliamentary, judicial, public service and police reforms, as well as '[o]ther legislative, structural, political and economic reforms as needed' (Republic of Kenya 2008b, 4). These agreements did not provide any details, but left it for subsequent negotiations to flesh out the reform programme. During the discussion on long-term issues, the parties committed to constitutional, institutional and land reform, including police, parliamentary, judicial, executive and civil service reform (Republic of Kenya 2008a). To that end, they agreed to establish the Commission of Inquiry into the Post-Election Violence (CIPEV) and the Truth, Justice and Reconciliation Commission (Republic of Kenya 2008; 2008d). They also agreed on the modalities for the constitutional review process and the principles for the entire reform process. Two months later, the parties added an ambitious implementation matrix.

The agreements on CIPEV and the TJRC deal explicitly with large-scale human rights abuses and issues of justice. They established CIPEV to investigate the large-scale violence that occurred in relation to the 2007 elections, while the TJRC got a broader mandate covering politically motivated violence, assassinations, community displacements, settlements, evictions, major economic crimes, in particular grand corruption, historical land injustices, and the illegal or irregular acquisition of land in the entire post-colonial period (Republic of Kenya 2008c; 2008d).

The CIPEV and TJRC agreements were negotiated with the assistance of a technical expert from the International Center for Transitional Justice, Priscilla Hayner. She worked with the parties on discussing issues of justice and formulating the terms of reference for both the CIPEV and the TJRC. In general, contentious and 'undecidable' issues were transferred out of the negotiations' political arena to different expert commissions: the election results to IREC, the post-election violence to CIPEV, the post-colonial grievances to the TJRC and national unity to the National Cohesion and Integration Commission.[19]

Kenya Dialogue: Implementation phase (13 March 2008–4 March 2013)

The ten agreements completed in the Negotiation phase designed, legitimised and gave momentum to a large-scale reform process, which Kenya embarked upon in the Implementation phase. The Negotiation and Implementation phases overlapped, as the latter began with the establishment of the first commission of inquiry on 13 March 2008 although negotiations continued until the last agreement was signed on 23 May 2008. For the purposes of this analysis, the Implementation phase ended with the general elections in March 2013, when the power-sharing government was replaced by a majority government.

The main modality for implementation and reform was to establish and empower non-judicial independent expert commissions to investigate a given problem and produce a set of recommendations and sometimes draft legislation. The negotiations established four expert commissions: IREC, CIPEV, TJRC and the National Cohesion and Integration Commission. The Implementation phase gave rise to additional commissions, such as the Commission of Experts tasked with drafting the new constitution, the Commission for the Implementation of the Constitution, and the Land Commission, while IREC, CIPEV and the TJRC recommended the establishment of a number of other commissions, such as the Independent Electoral and Boundaries Commission and the National Taskforce on Police Reforms. The 2010 Constitution established ten new commissions and institutions in areas previously associated with the executive.[20]

Mirroring the use of international, technical experts in the Negotiation phase, IREC, CIPEV and the TJRC had a 'hybrid' composition that included non-national commissioners. This feature responded to the low levels of public confidence in state institutions and the history of previous commission recommendations, which were never implemented. The shock of the post-election violence created a new path for Kenya's commissions of inquiry. Commissioners, NGOs and donors wanted the new commissions to be different: they were going to be implemented.[21]

The Commission of Inquiry into the Post-Election Violence

CIPEV turned out to provide the major link between the Dialogue and the process of ICC involvement, which had operated relatively independently of each other during the Negotiation phase. During the Implementation phase, CIPEV's interpretations, recommendations and relationship with Annan and the Panel set in motion a process of further ICC involvement.

CIPEV was created to investigate the facts and circumstances of the post-election violence, including the actions or omissions of state security agencies. It was also tasked with recommending measures to prevent, control or eradicate future political violence, to bring to justice those responsible, and to eradicate impunity and promote national reconciliation (Republic of Kenya 2008g). CIPEV interpreted its mandate in terms of criminal justice and the rule of law, but also considered the transitional issue of whether to grant amnesties. It advised against blanket amnesties, but found that minor offenders could be amnestied in exchange for confessions that could lead to the arrest and prosecution of major offenders (Republic of Kenya 2008g, 469).

Chaired by Justice Philip Waki, CIPEV (also called the Waki Commission) began work on 3 June 2008 and released its report on 16 October 2008. The report came to form the dominant narrative of Kenya's post-election violence, identifying at the 'heart of the post-election violence' a 'cycle of impunity' linked to the political use and institutionalisation of violence following the introduction of multiparty democracy in 1991 (Republic of Kenya 2008g, ix). The inquiry found the violence to have been 'spontaneous in some geographic areas and a result of planning and organization in other areas, often with the involvement of politicians and business leaders' (Republic of Kenya 2008g, viii). Furthermore, members of the state security agencies were also guilty of acts of violence and gross human rights violations. All of this took place in the context of lawlessness stemming from an apparent collapse of 'overwhelmed' security forces.

CIPEV considered its evidence to provide 'a firm basis' for further investigations (Republic of Kenya 2008g, 17). Although it did not reveal their names, it had collected material against 'powerful individuals in politics, government, business, the police and elsewhere' who appeared to have played a role in the post-election violence. To safeguard the integrity of this evidence, on 17 October 2008 CIPEV placed it in the custody of the mediation panel.

Among CIPEV's recommendations was the establishment of a Special Tribunal of Kenya (STK) to prosecute those responsible for the post-election violence. A hybrid tribunal, the STK was to be anchored in the Constitution and staffed with Kenyan and international personnel. CIPEV intended that its evidence should be handed to the STK upon its establishment. Importantly, if the government failed to set up the latter, 'consideration will be given by the Panel to forwarding the names of alleged perpetrators' to the ICC Prosecutor to conduct further investigations (Republic of Kenya 2008g, 18). This recommendation constructed an anti-impunity mechanism to propel the establishment of the STK: failure to establish the STK would trigger the internationalisation of a criminal accountability process.

Reception of the CIPEV report

Given its recommendation to prosecute the perpetrators of the recent political violence, CIPEV's report sparked a wider peace/justice debate on the merits of criminal accountability for the post-election violence. Kenya's peace discourse associated peace with non-criminal processes and equated justice with violence, holding that violence may erupt again if leaders were held accountable. For instance, Ngunyi (2008) argued that:

> the Waki [Commission's] approach is wrong … not because I support the killers, but because I support restoration as opposed to protracted punishment.

> This is how we will protect the next generation from our tribal madness. But if we replay our madness in the prolonged tribunal trials, we will infect our children with the hate....
>
> The country is currently fragile. In fact, the coalition government is just a 'ceasefire' arrangement. A tribunal or The Hague will definitely unsettle this balance. The question is: can we afford to disturb the fragile equilibrium? ... Taking people to The Hague without correcting the source of the hate is futile to the extreme. So long as the presidency remains powerful and coveted, we will continue to kill each other for it.

The peace discourse saw criminal justice as an appropriate response during ordinary times, but did not consider the post-election period as ordinary times in Kenya. Thus, non-criminal processes were a necessary but bitter pill to swallow: 'the alternative is either to swallow injustice as the price of calm or tread forward to a future replete with January-like massacres and Waki reports' (Kimani 2008).

The peace discourse was also mobilised by those who had most to lose from a justice process. For instance, Ruto argued that a tribunal 'defeats the whole purpose of unity' (Munene *et al.* 2008), while the president encouraged everyone to 'temper justice with reconciliation' (Standard Team 2008). Ordinary people sought to de-code the positions of the political elite, interpreting 'reconciliation' and 'healing' as implying impunity. Thus, Kibaki's remarks were widely understood to indicate his opposition to establishing the proposed hybrid tribunal.

Proponents of the justice discourse supported CIPEV's impunity narrative and worried that 'politicians will certainly break this country if they go unpunished' (Kenyans for Peace with Truth and Justice 2008). They hoped that prosecution would deter future violence. According to Makau Mutua (2008):

> Perpetrators must be held accountable no matter who they are. It does not matter if such a step puts the Coalition Government at risk. To do otherwise is to admit that the Coalition Government is out to protect mass killers and barbarians. Impunity should have no place in Kenya. Appeasement this time will mean the end of the country next time.

Kenyans for Peace with Truth and Justice (2008) opposed the idea of a hybrid tribunal and advocated a completely international process. Upon the release of the CIPEV report, the NGO coalition called upon the 'International Community to immediately begin the process of taking perpetrators to the International Criminal Court' rather than to 'call this a Kenyan problem requiring a Kenyan solution'.

At this point in time, the call for a formalised justice process somewhat echoed popular sentiments. A countrywide opinion survey conducted in October–November 2008 found that 58 per cent of Kenyans felt that human rights violators 'should be held accountable and face consequences for what they have done' while 37 per cent favoured amnestying them (Afrobarometer

2010, 7). A month later, a different poll found that 81 per cent of Kenyans 'strongly' or 'somewhat' agreed that the coalition government must prosecute those political leaders responsible for the post-election violence' (South Consulting 2009, para. 34). Within communities at the centre of the post-election violence, however, there was less support for a formal accountability process (Lynch 2011; Wolf 2013).

The elite reception of the CIPEV report was characterised by contradictory developments. The government and parliament formally approved the report in December 2008 and January 2009, respectively, but inside the GNU there were divergent views on the merits of a special tribunal. The ODM took a formal decision to reject the report in October 2008, opposing Odinga's position. Rift Valley MPs felt 'betrayed' by his public support for the recommendations (Munene *et al.* 2008).

The Special Tribunal of Kenya

The STK was not created. The Constitution of Kenya (Amendment) Bill 2009, which was to anchor the tribunal in the Constitution, was put to parliament on 12 February 2009. Although a small majority of MPs voted in favour of the Bill (101 to 93 votes), it failed to obtain the two-thirds majority (145 votes) required for constitutional amendments. Without this amendment, the Tribunal's investigations and judgements could be challenged as unconstitutional, and there was therefore little point in deliberating the establishment of the Tribunal as per the Special Tribunal of Kenya Bill 2009.

In the vote, sceptics and supporters of a special tribunal were almost equally distributed across the parties. This suggests that MPs voted according to parameters other than their party line. Even smaller parties, such as Safina and NARC, were split on the issue. In Uhuru Kenyatta's party, the PNU-affiliated KANU party, eight MPs approved and four rejected the Bill. Table 5.1 details the party affiliation of the 195 vote-casting MPs.

The vote was adjourned twice due to a lack of quorum, a problem created deliberately by those opposed to the Bill. For instance, Danson Mungatana, Assistant Minister for Medical Services argued, 'We do not need this kind of

Table 5.1 Party affiliation of MPs voting on the Constitution of Kenya (Amendment) Bill 2009

Position on the Constitution of Kenya (Amendment) Bill 2009	*ODM*	*PNU*	*ODM-Kenya*	*PNU-affiliated parties*	*ODM-affiliated parties*	*Non-affiliated parties*	*Sub-total*
For	45	29	5	17	1	4	101
Against	46	17	10	14	2	4	93

Sources: Parliament of the Republic of Kenya (2009b, 4960–4961; 2010b). One unnamed MP abstained and 28 MPs did not vote.

law right now. At the very minimal, we should deny this House the quorum. Otherwise, those who come to the House should vote against this Constitution of Kenya (Amendment) Bill' (Parliament of the Republic of Kenya 2009a). The vote was essentially about the desirability of a justice process and the state's ability to manage a process that reached deep into the political establishment. It was less about the STK and more about whether accountability could or should be handled nationally. Interestingly, those MPs who debated the Bill shared a narrative about the problems of the country's politics, but disagreed about the remedy.

Deliberation centred on five themes: impunity, the independence of the ICC, sovereignty, ethnicity and victims/witnesses.[22] STK sceptics remembered past inquiries into political violence and corruption that had had no formal accountability consequences. They saw continuity rather than change in Kenya and worried that the pursuit of highly placed individuals would lead to new violence and displacement. The Bill's supporters saw the history of impunity as the impetus for reform. By creating an STK, parliament would take responsibility for changing Kenya's future course, protect its sovereignty and ensure national ownership. In contrast, ICC involvement signalled state failure. The arguments for and against the proposed constitutional changes are displayed in Table 5.2, organised along the five themes.

Subsequent to the failed amendment vote, at the end of July 2009, the cabinet discussed the issue of justice. It saw five options for action: referring the post-election situation to the ICC; establishing the STK by other means; prosecuting the crimes in a special division of the High Court (akin to Uganda's ICD); prosecuting the crimes in the ordinary justice system based on the International Crimes Act; or withdrawing from the Rome Statute and repealing the International Crimes Act 2008 (Alai and Mue 2010, 7n). These alternatives internationalise or hybridise justice, 'upgrade' the existing justice system, preserve the status quo or neutralise pressure from the Rome Statute and the ICC.

Cabinet took the most status-quo-orientated path, deciding that a reformed police and judiciary would investigate and prosecute the post-election violence. The decision confirmed the fears of those who opposed the STK because they lacked confidence in Kenya's capacity to handle the problem domestically. It also fell short of the expectations of STK supporters, who had argued that a domestic institution should spearhead reform. Gitobu Imanyara, who had voted against the Bill, later initiated a second bill to establish the tribunal; this initiative stalled in November 2009 following four consecutive attempts to reach the parliamentary quorum (Alai and Mue 2010, 3). One of the quorum saboteurs, Isaac Ruto (quoted in Omanga and Ndegwa 2009) explained, 'This Bill has been recycled so many times. Parliament cannot be asked the same question all the time. We made it clear we are not interested in this Bill.' Clearly, parliament had moved on. But where to?

Table 5.2 Arguments pertaining to the Constitution of Kenya (Amendment) Bill 2009

Against the Bill	*For the Bill*
A history of impunity I urge my fellow legislators to agree with me that it is an exercise in futility to put it in this Constitution that we are going to set up a tribunal and yet in the end, there will be no conviction or nothing will happen in this country. We have many examples (Asst Min. for Medical Services, Hon. Mungatana).	**A history of impunity can now be corrected** [I]n the year 2007, we saw the cumulative effects of impunity. It is actually my view that, if we do not deal decisively with that impunity, we can as well forget about ever having any peaceful elections in this country! (Hon. Baiya).
That tribunal is being set up for the small people. This country has a history of punishing the small people when the big ones have committed the crimes! (Applause) We are putting up a tribunal for the young man who blocked the road. We are not putting up a tribunal for the person who paid the people who blocked the road! (Applause) (Hon. Jirongo).	[T]he reason we are seeking to establish those institutions of the Tribunal is because we have within our national institutions, been unable so far to effectively deal with the post-election violence. So, we are acknowledging that our institutions have fallen short and we are also acknowledging that ahead of constitutional reforms, we need to take certain bold steps (Min. for Justice, National Cohesion and Constitutional Affairs, Hon. Karua).
Impunity will undermine justice by the STK In my view, the perpetrators of post-election violence, who are in the Government, are busy building war chest to do two things: First, to make sure that they defeat any tribunal that will be set up in this country. Second, to make sure that they are ready to take over power, again, by paying young people [to perpetrate violence] (Hon. Jirongo).	**The STK is confronting impunity** This gallery ought to be full watching us amending the Constitution so that we tell Kenyans: "Never again will you touch me because of casting my ballot." … Never again are we going to remove a child from the back of a mother and throw it into a burning church because if you do, the Kenyan law will drop on you like a tonne of bricks (Min. for Nairobi Metropolitan Development, Hon. Kilonzo).
If for one reason, one of the two Principals is either by mischief or truth, actually investigated and considered to be one of the suspects to be taken to court, what will happen to this country? Mr. Temporary Deputy Speaker, Sir, there will be war and acrimony. Let us not forget that what we have now is as a result of the two Principals and that is the truth (Dr Machage).	Instead of running away from taking responsibility, and passing it to other people, I would like to urge hon. Members to show leadership and do what is right by creating institutions and mechanisms that will sort out our problems, however big they might be (Min. of State for Development of Northern Kenya and Other Arid Lands, Hon. I.E. Mohamed).

continued

Table 5.2 Continued

Against the Bill	*For the Bill*
The ICC as independent justice dispenser If we are genuine and we want those people to be punished, we should allow them to go [to The Hague]. That way they will not be able to mobilise their supporters. They will not be able to pay them with the money that they are looting the country today. Justice shall come to prevail! (Applause) (Hon. Jirongo).	**The ICC's independence does not guarantee accountability** [I]t is not guaranteed that if we do not act domestically, one Moreno-Ocampo … will be on the next flight to Nairobi. It may not be so! It is actually highly probable that our failure to act now; our failure to institute a domestic process to handle this matter, might actually suspend ad infinitum our ability and resolve to face, head on, the question of impunity (Applause) (Hon. Namwamba).
	[Y]ou may take the men and women, [whose] names are in the envelope, to the Hague. Well and good! They could be ten, 15, 20 or 30; … But by dealing with those that bear the greatest responsibility to these issues, you have not dealt with the person in the village whose brother or son was hacked to death or wife and daughter were raped and he knows by who (Min. for Foreign Affairs, Hon. Wetangula).
The STK does not ensure sovereignty Those who are talking about passing this Bill as a way of retaining Kenya's sovereignty, should know that we lost it long ago. The moment we called in foreigners to intervene in the issues that we had, our sovereignty was gone.… The argument that by passing this Bill we are safeguarding our sovereignty is a lie (Dr Eseli).	**Kenya retains her sovereignty with the STK** Kenya should manage its own affairs and take charge of its sovereignty. We cannot surrender or cede it to any other nation or agency. We must protect that treasured right.… The fight for Independence came with responsibility that we have the capacity to clean our own house (Hon. Lekuton).
Rwanda is still surviving. Has she lost her sovereignty? Have they? Has Germany lost her sovereignty just because their citizens are still being tried for the holocaust cases? No! (Asst Min. for Roads, Dr Machage).	People have offered to be killed to defend their own sovereignty, yet in this House we seem to have a few people who think that the alternative to the amendment to the Constitution is to allow those involved in the skirmishes of last year to be taken to the Hague. In the same token, if they are taken to the Hague, we shall cede our own sovereignty, and we will cease to be sovereign (Min. for Environment and Mineral Resources, Hon. Michuki).

Ethnicity [If the ICC takes charge] Kenyans will not say that a certain community whose judge was a member of the local or magistrate court, has sentenced our own member. We cannot hide our heads in the sand like an ostrich. Tribalism is rife in Kenya! (Asst Min. for Roads, Dr Machage).	**Ethnicity** We defecated in our house and, therefore, must clean it. In cleaning it, I want to urge all leaders to stop wearing ethnic blinkers in this matter. This thinking of "our man or woman" when we are faced with a calamity that can consume the very foundations of our country, is myopic, parochial and unhelpful to this country (Min. for Foreign Affairs, Hon. Wetangula).
The STK will endanger witnesses We know from history what transpired over the Ouko Inquiry. Witnesses died like flies and by the time the Commission was being disbanded, it had been so discredited. Even after disbanding it, witnesses continued to die. I do not know if we are very sure of what we are doing here (Dr Eseli). One fact we know is that some witnesses who testified at the Waki Commission are known. They are out there. They are afraid and tormented. Maybe some of them are already dead.… Let the international community take charge of the full process (Applause) (Asst Min. for Roads, Dr Machage).	**The STK will ensure victim participation and ownership** If you deny Kenyans that right [to prosecute serious offences], you are telling them to go international, to seek protection. However, they do not have the capacity. They do not have the wealth we have. They do not have the salaries we earn, so that they can hire the sort of lawyers who understand these [international] offences (Min. for Nairobi Metropolitan Development, Hon. Kilonzo).

Sources: Parliament of the Republic of Kenya (2009b; 2009c). The summary excludes statements by MPs who did not vote according to their stated views.

Further discussion of ICC involvement at Stage 2, Preliminary Examination

The ICC's preliminary examination lasted a bit more than two years. Over the course of this involvement stage, the power-sharing government, the Panel and the OTP developed different views on the desirability of further ICC involvement. The Prosecutor and the chief mediator became increasingly committed to the idea of ICC prosecution, while the government wanted to keep the process within Kenya.

The GNU at first sought to avoid engagement with the ICC and ignored the latter's request for information, but changed this approach after it failed to establish the STK. Sensing the imminence of a full ICC investigation, it sent a high-level delegation to Geneva and The Hague in July 2009 to request more time to establish a domestic mechanism (Office of the Panel of Eminent African Personalities 2014, para. 107; OTP 2009b).[23] The seven-member delegation included a Dialogue negotiator from each side, Kilonzo and Orengo, who had both advocated for the STK. The delegation first met with Annan in Geneva, expressing concern that another attempt at establishing the STK may not attract the required support in Parliament (Correll 2009, 2). The delegation then proceeded to The Hague, meeting the Prosecutor 'to ask for time from the ICC to have a local mechanism' (Orengo 2011, 22).

The meeting between the government delegation and the Prosecutor was effectively a negotiation, resulting in an agreement-type official statement of minutes, signed by the Prosecutor and three government representatives. The ICC granted the government 12 months to establish a criminal accountability mechanism, in return for which the government promised a report on the current status of investigations and prosecutions, information on witness protection measures and information on modalities for conducting national investigations and prosecutions. However, 'if there is no parliamentarian agreement, and in accordance with the Kenyan commitment to end impunity … the Government of Kenya will refer the situation to the Prosecutor' (OTP 2009a, 2; see also ICC 2009b, para. 49).

During Stage 2, the mediator and the ICC Prosecutor became increasingly committed to the idea of high-level ICC involvement. Annan saw ICC involvement as an integrated part of a larger peacebuilding project to steer Kenya onto a path of reconciliation and non-impunity. In March 2009, a year before the OTP launched its investigation, ICC officials participated in a high-level conference on implementation of the outputs of the Negotiation phase. More pro-actively, in July 2009, following the government dispatches to Geneva and The Hague, the Panel handed CIPEV's evidence to the Prosecutor. The decision was potentially destabilising, as CIPEV's list of suspects included at least two senior cabinet ministers. The Panel justified its decision in a note, explaining that CIPEV's evidence would be an 'important element' in the Prosecutor's assessment of Kenya's ability to bring perpetrators to justice domestically (Correll 2009, 2).

Annan translated Kenyan affairs to Moreno-Ocampo, 'explain[ing] how for instance in Kenya there is no opposition between a truth commission and justice' (ICC 2009a, 3–4). Annan also devised a 'three-pronged approach' to justice in

Kenya, which became associated with the Prosecutor: ICC prosecution of those most responsible, national accountability proceedings for other perpetrators and reforms and transitional justice instruments such as the TJRC (ICC 2009a, 3–4; see also Alai and Mue 2010). The Prosecutor (quoted in Council on Foreign Relations 2010) increasingly came to see the ICC as 'an independent part of the Kenyan justice system'. In the context of criticism of his involvement in Uganda and Darfur, Kenya was to provide the world with an exemplary case of international justice and would 'show [other countries] how to manage past violence and how to create a peaceful process for the upcoming elections in 2012' (OTP 2009b).

With no domestic justice process in sight, it was difficult to see how Kenya fulfilled its duty to prosecute. The Prosecutor met with Kibaki and Odinga, who offered to cooperate with the ICC. Although the government–OTP 'agreement' gave the GNU a July 2010 deadline for establishing a domestic mechanism, the Prosecutor requested CIPEV's evidence from the Panel and filed a request for authorisation of an investigation on 26 November 2009 (Office of the Panel of Eminent African Personalities 2014, 107; OTP 2009c). Having received no government referral, the Prosecutor invoked his Article 15 authority to investigate *proprio motu*, on his own initiative.

During two press conferences about his plans to investigate the post-election violence, the Prosecutor downplayed the imposed and interventionist nature of his activities. He conceptualised the ICC as 'a part – an independent part – of the legal and judicial system of Kenya' (OTP 2009c). The ICC was on the side of Kenyans:

> The Kikuyu, the Luos, the Luhya, the Kalenjin, the Swahili, the Kisii, the Maasai, the Kamba and all the other tribes of Kenya should feel that they are part of a bigger, global community; that we are their brothers and sisters. (OTP 2009d, 1)

In this imagined community of international justice, however, vulnerabilities differed. The ICC Prosecutor had requested information from the government regarding the status of witness protection and had also met with the Minister for Internal Security and the Attorney-General. Yet he publicised his intentions to investigate before Kenya's witness protection programme had become functional (South Consulting 2010b, 14). Prior to the Investigation stage, populations in the Rift Valley and Nairobi reported that 'senior and powerful politicians' were urging them not to participate in any future investigative process (South Consulting 2010b, 14). Victims were promised parcels of land and scholarships for their children in exchange for their silence. Amidst an 'escalation in threats to potential witnesses', the death of two potential witnesses and intimidation of others had 'forced' many potential witnesses 'into hiding locally or abroad' (South Consulting 2010b, v). Human rights organisations experienced an increased demand for protection (South Consulting 2010a, 9). In this context of insecurity, the Prosecutor announced plans to visit the sites where crimes were committed and to meet with the victims (OTP 2009c, 2).

ICC Stage 3: Investigation (31 March 2010–14 December 2010)

On 31 March 2010, PTC II authorised, by majority, an investigation into the situation in Kenya in relation to crimes against humanity committed between 1 June 2005 and 26 November 2009 (ICC 2010a). The OTP invited those who felt they would be suspected of crimes to come to The Hague to give their side of the story and William Ruto, who was on CIPEV's list of suspects, took this opportunity several times (ICC 2010c). In spite of the witness intimidation, the Prosecutor remained committed to using Kenya as an example. He argued that ICC prosecutions would

> send a clear message for the 15 elections to come in the region: violence during electoral times cannot be a tool to retain or to gain power; but it is a sure avenue towards a one-way ticket for prison in The Hague.
>
> (ICC 2010b, para. 4)

During the Investigation stage, popular support for ICC involvement decreased from 68 to 57 per cent in Kenya, but was arguably still relatively high (Wolf 2013, 158). This national average occluded variation among Kenya's ethnic communities, which, however, became more pronounced in the Indictment stage. Between 13 and 35 per cent of Kalenjin voters supported the ICC process during Stage 4 involvement, with support decreasing to 28 per cent of voters in Kenyatta's Mount Kenya communities (Wolf 2013, 160). Between 74 and 90 per cent of Luo voters supported the ICC process during the same period of time.

The Prosecutor appeared to wait for the constitutional referendum to have taken place before he announced his six suspects. Constitutional reform was an important transitional project and it took place during the Investigation stage. In the first part of the Implementation phase, the Committee of Experts had drafted a new Constitution, based on an earlier participatory constitutional reform process. The new draft Constitution was put to the people on 4 August 2010 and approved by 68.6 per cent of the voters. The referendum had a 72 per cent turnout and was largely peaceful. The new Constitution sought to 'alter significantly the configuration of political power' by introducing a bicameral legislature with a National Assembly and Senate, a devolved system of local government, gender quotas and a detailed electoral framework (Long *et al.* 2013, 143; see also Murray 2013). It delegated executive power to new institutions and required the vetting of all magistrates and judges.

ICC Stage 4: Indictment (15 December 2010–10 September 2013)

On 15 December 2010, the OTP issued summons to appear for six individuals, who were quickly nick-named the 'Ocampo Six'. The Prosecutor had built two cases. In the first case, he charged Henry Kosgey (Minister for Industrialisation and Chairman of the ODM), William Ruto (Minister of Higher Education) and Joshua Arap Sang (a radio executive) with crimes against humanity. In the second case, he charged Uhuru Kenyatta (Deputy Prime Minister and Minister of Finance), Francis Kirimi Muthaura (Cabinet Secretary and head of the Civil Service) and Mohammed Hussein Ali (former Police Chief) with crimes against humanity. With the exception of Sang, these persons were among Kenya's most powerful persons. The OTP indicted three suspects from each side of the conflict's communal and party-political divide: his first case targeted Kalenjin ODM officials and sympathisers, while the second case concerned PNU and PNU-affiliated politicians and top government officials. In April 2011, PTC II confirmed the charges against Ruto, Sang, Kenyatta and Muthaura – the 'Ocampo Four'.

Legal and political mobilisation against the ICC

Following the indictments, the government and parliament used considerable political and financial capital to postpone or eliminate the ICC cases. It sought to fight off the ICC intervention legally and politically. On 31 March 2011, the government submitted an admissibility challenge to the PTC, arguing that the criteria for admissibility were no longer met: the country had adopted a new Constitution and embarked on 'fundamental and far-reaching constitutional and judicial reforms' that would enable Kenya's prosecution of the cases (ICC 2011a, 3). It highlighted that the new Constitution strengthened fair-trial rights, gave effect to judicial reforms that would enable prosecution without an STK and guaranteed the independence of investigative institutions.

The government also highlighted the complementary nature of the ICC's jurisdiction and argued that the ICC's selective approach contributed to a lesser and biased justice: the focus on six individuals 'will have the [most unfortunate] effect of letting it seem that by their standing trial in The Hague, the whole tragic history of 2007/8 is put to rest' (ICC 2011a, 6). Furthermore, only 'by trying people in Kenya itself, and ensuring an even-handed investigation and prosecution of all those on whom suspicion rightly falls, may the national process of dealing with the tragedy be properly balanced'. A domestic process would build public confidence in the police and the judiciary.

The admissibility challenge failed. Tasked with judging whether the cases had become inadmissible, PTC II applied the narrow complementarity test: were Ruto, Sang, Muthaura and Kenyatta being investigated or prosecuted by Kenya? Kenya's Director of Criminal Investigation had informed the PTC that there had been a pending case against Ruto prior to the Indictment stage. Once the Prosecutor revealed his suspects, the government explained, the police commissioner had initiated investigations relating to 'the Ocampo six and other high ranking citizens' (ICC 2011b). PTC II inferred from this explanation that 'a situation of inactivity' remained; it wanted to see details of '*current* investigative steps undertaken' (ICC 2011b, para. 68, 70, emphasis in original). In the narrow world of the admissibility test, it did not matter that Kenya was reforming its justice system. What mattered was concrete investigations of the conduct of particular individuals whom the OTP had identified as bearing the most responsibility. The Kenyan government had requested a hearing in which it could argue its case before the PTC, but this request was refused.

The activities in the political domain entailed mobilisation of parliament within and regional governments without. A week after the 'Ocampo Six' were indicted, parliament adopted a motion that requested the government to withdraw from the Rome Statute, repeal the International Crimes Act and carry out national investigations (Parliament of the Republic of Kenya 2010a). Only one MP opposed the motion – Martha Karua, who was no longer Justice Minister. The government did not act on the MPs' request.

External political mobilisation involved the bold steps of obtaining AU support for a deferral request to the UN Security Council, which would then submit an Article 16 deferral request to the ICC. In advance of the AU summit in January 2011, key government ministers criss-crossed the continent in a campaign of 'shuttle diplomacy'. Travelling to states such as Botswana, Djibuti, Egypt, Ghana, Lesotho, Libya, Nigeria, South Africa and Uganda, cabinet members argued that Kenya was going to establish a mechanism for the domestic prosecution of those responsible and that an ICC trial during the 2012 elections was likely to spark a new round of violence (Irungu 2011).

The regional strategy was successful in terms of obtaining AU Assembly endorsement of a deferral request to the UN Security Council 'to allow for a National Mechanism' (Assembly of the African Union 2011). The AU Assembly therefore 'request[ed] the UN Security Council to accede to this request in support of the ongoing peace building and national reconciliation processes, in order to prevent the resumption of conflict and violence' (Assembly of the African Union 2011). The Security Council discussed the matter informally in March and April 2011, but could not agree on a common position (Security Council Report, n.d.; Xinhua News Agency 2011).

The matter was kept off the formal Security Council agenda until 16 May 2013, when the Council discussed a Kenyan request for dialogue with Council members on the ICC intervention. Several dialogues took place during 2013, and on 15 November Morocco, Rwanda and Togo requested a vote on a draft resolution asking the ICC to defer the prosecution of Kenyatta and Ruto, now the president and vice president. The draft resolution invoked Kenya's responsibility for international peace and security, reform process and role in fighting terrorism in the Horn of Africa (UN Security Council 2013). It was not adopted as it lacked one affirmative vote; seven Council members voted in favour of the resolution (Azerbaijan, China, Morocco, Pakistan, Russia, Rwanda and Togo), while eight abstained (Argentina, Australia, Guatemala, Luxembourg, South Korea, and the Western permanent members) (UN 2013). Disappointed about the outcome, Kenya criticised the Council for being 'no institutional destination for solving complex and fluid international security and political problems' (UN 2013).

The 2013 general elections

On 4 March 2013, Kenya held the first general elections since the 2008 crisis. The new constitutional dispensation meant that the country was electing representatives for the county councils, senate and national assembly as well as governors, women MPs and the president. Three party coalitions were in the running: the Amani Coalition, the Coalition for Reform and Development, and the Jubilee Alliance. Odinga (ODM) ran for president under the Coalition for Reform and Development umbrella, while the Jubilee Alliance fielded Kenyatta (now in the National Party) as president and Ruto (now in the United Republican Party) as his running mate.

Kenyatta won the presidential elections with 50.07 per cent of the vote, just enough to avoid a second round of elections. Odinga won 43.31 per cent of the vote, and Mudavadi of the Amani Coalition drew less than 4 per cent. The elections had a turnout of almost 86 per cent. Odinga initially cried foul, challenging the election result in court. An exit poll had estimated a tie, with 41 per cent support each for Kenyatta and Odinga (Long *et al.* 2013, 147). Odinga accepted the Supreme Court ruling when it validated the election results. Kenyatta became president and Ruto vice president. The Jubilee partnership had surprised many because the two leaders represented ethnic communities that had fought in Kenya's violent election-related struggles since 1992 (Lynch 2014; Wolf 2013). The 2008 post-election violence pitted Kalenjin and Luo against Kikuyu. This included violence and retaliation by ethnic militias.

The partnership between Kenyatta and Ruto made sense in the light of high-level ICC involvement: indicted for organising crimes against humanity, they could fight the ICC cases most effectively by commanding the state. They maximised their chances of achieving the highest offices by uniting their political capital and ethnic voting bases. Dubbed 'UhuRuto' during the election campaigns, their high-risk plan succeeded: on 13 March 2015 the Trial Chamber withdrew the charges against Kenyatta and on 5 April 2016 it decided by majority to terminate the case against Ruto and Sang. Both decisions centred on the evidence available to the OTP. The first derived from the Prosecutor's assessment that she had insufficient evidence to prove Kenyatta's guilt beyond reasonable doubt (ICC 2015). In the second decision, the judges found that Ruto and Sang had no case to answer under the original charges, given the evidence presented by the Prosecutor (ICC 2016). The Chamber vacated the charges against Kenyatta, Ruto and Sang, thereby enabling their future prosecution if new evidence emerges. It denied them an acquittal because of witness interference and intimidation 'at a disturbing scale' (ICC 2016, para. 141).

The Kenyan peace process took place within the 'new world' of peace and justice, as Kenya had commitments to the Rome Statute and the ICC launched a preliminary examination into the post-election situation early in the Negotiation phase. Yet this world was less present to ODM and PNU negotiators during the Negotiation phase than to their Ugandan counterparts as well as the Kenyan unity government during the Implementation phase. The conflict parties overcame their incompatibility by agreeing to share power, having delegated the issue of criminal accountability to CIPEV. Yet the ICC intervention affected the peace process, particularly during the Implementation phase. This part of the peace process began with plans to establish a hybrid Tribunal and ended with the democratic election of two indictees. The next chapter investigates exactly how ICC involvement shaped the Kenyan peace process and explains how and why it succeeded in building a political settlement.

Notes

1 For in-depth analysis of the violent election-related crisis, see Boone (2012), Cheeseman (2008), Harbeson (2012), Kanyinga and Long (2012) and Lynch (2011).
2 Interview with member of the mediation team, October 2010.
3 Interview with member of the mediation team, October 2010.
4 Interview with member of the mediation team, October 2010; see also Kanyinga and Walker (2013) and Lindenmayer and Kaye (2009, 5).
5 ODM's Kenneth Marende and Farah Maalim won the respective positions of Speaker and Deputy Speaker over PNU candidates Francis Kaparo and Gitobu Imamyara.
6 Interview with member of the mediation team, October 2010.
7 Interview with member of the mediation team, May 2011; see also HD (2009, 10).
8 Interview with member of the mediation team, May 2011.
9 Interview with member of the mediation team, May 2011.
10 Interview with member of the mediation team, October 2010.
11 Interview with member of the mediation team, May 2011.
12 Interview with member of the mediation team, May 2011.
13 Interview with Mutula Kilonzo, May 2011.
14 Interview with member of the mediation team, October 2010.
15 Interview with member of the mediation team, May 2011.
16 Interview with member of the mediation team, October 2010.
17 Interview with Mutula Kilonzo, May 2011.
18 Interview with Mutula Kilonzo, May 2011.
19 This commission was initially named the National Ethnic and Race Relations Commission.
20 These were: The Commission on the Implementation of the Constitution, the Auditor General, the Controller of Budgets, the National Police Service Commission, the National Land Commission, the Salaries and Remuneration Commission, the Commission on Revenue Allocation, the Public Service Commission, the Kenya National Human Rights and Equality Commission, and the Independent Electoral Boundaries Commission (Long *et al.* 2013, 143).
21 Interviews with Justice Waki and with member of the Committee of Experts, May 2011. See also Wanjala (2013).
22 It can neither be ruled out nor detected if arguments for or against the STK were motivated by a wish to evade criminal responsibility or that the absence of participation in the debate by many GNU ministers reflected this intention.
23 Interview with Mutula Kilonzo, May 2011.

References

Africa Forum. 2008. *Mission Report: Africa Forum Peace Mission to the Republic of Kenya, 7–12; 14–19; and 22–26 January 2008*. Pretoria: The Africa Forum.

Afrobarometer. 2010. *Kenyans and the Coalition Government: Disappointment in Spite of Relative Peace*. Afrobarometer Briefing Paper No. 91. www.afrobarometer.org.

Alai, Christine, and Njonjo Mue. 2010. *Kenya: Impact of the Rome Statute and the International Criminal Court*. ICTJ Briefing. New York: International Center for Transitional Justice.

Assembly of the African Union. 2011. *Decision on the Implementation of the Decisions on the International Criminal Court, Doc. EX.CL/639(XVIII)*, January 30–31. Assembly/AU/Dec.334(XVI). African Union.

BBC. 2008, February 29. 'Kenyans Celebrate Historic Deal.' *BBC*.

Boone, Catherine. 2012. 'Land Conflict and Distributive Politics in Kenya.' *African Studies Review* 55 (1): 75.

Centre for Humanitarian Dialogue. 2009. *The Prisoner of Peace: An Interview with Kofi A. Annan*. Geneva: Centre for Humanitarian Dialogue.

Cheeseman, Nic. 2008. 'The Kenyan Elections of 2007: An Introduction.' *Journal of Eastern African Studies* 2 (2): 166–184. doi:10.1080/17531050802058286.

Correll, Hans. 2009. *Note on Handover of CIPEV Materials to the Prosecutor of the ICC*. Kenya National Dialogue and Reconciliation, Statement by the Legal Advisor to the Panel of Eminent African Personalities. www.dialoguekenya.org/pressmedia/29-Jul-2009.

Council on Foreign Relations. 2010. *Pursuing International Justice: A Conversation with Louis Moreno-Ocampo (5 February 2010)*. Cfr.org.

East African Standard. 2008a, January 10. 'LSK to Sue Perpetrators of Post-Election Violence.' *The East African Standard*.

East African Standard. 2008b, January 26. 'Rights Group Seeks Evidence on Killings.' *The East African Standard*.

Elklit, Jørgen. 2011. 'The Role of International Organisations during Electoral Crises: The Case of Kenya 2007–08.' *Representation* 47 (4): 399–415.

Frazer, Jendayi. 2008. *Press Briefing by Ambassador Jendayi Frazer*. The White House, Office of the Press Secretary.

Government of Kenya. 2008a. *Former African Heads of State in Talks with President Kibaki*. State House. www.statehousekenya.go.ke/.

Government of Kenya. 2008b, January 4. *President Kibaki in Talks with Archbishop Tutu, Says He Is Ready for Dialogue*. State House. www.statehousekenya.go.ke/.

Harbeson, John W. 2012. 'Land and the Quest for a Democratic State in Kenya: Bringing Citizens Back In.' *African Studies Review* 55 (1): 15.

Hirondelle News Agency. 2008, January 23. 'International Criminal Court Observing Violence Closely.' *Hirondelle News Agency*.

International Criminal Court. 2009a. *Mr Louis Moreno-Ocampo, Prosecutor of the International Criminal Court. Seventeenth Diplomatic Briefing. Statement*. The Hague: International Criminal Court.

International Criminal Court. 2009b. *Report of the International Criminal Court to the UN General Assembly, 64th Session*. New York: UN.

International Criminal Court. 2010a. *Decision Pursuant to Article 15 of the Rome Statute on Authorization of an Investigation into the Situation in the Republic of Kenya*. The Hague: International Criminal Court.

International Criminal Court. 2010b. *Mr Louis Moreno-Ocampo, Prosecutor of the International Criminal Court. Eighteenth Diplomatic Briefing. Statement*. The Hague: International Criminal Court.

International Criminal Court. 2010c. *Prosecutor's Application Pursuant to Article 58 as to William Samoei Ruto, Henry Kiprono Kosgey and Joshua Arap Sang*. Public Redacted Version of Document ICC-01/09–30-Conf-Exp. The Hague: International Criminal Court.

International Criminal Court. 2011a. *Application on Behalf of the Government of the Republic of Kenya Pursuant to Article 19 of the ICC Statute*. ICC 01/09–01/11 and ICC 01/09–02/11. The Hague: International Criminal Court.

International Criminal Court. 2011b. *Decision on the Application by the Government of Kenya Challenging the Admissibility of the Case Pursuant to Article 19(2)(b) of the Rome Statute*. The Hague: International Criminal Court.

International Criminal Court. 2015. *Decision on the Withdrawal of Charges against Mr Kenyatta*. Doc. ICC-01/09–02/11. The Hague: International Criminal Court.

International Criminal Court. 2016. *Decision on Defence Applications for Judgments of Acquittal*. ICC-01/09–01/11 (5 April 2016). The Hague: International Criminal Court.

Irungu, Albert. 2011, March. 'ICC Debate Heats up but No Light.' *Katiba News*.

Juma, Monica Kathina. 2009. 'African Mediation of the Kenyan Post-2007 Election Crisis.' *Journal of Contemporary African Studies* 27 (3): 407. doi:10.1080/02589000903187016.

Juma, Yassin. 2008, January 8. 'Kufuor Arrives for Talks.' *NTV*. www.youtube.com/watch?v=DC5qPKADsho.

Kanyinga, Karuti. 2011. 'Stopping a Conflagration: The Response of Kenyan Civil Society to the Post-2007 Election Violence.' *Politikon* 38 (1): 85.

Kanyinga, Karuti, and James D Long. 2012. 'The Political Economy of Reforms in Kenya: The Post-2007 Election Violence and a New Constitution.' *African Studies Review* 55 (1): 31.

Kanyinga, Karuti, and Sophie Phillipa Rendall Walker. 2013. 'Building a Political Settlement: The International Approach to Kenya's 2008 Post-Election Crisis.' *Stability: International Journal of Security and Development* 2 (2): 1–21. doi:10.5334/sta.bu.

Kenya, Government of. 2008a. "President Holds Talks with US Assistant Secretary for African Affairs." *State House*, January 5. www.statehousekenya.go.ke/.

Kenya, Government of. 2008b. "Ghanaian President Arrives in Kenya." *State House*, January 8. www.statehousekenya.go.ke/.

Kenyans for Peace with Truth and Justice. 2008. *Kenyans for Peace through Truth and Justice Urges Full Implementation of the Waki Report*. Press Statement. www.pambazuka.org/en/category/elections/51717.

Khadiagala, Gilbert M. 2009. 'Forty Days and Nights of Peacemaking in Kenya.' *Journal of African Elections* 7 (2).

Kimani, Martin. 2008, October 26. 'Waki Report – Govt Must Fly close to the Sun.' *The East African*.

Lindenmayer, Elisabeth, and Josie Lianna Kaye. 2009. *A Choice for Peace? The Story of Forty-One Days of Mediation in Kenya*. New York: International Peace Institute.

Long, James D, Karuti Kanyinga, Karen E Ferree, and Clark Gibson. 2013. 'Choosing Peace over Democracy.' *Journal of Democracy* 24 (3): 140.

Lynch, Gabrielle. 2011. *I Say to You: Ethnic Politics and the Kalenjin in Kenya*. Chicago: University of Chicago Press.

Lynch, Gabrielle. 2014. 'Electing the "Alliance of the Accused": The Success of the Jubilee Alliance in Kenya's Rift Valley.' *Journal of Eastern African Studies* 8 (1): 93–114.

Magella, Robert. 2008, February 18. 'Share Both Power and Responsibility – Condoleezza Rice.' *NTV*. www.youtube.com/watch?v=Nn7nmjiL15Y.

Mamdani, Mahmood. 2010. 'Responsibility to Protect or Right to Punish?' *Journal of Intervention and Statebuilding* 4 (1): 53–67.

Munene, Mugomu, Lucas Barasa, and Sam Kiplagat. 2008, October 25. 'Secret Dossier That May Nail Key Suspects.' *Daily Nation*. http://allafrica.com/stories/200810260008.html.

Murray, Christina. 2013. 'Kenya's 2010 Constitution.' In *Jahrbuch Des Offentlichen Rechts. Neue Folge, Band 61*, edited by Peter Häberle, 747–788. Tübingen: Mohr Siebeck.

Mutua, Makau. 2008, October 25. 'Here's a Chance for the Country to Remake Itself (Opinion).' *Daily Nation*.

Nation Team. 2008, January 29. 'Country Celebrates Peace Agreement.' *Daily Nation*.

Ngunyi, Mutahi. 2008, October 18. 'Waki Report Not Good for the Country.' *Daily Nation*.

Nzioka, Patrick. 2008, January 23. 'ODM to File Complaint against Govt at The Hague.' *Daily Nation*.

Office of the Panel of Eminent African Personalities. 2014. *Back from the Brink: The 2008 Mediation Process and Reforms in Kenya*. African Union.

Office of the Prosecutor. 2008. *OTP Statement in Relation to Events in Kenya*. The Hague: International Criminal Court.

Office of the Prosecutor. 2009a. *Agreed Minutes of the Meeting between Prosecutor Moreno-Ocampo and the Delegation of the Kenyan Government, The Hague, 3 July 2009*. The Hague: International Criminal Court.

Office of the Prosecutor. 2009b. *ICC Prosecutor: Kenya Can Be an Example to the World*. Press Release. The Hague: International Criminal Court.

Office of the Prosecutor. 2009c. *Kenyan Authorities Committed to Cooperate as ICC Prosecutor Informs Them That in December He Will Request ICC Judges to Open an Investigation into Post-Election Violence*. The Hague: International Criminal Court, 1–3.

Office of the Prosecutor. 2009d. *Press Conference by the Prosecutor of the International Criminal Court, Louis Moreno-Ocampo, Thursday, November 26 2009, Nairobi and The Hague*. The Hague: International Criminal Court.

Omanga, Beauttah, and Alex Ndegwa. 2009, November 17. 'Debate on Imanyara Bill Stalls as MPs Stay Away.' *The Standard*.

Orengo, James. 2011. 'Get Me Right, I'm No Raila Stooge. The Big Interview: James Orengo.' *The Nairobi Law Monthly* 2 (5): 20–23.

Parliament of the Republic of Kenya. 2009a. '3 February 2009.' *Hansard*. Nairobi: Parliament of the Republic of Kenya.

Parliament of the Republic of Kenya. 2009b. '12 February 2009'. *Hansard*. Nairobi: Parliament of the Republic of Kenya.

Parliament of the Republic of Kenya. 2009c. '27 January 2009'. *Hansard*. Nairobi: Parliament of the Republic of Kenya.

Parliament of the Republic of Kenya. 2010a. '22 December 2010.' *Hansard*. Nairobi: Parliament of the Republic of Kenya.

Parliament of the Republic of Kenya. 2010b. 'Members of The 10th Parliament.' Nairobi: Parliament of the Republic of Kenya. www.parliament.go.ke/parliament/index.php?option=com_content&view=articl.

Preston McGhie, Meredith, and E Njoki Wamai. 2011. *Beyond the Numbers: Women's Participation in the Kenya National Dialogue and Reconciliation*. Geneva: Centre for Humanitarian Dialogue.

Rashid, Ronald. 2008a, February 18. 'Is Rice and Koffi [sic] the Recipe for Kenya's Peace Meal?' *NTV*.

Rashid, Ronald. 2008b, February 26. 'Annan Suspends Peace Talks.' *NTV*.

Republic of Kenya. 2008a. *[Agreed] Statement of Principles on Long-Term Issues and Solutions (23 May 2008).* Nairobi: Republic of Kenya.

Republic of Kenya. 2008b. *[Agreement on] Agenda Item Three: How to Resolve the Political Crisis (14 February 2008).* Nairobi: Republic of Kenya.

Republic of Kenya. 2008c. *[Agreement on a] Commission of Inquiry on Post-Election Violence (4 March 2008).* Nairobi: Republic of Kenya.

Republic of Kenya. 2008d. *[Agreement on a] Truth, Justice and Reconciliation Commission.* Nairobi: Republic of Kenya.

Republic of Kenya. 2008e. *Annotated Agenda and Timetable (1 February 2008).* Nairobi: Republic of Kenya.

Republic of Kenya. 2008f. *Modalities for the Kenyan National Dialogue and Reconciliation.* Nairobi: Republic of Kenya.

Republic of Kenya. 2008g. *Report of the Commission of Inquiry into the Post-Election Violence.* Nairobi: Government of Kenya.

Rice, Condoleezza. 2008. *Statement on Kenya Political Situation.* Department of State, Office of the Spokesman. http://2001-2009.state.gov/secretary/rm/2008/02/101291.htm.

Security Council Report. n.d. *Chronology of Events: Kenya. Security Council Report.* www.securitycouncilreport.org/chronology/kenya.php?print=true.

South Consulting. 2009. *Kenya National Dialogue and Reconciliation Monitoring Project, National Baseline Survey (January 2009).* Nairobi: Kenya National Dialogue and Reconciliation.

South Consulting. 2010a. *Kenya National Dialogue and Reconciliation Monitoring Project: Review Report, October 2010.* Nairobi: Kenya National Dialogue and Reconciliation.

South Consulting. 2010b. *Kenya National Dialogue and Reconciliation Monitoring Project: Status for Implementation of Agenda Items 1–4. Progess Report for January–March 2010.* Nairobi: Kenya National Dialogue and Reconciliation.

Spiegel Online. 2008, February 18. 'A Grand Coalition Government for Kenya? "The Most Neutral Solution Possible".' *Spiegel Online.* www.spiegel.de/international/world/a-grand-coalition-government-for-kenya-the-most-neutral-solution-possible-a-536031.html.

Standard Team. 2008, December 9. 'Amnesty for Waki List?' *The Standard.* www.standardmedia.co.ke/business/article/1144001298/amnesty-for-waki-list.

The Elders. 2008, February 4. *Message to Kenyans by The Elders' Chair Desmond Tutu.* Press Release, The Elders.

UN Department of Political Affairs. 2008. 'Crisis Mediation in Kenya: A Support Role by the UN.' *Politically Speaking,* 4–5. New York: United Nations.

UN News Centre. 2008, January 31. *Ban Ki-Moon to Visit Strife-Torn Kenya.* Press Release, UN News Centre.

UN Security Council. 2013. *Azerbaijan, Burundi, Ethiopia, Gabon, Ghana, Kenya, Mauritania, Mauritius, Morocco, Namibia, Rwanda, Senegal, Togo and Uganda: Draft Resolution.* UN Doc S/2013/660. New York: United Nations.

United Nations. 2013, November 15. *Security Council Resolution Seeking Deferral of Kenyan Leaders' Trial Fails to Win Adoption, with 7 Voting in Favour, 8 Abstaining.* UN Meetings Coverage and Press Releases, UN.

US Embassy Kampala. 2008. *Museveni Steps into Kenyan Political Process.* 08Kampala97, 08Kampala9. wikileaks.org.

Wachira, Patrick. 2008, February 29. 'Kibaki Pledges to Unite and Reconcile Kenyans.' *East African Standard.*

Wanjala, Robert. 2013, August 16. 'Concerns over Bid to Amend Kenya's Rights Report.' *Institute for War and Peace Reporting.*

Wolf, Thomas P. 2013. 'International Justice vs Public Opinion: The ICC and Ethnic Polarisation in the 2013 Kenyan Election.' *Journal of African Elections* 12 (1): 143.

Xinhua News Agency. 2011, April 8. 'UN Security Councils Fails to Come to an Agreement on Kenya Case.' *Xinhua News Agency.*

6 Political authority, justice and power-sharing

As the Prosecutor of the International Criminal Court, I am an independent part of the Kenyan justice system.
Louis Moreno-Ocampo, remarks at 'Kenya National Dialogue and Reconciliation Two Years On: Where are We?' Nairobi, December 2010

The Kenya National Dialogue and Reconciliation is rarely analysed as a case of judicialised peace and has sparked limited scholarly debate about the role of the ICC in peace processes. As the Prosecutor chose to indict Kenyan individuals more than two years after the negotiations ended, the assumption has been that the ICC's intervention could have affected the 2013 elections but not the 2008 negotiations. Such an approach equates ICC involvement with the Indictment stage and overlooks the effects of ICC involvement at the earlier active stages. A broader understanding of judicialisation by the ICC as a differentiated process with interactive and constitutive effects enables the analysis of involvement impact associated with aspects of the ICC's justice intervention other than the Prosecutor's indictments. At the same time, although they took place in the Implementation phase, the Kenya indictments enable, in the following chapter, a comparative analysis of high-level effects in Uganda and Kenya.

The previous chapter investigated the processes of peacemaking and ICC involvement in Kenya, analysing developments separate to each process as well as their interaction. In the present chapter, this account is subjected to further analysis by means of investigating how ICC involvement affected the Kenyan peace process, identifying which significant peace process features were not affected by ICC involvement, and understanding how and why the Kenya Dialogue achieved a political solution. The chapter has two parts, the first one focusing on how ICC involvement did and did not affect the peace process. The second part explains how and why the peace process achieved a political settlement. It ends by exploring these findings by means of counter-factual analysis, imagining whether a high level of ICC involvement would have affected the Kenyan conflict parties' ability and willingness to transcend their incompatibility.

Part 1 How ICC involvement did and did not affect the peace process

This part of the chapter examines whether and how the process of ICC involvement affected the peace process and its political settlement. Operationalising the notions of interactive and constitutive involvement effects, it first argues that the ICC intervention had no significant effects on the conflict principals' ability to reach a political solution and did not contribute to the marked legalisation of the Negotiation phase. It did, however, interact with the peace process to shape the politics of the Negotiation and Implementation phases in other ways. To understand these effects of ICC involvement, the chapter analyses how ICC involvement constituted a centrifugal effect on the GNU, which was nevertheless balanced by the centripetal provisions of the power-sharing agreement. Thereafter it investigates the delegation of discursive authority and the extent to which ICC involvement shaped the meaning and nature of justice.

Legalisation of the Negotiation phase

The Negotiation phase of the Kenya Dialogue, and particularly the discussions on Item 3 of the agenda, were legalised in the sense of being framed by law. The ICC was not the source of this process of legalisation, however, as it derived from the perspectives and decisions of the conflict parties and the mediation team. The conflict parties consciously built their respective negotiation teams to include legal competences (Karua, Kilonzo, Wetang'ula and Orengo were lawyers) and brought in party lawyers to argue their case vis-à-vis the electoral outcome. The governance negotiations were shaped by the possibilities and constraints of the Constitution, with the parties taking diverging positions on some of its provisions. For instance, the PNU opposed a power-sharing for constitutional reasons, arguing that such an arrangement would only be appropriate where the constitutional order had collapsed and that this did not pertain to Kenya (Office of the Panel of Eminent African Personalities 2014, para. 64). Seeing itself as the most rule-of-law-orientated party, PNU negotiators felt that a constitutional amendment to enable the coalition government was 'inappropriate' (Office of the Panel of Eminent African Personalities 2014, 66). To overcome the stalemate on power-sharing, the issue was delegated to the Legal Working Group, led by Annan's former legal advisor at the UN Secretariat, Hans Correll. As the group was formed before there was political agreement on power-sharing, legalisation was used as a mediation technique to depoliticise the negotiations.

The crucial meeting between the two principals and the mediators on 28 February 2008 took the Legal Working Group's draft bill as the point of departure. The two negotiation teams were actively kept away from this meeting to put pressure on Kibaki and Odinga and liberate the draft from the political arguments that constituted its context. During this meeting, Kibaki and Odinga relied on their respective lawyers to assist their perusal of the draft, although the meeting was essentially about the political decision to share power. The peace process outcome was understood as having to conform to the rule of law and the laws of Kenya, although this was only possible if the Constitution was adjusted.

The decision to agree on the political settlement

Involvement by the world court did not hinder the parties' ability to reach a negotiated solution, but it also cannot be said to have facilitated it. Involvement was in the Preliminary Examination stage when the parties agreed to share power and overcame their sticking point. The OTP's examination and monitoring of the Kenyan violence did not have any effect on the negotiators, who were preoccupied with more immediate issues surrounding a potential power-sharing solution. To the negotiators, ICC investigation and indictment were a potentiality, a future possibility whose importance dwarfed in comparison to the immediate goals of ending the violence, transcending the governance stalemate and preventing further population displacement.

When the parties decided to share power, criminal accountability had not yet become a personal matter. Negotiators and principals did not have to take into account the fates of particular individuals, including themselves. According to Kilonzo, Ruto 'would have taken extreme exception' if the Court and its justice mandate had featured in the negotiations on power-sharing.[1] It cannot be assumed that Ruto would not have taken the Dialogue negotiations hostage had he been indicted before tackling Item 3 of the agenda. In fact, Ruto 'started taking exception much later', when he was indicted during the Implementation phase.[2]

ICC involvement constituted a permissive context for the power-sharing deal, although it neither hindered nor facilitated it. In order to be able to argue that ICC involvement *facilitated* the principals' ability to settle the conflict, the analysis would have to yield one of the following indications: the conflict parties would have considered the prospect of an ICC investigation or they would at least have noticed that the situation was monitored by the OTP. This does not appear to have been the case. The prospect of actual ICC involvement was also absent from the parliamentary debate that domesticated the Rome Statute through the International Crimes Act in May 2008. Neither the Attorney-General nor MPs entertained the idea that the ICC would actually investigate the 2008 post-election violence (Parliament of the Republic of Kenya 2008). Instead, references were made to other cases of international justice or historical incidents of violence in Kenya, such as the Wagalla massacre.

Centrifugal impact on the government of national unity

The political settlement experienced both centrifugal and centripetal forces, which simultaneously pulled the coalition government apart and kept it together. One centrifugal pull stemmed from the high level of ICC involvement, which split the ODM, divided the political class and constituted an obstacle to implementation of the agreed solutions to the underlying conflict. This centrifugal effect, however, was balanced by the centripetal structures of the power-sharing arrangement.

In Kenya, the divisive nature of international justice had an interactive, centrifugal effect on the GNU. The divisiveness had been observed by Kenya National Dialogue and Reconciliation monitors (South Consulting 2009) and demonstrated in the vote on the Constitution of Kenya (Amendment) Bill 2009, where it became clear that political parties lacked authority over their MPs. As a consequence, they could not provide the institutional structure to forge elite agreement on how to reform Kenya and could not be relied upon to promote issues that could secure a long-term peace. In a related development, the ODM split along Kalenjin/non-Kalenjin lines once the Prosecutor identified his Ocampo Six.

Odinga supported ICC involvement and spoke out against the government's shuttle diplomacy, although earlier he had supported amnesty for the post-election violence. As the Prosecutor's ODM case charged only persons who identify as Kalenjin (Ruto, Sang and Kosgey), there was a sense among Kalenjin politicians and ordinary people that Odinga was disloyal (Wolf 2013, 153). Furthermore, Luo grassroots were involved in the violence, yet no Luo politician was indicted. To Kalenjins in the Rift Valley and their MPs, Odinga was working through his 'Western allies', the US president (who was of Luo descent) and the ICC Prosecutor; this conspiracy was boiled down to 'the 3 O's' – Odinga, Obama and Ocampo (Lynch 2014, 106). These feelings of being unfairly singled out prompted a new ethnic constellation in Kenyan politics, as Kalenjin MPs found common ground with Kikuyu and Meru MPs: within a week of the Prosecutor's announcing his two cases, analysts observed the contours of the political alliance, which became the Jubilee union (analysed below). In spite of these new political constellations, the disaffected MPs remained in the ODM; this weakened the party and unbalanced the GNU.

Further unbalancing the political settlement was the fact that the PNU opposed internationalisation, while key ODM politicians supported an ICC process (Nichols 2015, 218). PNU ministers qua the government challenged the admissibility and requested a deferral of proceedings by the Security Council, while ODM politicians such as Odinga, Orengo and ODM Secretary-General Anyang' Nyong'o disowned these steps. Signifying the split, the Committee for the Management of Coalition Affairs, a conflict management organ established in the political settlement, disintegrated.

These centrifugal factors were balanced by the centripetal design of the power-sharing agreement. According to the National Accord and Reconciliation Act (2008), the GNU would be dissolved if one of the GNU parties decided to leave the coalition. As the National Accord and Reconciliation Act stated in the preamble that 'neither side is able to govern without the other'. If the ODM left the coalition, the PNU would also be out of power as the Act would trigger a new election. As a result, instead of formally leaving the coalition, ODM politicians on several occasions stayed away from cabinet meetings and parliamentary committees, and the two principals stopped communicating (BBC 2010; Wafula

2011). Calls by PNU or ODM ministers to withdraw from the coalition were cancelled or never effectuated (Mureithi 2011). The PNU tried to reinterpret the National Accord and Reconciliation Act to allow dissolution of the coalition without fresh elections, but this attempt did not succeed: the text of the Act was unambiguous in its description of the consequences of coalition dissolution so it could not sustain such an interpretation.

Amidst these centrifugal and centripetal forces, how did the state of power-sharing affect the reform process? Qualitative and quantitative analysis provides a mixed picture. When interviewed in April and May 2011, implementers and close observers argued that the reform agenda had slowed down since December 2010, partly because the government was preoccupied with political and legal mobilisation against the ICC process.[3] Monitors of Dialogue implementation (quoted in Nichols 2015, 216) observed similarly that ‘conflicts within the coalition and in the parties that make up the coalition have the potential of deflecting attention away from reforms to short-term interests’. Others pointed out that the reform process benefitted from taking place ‘under the radar’ as public attention focused on the ICC.[4] Sriram and Brown (2012, 222) even suggest that ‘the mere possibility of ICC involvement’ catalysed pressure for reform. Nichols (2015) analyses parliamentary deliberation of all major reform bills and concludes, in contrast, that ICC involvement had minimal effect on constitutional, judicial and security sector reform.

A similar approach maps the landscape of Kenya’s reform process by means of the number of bills introduced during the tenth Parliament. This exercise shows that a high level of ICC involvement cannot be described as having slowed the general process of reform. In fact, the period covering the Indictment stage saw the introduction of a relatively large number of bills. Figure 6.1 illustrates the number and frequency of bills and indicates relevant ICC milestones.

Figure 6.1 indicates a higher level of formal government activity in 2011 and 2012. This development is likely to stem from 49 new laws written into the 2010 Constitution. By August 2011, Parliament had passed all the bills which were listed in the Constitution as requiring enactment within a year of its promulgation, although this occurred in a ‘last-minute rush’ (South Consulting 2012, para. 7; see also Manji 2012). Once the deadline was met, however, the pace of passing bills slowed down.

The resilience of the reform agenda derived from its organisational form. The many expert commissions tasked with reviewing, reforming and creating institutions could work relatively independently of the politics of ICC indictment: the split in the ODM, the new political alliances, the anti-ICC rallies of the Jubilee Alliance, the admissibility challenge and the shuttle diplomacy. By depoliticising the reform process in a series of commissions and committees, it was to some extent insulated from the instability at the centre of the GNU. This strategy worked well to propel constitutional, electoral and judicial reforms. As Kanyinga and Long (2012, 47) argue with regard to constitutional reform, the Committee of Experts ‘helped protect the [constitutional revision] process from interests capable of undermining it’.

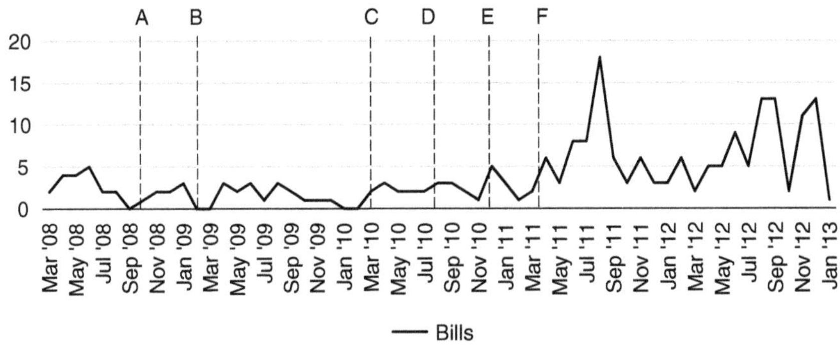

Figure 6.1 Bills introduced during the tenth Parliament (March 2008–February 2013).

Source: www.parliament.go.ke

Note
The data captures the date of introduction of a bill to Parliament, not its reading. The relevant milestones are as follows: CIPEV report (A), STK vote (B), OTP commences investigation (C), constitutional referendum (D), OTP charges six (E) and PTC confirms the charges against four individuals (F).

The reform process progressed in general, but some areas of reform and remedy were sabotaged or marginalised: domestic criminal accountability, land reform as a form of social justice and inter-communal reconciliation. These policy issues were some of the most difficult and politically costly challenges facing Kenya, while also of importance to the prevention of a recurrence of conflict. To understand these casualties, the chapter turns to the nature and role of justice during the peace process, including the impact of ICC involvement on the nature of justice in Kenya.

Changing meanings and parameters of justice

ICC involvement contributed to a gradual narrowing of the meaning of justice, whereby justice came to signify criminal and procedural justice while social justice issues were marginalised. This affected the implementation of land reform, which was furthermore not linked to reconciliation. At the same time, the internationalisation of justice enabled the non-implementation of domestic criminal justice.

Narrowing of justice

A constitutive effect of high-level ICC involvement was the narrowing of justice over the course of the Implementation phase. Representing a broad understanding of justice, the annotated agenda and negotiated agreements referred to social, procedural and criminal justice. Social injustice was seen as the root cause of conflict, procedural injustices were the trigger of violence and criminal justice was the appropriate response to this violence. Reconciliation and reform were remedies to resolve the conflict. As CIPEV released its report and the ICC proceeded up the trajectory of involvement, however, criminal justice became the focus of political mobilisation by the political class and civil society. As a consequence, policy commitments to social justice suffered from a lack of implementation. This affected land reform and reconciliation.

Issues of social justice appeared in the first agreement of the Negotiation phase, which encouraged local communities to 'stand up for justice and fairness' (Republic of Kenya 2008c, sec. 2(b)), but they also informed the negotiations in a wider sense. For instance, during the governance discussions, Machel reminded the negotiators that the issues on the table 'were much broader and deeper than the disputed presidential election' and that any political solution would need to see elections as part of a broader process (Office of the Panel of Eminent African Personalities 2014, para. 65). In fact, social injustices were understood to be the root causes of conflict. The *Statement of Principles on Long-term Issues and Solutions* and, to some extent, the agreement on how to resolve the crisis provide a narrative of these underlying injustices, such as poverty, exclusion, perceptions of historical injustices and the unequal distribution of resources. These agreements committed the parties to policies such as equitable development, alleviation of poverty and youth unemployment, and the broad reform process of land, constitutional, institutional and legal structures, including reforms of the police, parliament, judiciary, executive and civil service.

Procedural justice was associated with fairness and democratic legitimacy and was invoked by both parties: the ODM based their claims of a stolen election on procedural injustices such as electoral fraud, while the PNU based their right to the presidency on the constitutionality of the process: the Electoral Commission, the elections and the swearing-in ceremony. According to a member of the mediation team, 'It was actually relatively easy to get agreement that there needed to be a justice process, because both sides were looking at the other side at the table, thinking "We're gonna catch you out."'[5] Hence the two commissions of inquiry: the ODM wanted IREC to detect the PNU's procedural injustices, while PNU wanted CIPEV to investigate the ODM's protest violence.

Criminal justice was reflected right from the first agreement, which called for '[i]mpartial, effective and expeditious' investigation and prosecution of 'all cases of crime and police brutality and/or excessive use of force' (Republic of Kenya 2008c). Subsequent agreements reiterated this commitment or established CIPEV to carry it out. The abstract commitment to criminal justice was uncontroversial and shared by the negotiators and mediators. Annan maintained at all times that the post-election violence had to be prosecuted, either through Kenyan mechanisms or by the ICC (ICC 2010b, 4), and involved Priscilla Hayner as a technical expert on the issue of justice. A co-founder of the International Center for Transitional Justice, Hayner represented a justice actor at the forefront of international policy-making and central to the justice discourse. Her book on truth and reconciliation commissions (Hayner 2001) was described by the negotiators as 'our transitional justice bible'.[6]

The agreements' focus on criminal accountability does not relate to the ICC's Kenya involvement in an interactive or constitutive sense. In fact, the low level of this involvement during the Negotiation phase gave the mediators and negotiators the opportunity to be vague and unspecific with regard to criminal justice: although emphasising the imperative of accountability, the parties did not need to specify the forum for such a process or address the issue of justice in relation to the two conflict parties. The problem of justice was delegated to CIPEV, whose commissioners were at liberty to devise any kind of formula that entailed criminal accountability. Questions of criminal justice were postponed and placed in this expert body, just like the question of electoral victory was postponed and transferred to IREC (Elklit 2011).

Justice narrowed during the Implementation phase. Internationalisation and domestic legalisation shaped the notion of justice, to the extent that the political settlement became increasingly associated with criminal and procedural forms of justice while social justice issues were marginalised. Two inter-related factors contributed to this process of decontestation. First, CIPEV and the ICC Prosecutor interpreted the conflict as deriving from impunity, a narrative that was new to the Dialogue. Impunity was absent from the agreements on the first three agenda items, although later 'the fight against impunity' was identified as one of the values underpinning the reform and reconciliation processes (Republic of Kenya 2008a). Impunity was seen as secondary to the root causes of conflict, but during the Implementation phase CIPEV and the OTP constructed impunity as the main problem, the 'heart' of the conflict. This narrative was consolidated during the national debate on the STK. The TJRC was designed to provide the deep and structural perspective on the conflict, but its report was submitted only in May 2013 when the impunity narrative had become entrenched.

Finally, Kenyan NGOs pushed criminal and procedural justice issues and tended to forget about social justice. A survey of the statements and open letters of Kenyans for Truth with Peace and Justice during the Negotiation and Implementation phases reveal an overwhelming focus on procedural and criminal justice.[7] This advocacy material is concerned with international accountability, the judiciary and electoral reform. Issues of social justice and reconciliation are curiously absent from the NGO coalition's public discourse, given its aim of promoting truth, peace and justice. That said, this justice focus matched that of the wider population, as ordinary people called for criminal and procedural justice. Scholars identify a 'strong popular desire for accountability through prosecutions' (Brown and Sriram 2012, 246) and favouring of constitutional reform (Kanyinga and Long 2012).

The discursive focus on breaking the cycle of impunity did not translate into actual criminal accountability. As the ICC judges noted in 2016, 'The only serious prosecutorial effort to speak of [in Kenya] is that of the Office of the Prosecutor of this Court' (ICC 2016, para. 31). While procedural injustices were remedied through constitutional, electoral and legislative reform, nobody was held to account for organising or perpetrating the post-election violence. This non-implementation derived from internationalisation.

Internationalisation and local impunity

Kenya's status as a Rome Statute state party created opportunities for internationalising justice, which would have lacked in the absence of membership. The OTP quickly decided to monitor the situation, announcing this new focus one month into the post-election crisis. Membership also enabled CIPEV to create an anti-impunity mechanism that could shield an accountability process against domestic political sabotage: international delegation was a threat that aimed to propel a national process. Justice Waki explained, 'We said, if they [the politicians] try to scuttle this process, we will call in the international community and get it handled internationally.'[8] Had Kenya not ratified the Rome Statute, active ICC involvement would have to have been triggered by a Security Council referral – an unlikely prospect for the Kenyan violence given the scale and nature of violence in the Council's two ICC referrals to date, the crises in Darfur and Libya.

Towards the end of 2008 and during 2009, the symbolic power of international justice captured the imagination of large parts of the country. Designed as a stick, the idea of an ICC investigation became a carrot: people advocated 'Don't be Vague, go to The Hague', Kenyans for Peace with Truth and Justice lobbied against a Kenyan solution, and the Constitution of Kenya (Amendment) Bill 2008 was defeated by parliament. When a private members' bill sought to establish the STK in late 2009, only 18 MPs (8 per cent of parliament) were present during its first reading (Nichols 2015, 78; Office of the Panel of Eminent African Personalities 2014, 108). Even before the vote on the 2008 Bill, CIPEV's deadline for establishing the tribunal became the 'Hague deadline' in the media (see, e.g. Ohito *et al.* 2009), a term signifying the expectation that failure to establish the STK would trigger an ICC investigation.

To some extent, the STK represented an internationalisation of justice. To CIPEV commissioners, hybridity followed logically from the international peacemaking process at the heart of the transition: 'Since this [Kenya National Dialogue and Reconciliation] process has an international aspect, let also the judicial process have an international aspect.'[9] But where an STK would be established through Kenyan political processes, an ICC process was completely international.

The GNU was divided on whether to internationalise justice. Unlike in Uganda, ICC involvement did not have clear benefits for the government. The cabinet discussion in July 2009 indicates that it was wrestling with the issue of justice, considering both a self-referral and Rome Statute withdrawal. It settled on judicial reform, explaining that it aimed to provide 'the enabling environment for the ongoing reform agenda that encompasses the delivery of a new Constitution by next year, electoral reforms, boundary reforms, and land reforms' (Government of Kenya 2009). The cabinet assessed that a criminal accountability process would jeopardise these reforms. While many reforms were initiated and partly implemented, in particular constitutional, electoral and judicial reform, the government's assessment was borne out with regard to domestic accountability and land reform.

Domestic accountability became the main casualty of the internationalisation of criminal justice. From the moment Kenya lost the admissibility challenge, criminal justice became a purely international affair for the GNU. Given the ICC's same-person, same-conduct test, the admissibility process focused on whether Kenya was investigating or prosecuting the Ocampo Six. This translated into a lack of international pressure on Kenya to prosecute the many other alleged perpetrators of post-election violence. Indeed, Nichols (2015, 85) concludes that from January 2012 'the OTP had abandoned its attempts to encourage domestic prosecutions and instead focussed its attention on the trial of the Ocampo Four'. Had the PTC interpreted the government's admissibility submissions differently and returned jurisdiction to Kenya, the Court would have been able to review the national justice process. As the Prosecutor may request a review of the Court's admissibility decisions if new facts emerge (for instance, evidence of unwillingness to prosecute),[10] the ICC could have compelled the GNU to apply downwards pressure on the police and the judiciary.

Amidst their focus on the international justice process from December 2010 onwards, the government, parliament and civil society paid insufficient attention to domestic accountability. In 2011, monitors of the Implementation phase highlighted that only a few cases of post-election violence had gone to court and all of them had been dismissed because the investigations were 'poor or insufficient' and the prosecution 'unconvincing' (South Consulting 2011, 24). The following year, a task force established by the Director of Public Prosecution to review 6,000 cases of post-election violence reported that the bulk of cases were 'unprosecutable' for lack of evidence (Kenyans for Peace with Truth and Justice 2014, 8; Kenya National Commission on Human Rights 2012, 24).

As some actors in the GNU had interest in continuing the practice of impunity for political violence, pressure on the national justice system would have had to have come from civil society. However, domestic NGO advocacy for criminal justice focused on the ICC Prosecutor's high-profile intervention or the politics of judicial reform, rather than on the state's systematic failure to properly investigate and prosecute the post-election violence (e.g. Kenyans for Peace with Truth and Justice 2011; 2012). In November 2012, Kenya National Commission for Human Rights (2012, 24) concluded that the 'only measure of justice for victims of the post election violence is being pursued by the International Criminal Court'. Local impunity did not escape the notice of ordinary people, who continued to have low levels of confidence in the government's ability to conduct genuine investigations (South Consulting 2012, para. 8).

Land reform and reconciliation

The land issue was arguably the real 'heart' of Kenya's election violence (Harbeson 2012, 26), but the narrowing of justice during the Implementation phase resulted in the indefinite deferral of efforts to resolve it. This issue marginalisation happened in spite of the earlier inter-party agreement that the land issue 'has been a source of economic, social, political and environmental problems' for many years and that 'land reform is a fundamental need in Kenya' to be addressed 'comprehensively and with the seriousness it deserves' (Republic of Kenya 2008a, sec. 2(b)).

The negotiations on the long-term issues produced a comprehensive plan to transform land tenure relations, including addressing 'fundamental issues of land tenure and land use' in the constitutional review; harmonising land laws; considering links between land use, conservation, forestry and water resources in land policies; and strengthening local mechanisms for sustainable land rights administration and management (Government of Kenya 2008, 4–5). These ideas related to earlier, unsuccessful reform efforts (Harbeson 2012; Narh *et al.* 2016).

The 2010 Constitution created a socially just overall legal framework for land reform by establishing that land 'shall be held, used and managed in a manner that is equitable, efficient, productive and sustainable' (Article 40(1)). During the Implementation phase, however, the negotiators' ambitious plan for resolving land-based grievances was gradually side-lined, as justice came to mean procedural justice and anti-impunity. Land-related reform initiatives implemented land law reform rather than a deeper reform that would redefine the 'relationships between and within communities, and between communities and the state' (Boone 2007, 558). The new Kenyan land laws are neither redistributive nor transformational (Manji 2012, 126), but articulate a procedural notion of justice. For instance, they formalise and individualise land rights through land title registration and certification, but do not restructure landholding in a redistributive manner. According to Narh *et al.* (2016, 10), frictions between formalised processes of land rights 'smeared' onto an existing entrenched informal land tenure regime may even 'have increased land rights uncertainties and conflicts'.

Importantly, land reform was not linked to reconciliation. The power-sharing solution had not removed the need to reconcile local communities, but constituted the governance context within which Kenyans should deal with the local, long-standing and land-related tensions that had made the violence seem justified and meaningful to so many. Where the negotiations had produced a semi-specific agenda for beginning to address the land issue, they generated a handful of vague ideas about reconciliation. Unlike in the Juba Peace Talks, reconciliation was not understood as a form of justice that had to be consciously forged. Rather, it was implicitly conceived as the by-product of other reform initiatives: once control and impunity were wrested from the political elite, inter-communal reconciliation would follow.

Vague ideas about reconciliation pertained even to the TJRC. The negotiators 'did not discuss [its mandate] … in detail or at length' (Office of the Panel of Eminent African Personalities 2014, 124), but implicitly conceptualised the TJRC as a body for truth-telling and knowledge generation, rather than a vehicle for reconciliation. Its terms of reference mustered only to direct it to engage in 'activities' that 'it determines to advance national or community reconciliation' and to write recommendations that 'may' include measures to promote reconciliation (Republic of Kenya 2008b, 1, 2). Once implemented, the TJRC wrestled with the concept of reconciliation and 'saw its role in relation to reconciliation as that of laying the foundation for a long-term process' (Republic of Kenya 2013, 46). By 'uncovering the truth, providing a forum for individuals to share their experiences and by providing some accountability, the Commission will have placed the nation on a path to further reconciliation and national cohesion and unity' (p. 47). Reconciliation was seen to follow from truth-telling, acknowledgement and documentation.

The National Cohesion and Integrity Commission took more concrete steps to reconcile communities. This new body initiated an inter-communal peace process in 2010 in Nakuru in the Rift Valley, the region with the most politicised and most bitterly contested land allocation. It also initiated local peacemaking within and between other ethnic communities. The Nakuru County process resulted in a peace agreement between Kalenjin and Kikuyu elders in Nakuru that committed them to non-violence and established informal mechanisms for dispute resolution (HD 2014). However, Alice Nderitu, the mediator, finds that this first, successful local peace process is threatened by the persistence of land disputes (HD 2014, 37). In fact, rural inter-communal violence displaced 112,000 persons in 2012; 55,000 persons in 2013; and 216,000 in 2015 (Internal Displacement Monitoring Centre 2015, 6).

Delegation of discursive authority

Involvement by first the mediation Panel and then the ICC transferred discursive authority to these two actors. During the Negotiation phase, involvement by the Panel entailed the transfer of discursive authority from the conflict parties to the mediators. Annan successfully used this authority as part of his 'power mediation' of the governance negotiations (discussed below): he monitored and policed press releases by the conflict parties, approved statements by powerful external actors, and raised popular, MP and donor expectations by exaggerating the parties' agreement on power-sharing.

Active ICC involvement passed discursive authority from the mediation Panel to the ICC, a constitutive effect of involvement. Once he had authority to narrate the conflict and its resolution, the Prosecutor adopted a discourse of prevention, protection and assistance. His statements created a straightforward relationship between criminal accountability and peace, arguing, for instance, that '[j]ustice for the post-electoral violence in Kenya will ensure a peaceful election in 2012' (ICC 2010b, 4). This campaign supported the CIPEV narrative, which grounded Kenya's election-related violence in the institutionalisation of impunity. To show the deterrent effect of justice and the fight against impunity, Kenya was to be an 'example to the world' and to Africa (OTP 2009a). This construction of Kenya as a global example may have increased the ICC's stakes in Kenya's justice process to the extent that the Prosecutor and Annan became committed to the idea of ICC involvement.

To include Kenyans in the project of international justice, the Prosecutor argued that not only was the ICC an independent part of the Kenyan justice system, but also Kenyans 'should feel that they are part of a bigger, global [justice] community' (ICC 2010b, 4). 'The people from Nyanza, Rift Valley, Western, Central, Eastern, Coast and Nairobi Provinces must know that they are not alone' (OTP 2009b, 1). 'The whole international community is with the Kenyans' (OTP 2010). As such, the ICC intervention was constructed as helping Kenyans with something that was evidently difficult: holding to account those most responsible for the political violence and 'breaking the cycle of impunity'. The Registry's Outreach division supported this discourse of assistance. Among other initiatives, it launched a vernacular radio campaign, which sought to 'reach out to victims and affected communities' in Kiswahili, Luo, Kalenjin and Kikuyu languages (ICC 2010c).

The Jubilee campaign

The discourse by the Prosecutor and the Panel was contested by Kenyatta and Ruto's Jubilee Alliance. This counter-discourse was not an interactive or constitutive effect of ICC involvement, but it was made possible by the prior delegation of discursive authority to the ICC. Internationalisation enabled the Jubilee Alliance to construct a successful anti-international and anti-ICC discourse ahead of the 2013 elections. Kenyatta and Ruto used the high-level ICC intervention as an opportunity to win over the electorate, posing as victims of primarily foreign forces and portraying Odinga as the latter's insider and conspirator (Lugano 2017; Lynch 2014; Mueller 2014; Wolf 2013).

Wrong (2013) argues that the ICC cases gave UhuRuto 'a priceless fillip' in the general election. However, indictments can vilify or martyrise, depending on their discursive construction. Insurgent ICC indictees in Uganda, the DRC and CAR have not been able to turn their status into a political resource. In contrast, Sudan's al Bashir won 68 per cent of the vote in the 2010 elections, while the 2015 elections, which were boycotted by most opposition parties, returned 94 per cent to him. Mirroring al Bashir's domestic ICC strategy, Kenyatta and Ruto turned their ICC cases into a political resource by contextualising them in a discourse of sovereignty, national independence and unity. The ICC cases were portrayed as a foreign 'plot' to influence the outcome of the elections and the much-used phrase 'reclaiming sovereignty' became a 'code for throwing off the colonial yoke' (Wrong 2013; see also Lugano 2017). The ICC came to represent Western imperialism, a narrative aided by the Prosecutor's Africa bias. As a Limuru resident (quoted in Wolf 2013, 161) opined, 'The ICC is a tool of the West, used just to oppress Africa.'

The name of the Jubilee Alliance signified Kenya's independence anniversary in 2013, which marked 50 years of statehood. Carrying a Kiswahili name that means 'independence' and 'freedom', Uhuru Kenyatta was the son of the country's first president, the nationalist Jomo Kenyatta. In the discourse of the Jubilee Alliance, Uhuru represented *uhuru* and sovereignty, which was contrasted with Western imperialism. Indeed, the term 'Ocampo Six' derived from the 'Kapenguria Six', the 1950s name given to six nationalists (including Jomo Kenyatta) convicted in 1953 by the settler-colonial government for fomenting the Mau rebellion.

The Ocampo Six reminded Kenyans of the injustice of colonial state violence. As Gituku (2011) remarked, 'Luis Moreno-Ocampo probably does not know that another Kenyatta was the victim of massive perjury in another politically-instigated trial.' The Kapenguria trial took place in a state of emergency and was a show trial: the presiding judge was paid 20,000 pounds by the governor to ensure a conviction and key witnesses later admitted to having been bribed (Elkins 2005, 38–46). When Western ambassadors warned Kenyans against voting for two ICC suspects, they unwittingly confirmed the Jubilee discourse.

Temporal delegation

In matters of justice, ICC involvement delegated temporal authority to the ICC, although the Court was not the only grantor of time. During the Preliminary Examination stage, the Panel and the OTP decided whether to grant time, while the PTC became the grantor of time during the Indictment stage. The first time-frame for establishing a criminal accountability mechanism was set by CIPEV, which demanded that the government should establish the STK before February 2009. Failing this, incriminating material would be passed on to the OTP. The Commission set this deadline fearing that evidence would disappear and the environment would change if too much time passed before the commencement of an accountability process.[11] By transferring incriminating material to the Panel, CIPEV delegated temporal authority to the Panel. The account by Correll (2009, 1, emphasis added) illustrates the Panel's temporal authority:

> [After the Constitution of Kenya (Amendment) Bill was defeated,] the Panel deemed it appropriate that the Government *be given some additional time* beyond the date established by the Waki Commission to ensure that the necessary legislation for the establishment of the Special Tribunal could be enacted. In a letter dated 23 February 2009 sent by [Mr. Annan] … to the two Principals, he indicated that this *should be done within a reasonable period of time*. In a subsequent letter … the end of August 2009 *was set as the time limit*.

When the Panel passed the CIPEV evidence on to the OTP, it also transferred temporal authority to the ICC. The GNU therefore sent a delegation to The Hague to ask for more time. The OTP at first granted the government 12 months, but then went back on its offer by launching a *proprio motu* investigation. As Annan (quoted in Rice 2009) stated on the occasion, 'Justice delayed is justice denied.'

The third grantor of time was the PTC, a role built into its authorisation of the Investigation stage and judging of the admissibility proceedings. This role was signified by the government's admissibility challenge, which was basically a plea for more time.[12] Both PTC decisions centred on the idea that Kenya was not doing enough as per the time of these two decisions: the investigation was allowed because 'at present there is no domestic prosecution for the alleged crimes against humanity, nor is there any prospect of such prosecution' (ICC 2010a, para. 183), while the admissibility challenge was rejected for similar reasons. The Kenyan reform process was thus out of sync with the ICC process: it was one step behind the expectations of those interpreting the Rome Statute.

Part 2 How and why the peace process succeeded

The Kenya National Dialogue and Reconciliation process achieved a political settlement because the conflict principals used their agency and authority to agree on and internally enforce the proposed power-sharing solution. They did so within a context of hardliner opposition within the PNU and a mediation strategy that relied on a creative mix of muscle, politicisation of the law and legalisation of politics. After analysing the nature and role of political authority and the strategies of mediation, this part of the chapter examines the three transcendence strategies that enabled the political solution. It ends with a counterfactual analysis of the likely impact of high-level ICC involvement on the conflict parties' ability to settle the crisis, had the Indictment stage occurred during the Negotiation phase.

As conflict principals, Kibaki and Odinga had political authority to take and enforce decisions pertaining to Kenya's violent crisis. This authority derived from their positions as heads of the two largest parties and, respectively, leader of the opposition and the country's president. It was voluntarily delegated to the negotiation teams, but then referred back to the principals when Annan suspended the negotiation process to take matters to Kibaki and Odinga. Throughout the peace process, mediators and third-party actors confirmed and legitimised Kibaki and Odinga's positions of authority by pressuring and looking only to the two conflict principals and their delegations for a resolution of the conflict.

The conflict parties contained hardliners and moderates. Within the ODM, these factions converged on the agreeability of a power-sharing solution that would create a prime ministership for Odinga and a deputy prime ministership for another ODM politician. Within the PNU, however, hardliners opposed power-sharing. On 19 February, the PNU Parliamentary Group issued a statement that ruled out power-sharing and the creation of a post of prime minister (Office of the Panel of Eminent African Personalities 2014, para. 40–41). More dramatically, moments before Kibaki was to sign the power-sharing agreement, he was approached by PNU ministers who tried to dissuade him from going ahead with the deal (Office of the Panel of Eminent African Personalities 2014, para. 41). Kibaki, however, used his authority to overrule these hardliners.

Mediation with muscle

The conflict principals' political authority enabled them to overcome the sticking point, but before this happened the Panel's flexible mediation had guided and pushed the conflict parties to a turning point. During the negotiations on power-sharing, the Panel's 'pure' mediation evolved as 'power' mediation. Pure mediation uses 'reasoning, persuasion, the control of information and the suggestion of alternatives' to assist the antagonists in finding an acceptable agreement (Fisher and Keashly 1991, 33); this form had been used during the negotiations on the first two agenda items.

Power mediation builds on pure mediation by introducing the use of leverage or coercion by third parties, often 'in the form of promised rewards or threatened punishments' (Fisher and Keashly 1991, 33). The Panel's power mediation included the strategic use of public statements and the coordination and involvement of coercive external actors. It is thus an understatement to conclude that the political solution 'was neither dictated to them from above nor the result of coercion from outside forces' (Lindenmayer and Kaye 2009, 22).

The change in mediation strategy was indicated by Annan's communication to Parliament on 12 February 2008, during the opening of an informal all-party *kamukunji* meeting on progress in the Dialogue. As a way to pressure the conflict parties to agree on the idea of sharing power, Annan told parliament about the 'possible constitution of a grand coalition which could oversee reforms within two years' (quoted in Lindenmayer and Kaye 2009, 15). This implied a level of agreement that was not yet reached and raised the expectations of MPs, Kenyans and the wider world. Dialogue negotiators, particularly from the PNU, were outraged.

The Panel's 'mediation with muscle' also mobilised powerful external actors to lean on the conflict parties, as discussed in the previous chapter. However, unbeknown to the conflict parties at the time, third-party coercion was an integrated part of the mediation strategy, although this was likely kept from the conflict parties. Statements by the US – and probably other external actors too – were in fact approved by the Panel. The US embassy in Nairobi sent draft statements to the mediation team and Annan would approve them before they went out (Cohen 2008).

The Panel used legalisation, a different kind of muscle, as a strategy to overcome political stalemate and subjected the law to 'political instinct'. During the governance negotiations, the Legal Working Group was asked 'to turn an eventual political agreement into a legal framework acceptable to both sides' (Office of the Panel of Eminent African Personalities 2014, 40). Although the parties disagreed about solving the crisis through a power-sharing arrangement, Correll wanted the drafting to begin immediately and distributed a draft piece of legislation to them (Office of the Panel of Eminent African Personalities 2014, para. 40).

Politicisation of the law occurred to pave the way for power-sharing. As the draft national accords did not align with the Constitution, Annan and Correll proposed to amend the latter. PNU negotiators opposed this idea, with Karua accusing Annan of trying to engineer a 'civilian coup' by introducing a new executive post into the system (Cohen 2008). He responded by emphasising that 'what mattered was to be constitutional rather than do everything in accordance with the constitution' (Office of the Panel of Eminent African Personalities 2014, 67). The result was the Constitution of Kenya (Amendment) Act 2008, which removed constitutional obstacles to the power-sharing agreement.

Transcending incompatibility

To overcome the sticking point, mediators and the conflict parties succeeded in 'transcending [the] incompatibility' (Wallensteen 2012, 53; see also Ramsbotham *et al.* 2011, chap. 7). The incompatibility – rival claims to the right to rule – was transcended by means of three strategies. First, control over government was enlarged and shared between PNU and ODM politicians. This strategy made political power more elite inclusive. To accommodate intra-party dynamics and the need for positions for influential supporters, negotiations during the Implementation phase on who to appoint to positions of power resulted in the multiplication of cabinet roles and the creation of 17 new ministries (Schreiber 2016, 8). The GNU would end up with 40 ministers and 52 assistant ministers.

Second, the pool of executive power was enlarged to give some power to the prime minister and his two deputies. The prime minister got the authority to coordinate and supervise the execution of government functions and affairs, to control two deputies and to be a senior member of the cabinet; the role of the deputy prime ministers is not specified in the agreement or in the National Accords Act. As the president did not lose any of his previous functions in the bargain, the executive arrangement entailed resource enlargement rather than resource division.

A last transcendence strategy was to postpone resolution of the two most contentious and divisive issues – the 2007 election results and responsibility for the violence – by 'parking' them for some time in CIPEV and IREC. The hybrid character of these two commissions of inquiry and the highly regarded standing of their commissioners framed this strategy as the most appropriate response to the issues.

Counter-factual analysis

In the light of the experiences in Uganda, it is relevant to ask counter-factually whether a higher level of ICC involvement during the Negotiation phase would have impeded the ability to reach the power-sharing deal. In other words, if the peace process had been prolonged to the extent that the OTP would have charged six Kenyans with crimes against humanity during or before the Negotiation phase, would the conflict parties have agreed to deal with their incompatibility by means of a political solution? To think through this scenario, it is useful to recall the national reaction to the Indictment stage and imagine how it would have affected the Dialogue participants' negotiation of a political solution.

First, the government 'nationalised' the alleged guilt of the Ocampo Six, mobilising AU member countries to create support for an AU deferral request to the Security Council and submitting an admissibility challenge to the ICC. Parliament, for its part, instructed the government to withdraw from the Rome Statute. These actions suggest that a high level of ICC involvement was interpreted as an encroachment on Kenya's national sovereignty. Had the government still been paralysed, it may not have been able to mobilise regionally and legally, but it would likely still have 'nationalised' the indictments.

The nationalisation would have made the settlement unlikely. Agreement on power-sharing would have required that an illegitimate, non-functioning, PNU-led government that faced a perceived illegitimate, foreign intervention would have agreed to share power with the political party that was seen to have initiated the violence that caused the ICC intervention. As we saw, the PNU attributed the post-election violence to ODM mass action.

Second, the indictments split the ODM between those in favour of an international justice process and those who felt unfairly targeted, with aggrieved MPs remaining in the ODM because of the centripetal structures of the National Accord and Reconciliation Act 2008. In the absence of this Act, the party may have split: Odinga's supporters would have remained in the ODM, while those who sympathised with the 'victims' of the alleged 3 O-alliance would have gone elsewhere. In a context of ongoing political violence, this split would likely have fuelled violence between the Luo and Kalenjin communities. Lynch (2014, 106) reports that 'the idea that Odinga was to blame for taking Kenyatta and Ruto to The Hague was often extended to the Luo community more generally'. This projection was the result of a deliberate political strategy by the Kalenjin leadership, as it told people 'that it's the Luo who took them to the ICC and who betrayed them' (NGO activist, quoted in Lynch 2014, para. 106).

Violence only stopped once the principals agreed to form the GNU. In the imagined context of violence between grassroots and militias associated with the three main ethnic communities, settling the conflict may even have required three-way power-sharing negotiations between the Odinga-led ODM, Ruto's party and Kibaki's PNU. The success of such a process would depend on whether the issue of justice became a sticking point in the Negotiation phase. The next chapter explores the centrality of sticking points and the importance of politico-legal authority to transcend or resolve them.

Having analysed the impact of ICC involvement in the Juba Peace Talks and the Kenya Dialogue in this and the previous three chapters, the remaining part of the book seeks to identify and understand a set of more general characteristics pertaining to peace processes that are judicialised by the ICC's international justice interventions. Against the backdrop of theories of judicialisation and amidst little systematic analysis of claims of the peace/justice debate, it asks: what does ICC involvement do to peace processes, and why do we see such effects? The next chapter compares the effects of ICC involvement in Uganda and Kenya on the peace processes in Juba and Nairobi with a view to understanding how ICC involvement during ongoing conflict affects the conditions of possibility for negotiating a political solution. This comparison results in a theory of ICC impact on peace processes, which the last chapter tests deductively on a third case, while also discussing its main policy implication, the sequencing of peace and justice.

Notes

1 Interview with Mutula Kilonzo, a member of the PNU delegation, May 2011.
2 Interview with Mutula Kilonzo, May 2011.

3 Confidential interview with donor representative, May 2011; interview with Mutula Kilonzo, May 2011; interview with Justice Waki, May 2011.
4 Interview with member of the mediation team, May 2011.
5 Interview with member of the mediation team, May 2011.
6 Quoting Karua, Interview Preston McGhie, May 2011.
7 Between 4 February 2008 and 1 March 2013, Kenyans for Peace with Truth and Justice issued 27 letters and statements, according to their website. See http://kptj.africog.org/.
8 Interview with Justice Waki, May 2011.
9 Interview with Justice Waki, May 2011.
10 As per Article 19(10) of the Rome Statute.
11 Interview with Justice Waki, May 2011.
12 Interview with a defence councillor to one of the Ocampo Six, May 2011.

References

BBC. 2010, February 16. 'Kenyan Ministers "Boycott" Cabinet.' *BBC.*

Boone, Catherine. 2007. 'Property and Constitutional Order: Land Tenure Reform and the Future of the African State.' *African Affairs* 106 (425): 557–486.???

Brown, Stephen, and Chandra Lekha Sriram. 2012. 'The Big Fish Won't Fry Themselves: Criminal Accountability for Post-Election Violence in Kenya.' *African Affairs* 111 (443): 244–260.

Centre for Humanitarian Dialogue. 2014. *From the Nakuru County Peace Accord (2010–2012) to Lasting Peace*. Geneva: Centre for Humanitarian Dialogue.

Cohen, Roger. 2008, August 14. 'How Kofi Annan Rescued Kenya.' *New York Review of Books*.

Correll, Hans. 2009. *Note on Handover of CIPEV Materials to the Prosecutor of the ICC.* Kenya National Dialogue and Reconciliation, Statement by the Legal Advisor to the Panel of Eminent African Personalities. www.dialoguekenya.org/pressmedia/29-Jul-2009.

Elkins, Caroline. 2005. *Britain's Gulag: The Brutal End of Empire in Kenya.* London: Pimlico.

Elklit, Jørgen. 2011. 'The Role of International Organisations during Electoral Crises: The Case of Kenya 2007–08.' *Representation* 47 (4): 399–415.

Fisher, Ronald J. and Loraleigh Keashly. 1991. 'The Potential Complementarity of Mediation and Consultation within a Contingency Model of Third Party Intervention.' *Journal of Peace Research* 28 (1): 29–42.

Gituku, Ngari. 2011, March 11. 'How ICC Cases Mirror Those of Kapenguria.' *The Star.*

Government of Kenya. 2008, July 30. *Long-Term Issues and Solutions: Matrix of Implementation Agenda.* Nairobi: Government of Kenya.

Government of Kenya. 2009, 30 July. *Cabinet Prioritizes National Healing and Reconciliation.* Press Release. Nairobi, State House.

Harbeson, John W. 2012. 'Land and the Quest for a Democratic State in Kenya: Bringing Citizens Back In.' *African Studies Review* 55 (1): 15.

Hayner, Priscilla. 2001. *Unspeakable Truths: Confronting State Terror and Violence.* New York: Routledge.

Internal Displacement Monitoring Centre. 2015. *Towards a Comprehensive Response to Internal Displacement in Kenya: A Roadmap for Action.* Geneva: Internal Displacement Monitoring Centre

International Criminal Court. 2010a. *Decision Pursuant to Article 15 of the Rome Statute on Authorization of an Investigation into the Situation in the Republic of Kenya.* The Hague: International Criminal Court.

International Criminal Court. 2010b. *The Importance of Justice in Securing Peace.* Review Conference of the Rome Statute. The Hague: International Criminal Court.

International Criminal Court. 2010c, December 3. *The ICC Launches Outreach Programme Radio Campaign in Kenya.* Press Release. The Hague: International Criminal Court.

International Criminal Court. 2016, 5 April. *Decision on Defence Applications for Judgments of Acquittal.* ICC-01/09–01/11. The Hague: International Criminal Court.

Kanyinga, Karuti, and James D Long. 2012. 'The Political Economy of Reforms in Kenya: The Post-2007 Election Violence and a New Constitution.' *African Studies Review* 55 (1): 31.

Kenya National Commission on Human Rights. 2012. *Living and Voting with Dignity and Justice.* Nairobi: Kenya National Commission on Human Rights.

Kenyans for Peace with Truth and Justice. 2011, June 8. *Civil Society Statement on the Process of Vetting for the Chief Justice, Deputy Chief Justice and Director of Public Prosecutions.* http://kptj.africog.org/civil-society-statement-on-the-process-of-vetting-for-the-chief-justice-deputy-chief-justice-and-director-of-public-prosecutions/.

Kenyans for Peace with Truth and Justice. 2012, January 20. *KPTJ Press Statement on the Confirmation of Charges Decision.* http://africog.org/new/wp-content/uploads/KPTJ_Press_Statement_ICC_confirmation_of_charges_decision.pdf.

Kenyans for Peace with Truth and Justice. 2014. *A Real Option for Justice? The International Crimes Division of the High Court of Kenya.* Nairobi: Kenyans for Peace with Truth and Justice.

Lindenmayer, Elisabeth, and Josie Lianna Kaye. 2009. *A Choice for Peace? The Story of Forty-One Days of Mediation in Kenya.* New York: International Peace Institute.

Lugano, Geoffrey. 2017. 'Counter-Shaming the International Criminal Court's Intervention as Neocolonial: Lessons from Kenya.' *International Journal of Transitional Justice* 11 (1): 9–29.

Lynch, Gabrielle. 2014. 'Electing the "Alliance of the Accused": The Success of the Jubilee Alliance in Kenya's Rift Valley.' *Journal of Eastern African Studies* 8 (1): 93–114.

Manji, A. 2012. 'The Grabbed State: Lawyers, Politics and Public Land in Kenya.' *Journal of Modern African Studies* 50 (3): 467–492. 47c26.

Mueller, Susanne D. 2014. 'Kenya and the International Criminal Court (ICC): Politics, the Election and the Law.' *Journal of Eastern African Studies* 8 (1): 25–42.

Mureithi, Francis. 2011. 'PNU Drops Plan to Quit Coalition.' *The Star.* http://allafrica.com/stories/201103140690.html.

Narh, Peter, Cosmas K. Lambini, Matthew Sabbi, Van Dien Pham, and Trung Thanh Nguyen. 2016. 'Land Sector Reforms in Ghana, Kenya and Vietnam: A Comparative Analysis of Their Effectiveness.' *Land* 5 (8): 1–17.

Nichols, Lionel. 2015. *The International Criminal Court and the End of Impunity in Kenya.* Cham: Springer.

Office of the Panel of Eminent African Personalities. 2014. *Back from the Brink: The 2008 Mediation Process and Reforms in Kenya.* African Union.

Office of the Prosecutor. 2009a. *ICC Prosecutor: Kenya Can Be an Example to the World.* Press Release. The Hague: International Criminal Court.

Office of the Prosecutor. 2009b. *Press Conference by the Prosecutor of the International Criminal Court, Louis Moreno-Ocampo, Thursday, November 26 2009, Nairobi and The Hague.* The Hague: International Criminal Court.

Office of the Prosecutor. 2010. *ICC Prosecutor to Visit Kenya to Meet Victims and Listen to All Kenyans.* Press Release. The Hague: International Criminal Court.

Ohito, David, David Ochami, Isaac Ongiri, and Joseph Murimi. 2009, January 26. 'MPs in a Rush to Beat Hague Deadline.' *The Standard.*

Parliament of the Republic of Kenya. 2008. '7 May 2008.' *The Hansard.* Nairobi: Parliament of the Republic of Kenya.

Ramsbotham, Oliver, Tom Woodhouse, and Hugh Miall. 2011. *Contemporary Conflict Resolution: The Prevention, Management and Transformations of Deadly Conflict.* Oxford: Polity Press.

Republic of Kenya. 2008a. *[Agreed] Statement of Principles on Long-Term Issues and Solutions (23 May 2008).* Nairobi: Republic of Kenya.

Republic of Kenya. 2008b. *[Agreement on a] Truth, Justice and Reconciliation Commission.* Nairobi: Republic of Kenya.

Republic of Kenya. 2008c. *[Agreed] Statement (1 February 2008).* Nairobi: Republic of Kenya.

Republic of Kenya. 2013. *Report of the Truth, Justice and Reconciliation Commission.* Vol. 1. Nairobi: Government of Kenya.

Rice, Xan. 2009, July 9. 'Annan Hands ICC List of Perpetrators of Post-Election Violence.' *Guardian.*

Schreiber, Leon. 2016. 'Making Power Sharing Work: Kenya's Grand Coalition Cabinet, 2008–2013.' *Innovations for Successful Societies Reports.* Princeton, NJ: Princeton University.

South Consulting. 2009. *Kenya National Dialogue and Reconciliation Monitoring Project: Status of Implementation of Agenda Items 1–4. Third Review Report, July 2009.* Nairobi: Kenya National Dialogue and Reconciliation.

South Consulting. 2011. *The Kenya National Dialogue and Reconciliation (KNDR) Monitoring Project: Draft Review Report, April 2011.* Nairobi: Kenya National Dialogue and Reconciliation.

South Consulting. 2012. *Progress in Implementation of the Constitution and Preparedness for 2012.* The Kenya National Dialogue and Reconciliation Monitoring Project. Nairobi: Kenya National Dialogue and Reconciliation.

Sriram, C L, and S Brown. 2012. 'Kenya in the Shadow of the ICC: Complementarity, Gravity and Impact.' *International Criminal Law Review* 12 (2): 219–244.

Wafula, Caroline. 2011, March 9. 'ODM "Ready" for Dialogue over House Team Row.' *Daily Nation.*

Wallensteen, Peter. 2012. *Understanding Conflict Resolution.* 3rd edn. London: SAGE Publications.

Wolf, Thomas P. 2013. 'International Justice vs Public Opinion: The ICC and Ethnic Polarisation in the 2013 Kenyan Election.' *Journal of African Elections* 12 (1): 143.

Wrong, Michela. 2013, November 3. 'Indictee for President!' *International Herald Tribune.*

7 Impact of ICC involvement in Uganda and Kenya

A comparison

We keep saying rhetorically that there is no conflict between justice and peace, and that the two are complementary. In reality when you have a situation where the people who are to be held accountable are in positions of power, it's not easy.

Francis Deng, former UN Under-Secretary-General[1]

The peace processes in Juba and Nairobi began roughly three and five years after the Rome Statute came into force. As such, they took place in the same new world of international justice: the duty to prosecute had been institutionalised in the ICC, the Court was in its first decade, the Prosecutor was Luis Moreno-Ocampo, international justice NGOs were active and righteous, and peacemakers were grappling with the demands for international justice. Beyond international justice, Uganda and Kenya faced a similar wider political world. Kenya was more important than Uganda in terms of its geo-strategic location and economic position, yet the two countries had similar international relations: they did not generally wield a lot of influence, but were at times able to sway international decision-makers. Uganda kept the humanitarian situation in the north off the formal UN Security Council agenda, while Kenya successfully projected itself as a bastion of stability. Ugandan troops in Somalia and Kenya's 'frontline' role in the Global War on Terror made them Western counter-terrorism allies in the Horn of Africa.

Despite these similarities, the two peace processes experienced two very different external environments: the international community was united, focused and supportive of the Kenyan peace process, while it moved from being hostile to briefly supportive to impatient with the Ugandan process. International justice proponents adopted a wait-and-see approach to justice in the Kenyan peace process, satisfied that the issue of accountability was delegated to a commission of inquiry, but in the Juba Peace Talks they demanded an immediate criminal process and the repeal of Uganda's amnesty law. In the Ugandan negotiations, the question of accountability was so dominant that negotiators and mediators felt the presence of the ICC in the negotiating room, while Kenyan negotiators were oblivious to the Prosecutor's initiation of a preliminary examination. Furthermore, the ICC

Prosecutor launched a campaign to delegitimise negotiations with the LRA, while emphasising the preventative nature of his role in Kenya.

This chapter compares ICC involvement in the two peace processes to better understand how, when and why ICC involvement in situations of ongoing conflict affects peace processes. It has two parts. Part 1 compares the interactive and constitutive effects of ICC involvement in the two peace processes in order to identify patterns of effects. It analyses four processes associated with judicialisation by the ICC: the shaping of sticking points, delegation of politico-legal authority and of discursive authority, and decontestation of the meaning of justice. These involve both the legal constraints of hard law studied by liberal institutionalists and the discursive legitimisation of claims and narratives identified by constructivists. The focus on legal indeterminacy by critical legal studies explains judicial agency with reference to not only the Rome Statute but also actors' interpretations of the Statute. By investigating these interpretations, it is possible to develop an understanding of action and inaction by actors such as the ICC Prosecutor and the Security Council members.

Part 2 formulates a set of general findings about the impact of ICC involvement on peace processes. It discusses the difference that levels of ICC involvement make: it matters whether peace negotiations take place in the context of a low or high level of judicialisation. Furthermore, Stage 4 involvement constitutes a watershed for peace negotiations. Part 2 thereafter discusses the changing imperatives of different involvement stages and the differentiated resilience of the three peace process phases.

Part 1 Comparing the Juba Peace Talks and the Kenya Dialogue

At their most basic level, the Juba Peace Talks failed while the Kenya Dialogue succeeded: the Ugandan conflict parties could not commit to a political settlement, while their Kenya counterparts decided to enter into a political pact. Chapters 5 and 7 explained these outcomes in terms of sticking points, intra-party conflict, mediation strategies, temporality and discursive action. It became clear that the two peace processes interacted with the trajectories of ICC involvement and that this to some extent affected the negotiation outcomes.

The key difference between the two judicialised peace processes concerned the level of ICC involvement in the different conflict resolution phases. ICC involvement was already at a high level when the Pre-Negotiation phase began in the Ugandan process, while the entire first two phases of the Kenyan peace process took place in conditions of low ICC involvement. Only in the latter part of the Implementation phase did the Kenyan Dialogue experience a high level of ICC involvement. Figure 7.1 illustrates the two peace processes in their respective contexts of ICC involvement.

The concept of legalised politics, as we saw in Chapter 2, denotes the process of bringing politics into the domain of law and framing political negotiations by legal categories, obligations and proscriptions. It concerns a form

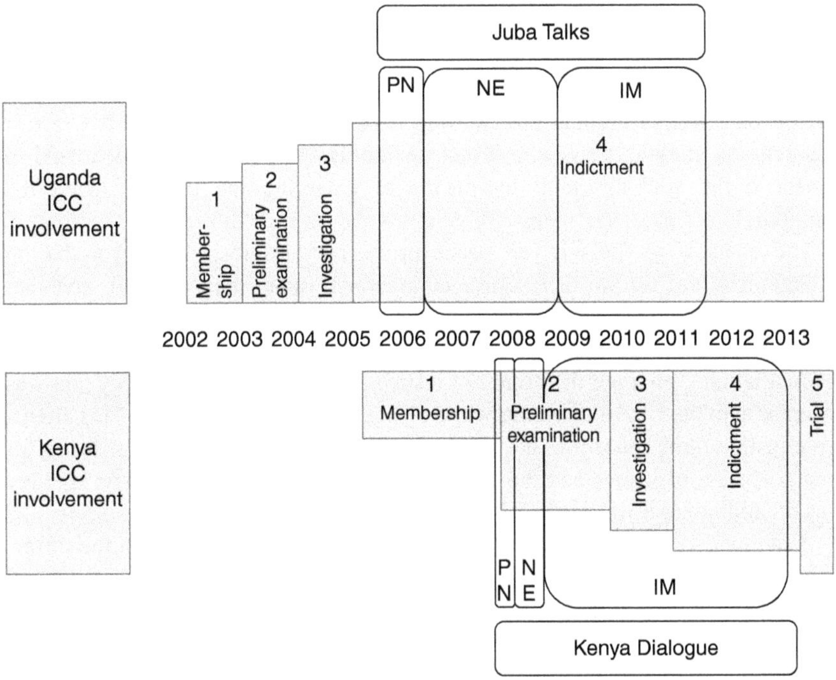

Figure 7.1 The processes of ICC involvement and peacemaking in Uganda and Kenya.

Note
Peace process phases are abbreviated as Pre-Negotiation (PN), Negotiation (NE) and Implementation (IM) phases.

of politics that is affected by interactions with a legal framework, while judicialised politics is shaped by judicial or court action. Liberal institutionalist, constructivist and critical insights into the relationship between law and politics suggest that international courts may affect peace processes in both interactive and constitutive ways.

In the Juba Peace Talks and the Kenya Dialogue, conflict resolution was judicialised in various ways by ICC involvement. At the same time, different non-ICC related processes of legalisation also took place. Comparing the two cases, four aspects of judicialisation come to the fore. Analysing these, it is possible to understand why the peace processes were affected in different ways by ICC involvement as well as how, when and why ICC intervention affects a peace process. The four aspects of legalisation are the Rome Statute's shaping of the sticking points, the delegation of politico-legal and discursive authority from the local to international levels, and the attempt to decontest the meaning of justice.

Shaping the sticking points

The peace processes had different sticking points, which reflected the two conflicts. In Kenya, the political crisis was about governance, and the sticking point in the Negotiation phase concerned the right to govern. In Uganda, the conflict had become one of civilian atrocity and insurgency, but due to the ICC arrest warrants the sticking point concerned justice. Both peace negotiations tried to transcend the sticking point by means of enlarging the pool of contested resources.

The analysis of the Kenyan peace process argues that the power-sharing arrangement was a form of resource enlargement rather than resource division: Raila Odinga gained executive power, but hardly at the expense of Mwai Kibaki. In the Ugandan negotiations, the alternative justice form, 'accountability and reconciliation', enlarged the notion of justice in order to design a policy that was acceptable to the LRA leadership while respecting the Rome Statute. This alternative justice form could not, however, accommodate the Prosecutor's desire for a narrow form of justice and the LRA commanders' desire for amnesty: if Kony was rehabilitated, it was at the ICC's expense, so to speak.

A comparison of efforts to overcome the sticking points brings out the difference that types and levels of legalisation make. In Uganda, there was a high level of international legalisation, while the Kenyan negotiations, which took place in the context of Stage 2 ICC involvement, were marked by a low level of international legalisation and a high level of local legalisation, including legalisation by negotiators, mediators and the conflict parties. In the Kenya Dialogue, this process of legalisation was a conscious response to a stalemate in the negotiations and the fact that decision-making power on this issue lay with the principals. The negotiations on power-sharing succeeded through a dynamic process of politicisation and legalisation: the political negotiations were suspended through a process of legal drafting in the lawyers' working group, while Correll and Annan introduced an amendment clause to the Constitution, effectively subjecting the latter to the political imperative of ending the violence. Importantly, the legal drafting process preceded Kibaki and Odinga's decision to share power. Indicating the awareness that the move was controversial, Annan justified the politicisation of the Constitution with it being an 'exceptional measure' for 'exceptional times' (Lindenmayer and Kaye 2009, 15).

In the Juba Peace Talks, legalisation was a response to the incompatibility between the ICC indictments and the position of the LRA leaders, but it happened without politico-legal dynamism. Stage 4 involvement legalised politics, but those with authority to politicise the Rome Statute sufficiently in order to overcome the sticking point were located outside the peace process and were not interested in politicising the law: in The Hague, the Prosecutor did not want to invoke his discretionary power in Article 53 to end a prosecution in the 'interests of justice' and, in New York, the Security Council did not want to invoke Article 16 to request a deferral of prosecution. The fact that the LRA preyed on civilians in three fragile states was not seen by the OTP and the Security Council as an exceptional situation calling for exceptional measures. The participants in the Juba process did politicise the Rome Statute by exploring its limits and boundaries and reinterpreting its concept of complementarity. However, these participants did not wield the required politico-legal authority to realise their justice proposal.

The findings from Uganda are comparable to the high-level Implementation phase in Kenya. Given the centrality of several indicted persons (Kenyatta, Muthaura and Ruto) to the implementation of the Kenya Dialogue, this last phase experienced a sticking point in the issue of justice; the Negotiation and Implementation phases thus each had their sticking point. The second sticking point did not prevent a political solution, since this had been reached in the Negotiation phase, but it constituted a centrifugal force in the power-sharing government, which at times threatened to tear apart the fragile ODM–PNU coalition as well as the internal coherence of the ODM. Furthermore, authority to remove this sticking point was located in The Hague and New York: the PTC could return the case to Kenyan jurisdiction while the Security Council could request a deferral of prosecution. The government therefore mobilised its resources to initiate admissibility proceedings in the PTC and obtain support from the AU and the Security Council. As a result, and explored further below, the government devoted so much attention to the ICC intervention that the Implementation phase became increasingly one-dimensional: reconciliation and land reform yielded to the government's international political and legal mobilisation against an ICC process. Table 7.1 summarises the differences in dealing with the three sticking points across the relevant peace process phases.

The proposed solutions to overcome the sticking points of the Negotiation phases of the Juba Peace Talks and the Kenya Dialogue relied on politico-legal authority for their effectuation and legitimacy.

Delegation of authority

Delegation is a key dimension of legalisation, denoting 'the extent to which states and other actors delegate authority to designated third parties – including courts, arbitrators, and administrative organizations – to implement agreements' (Abbott *et al.* 2000, 415). Central to the concept of delegation, therefore, is the act of granting authority to another entity to interpret and apply a particular set of rules. Bradley and Kelley (2008, 19) find that the 'legal effect' of delegation to the ICC is high because 'it can enforce its criminal judgments directly through the strong sanction of imprisonment'. This section looks at the effects of delegation to the ICC more broadly, examining the transfer of politico-legal and discursive authority.

Politico-legal authority

The source of sufficient politico-legal authority to overcome the sticking point in Kenya lay inside the peace process, personalised by the conflict principals as

Table 7.1 Sticking points and resolution efforts in Uganda and Kenya

	Uganda	*Kenya*	
Peace process	*Negotiation phase*	*Negotiation phase*	*Implementation phase*
ICC involvement	*Stage 4*	*Stage 2*	*Stage 4*
Sticking point	The imperative of prosecuting the LRA leaders at the ICC	The right to govern the country	The imperative of prosecuting key political actors at the ICC
Efforts to overcome the sticking point	Politicisation of the Rome Statute by Juba participants	Legalisation of the negotiations. Politicisation of the Constitution by Dialogue participants	Politicisation by Kenyan government (AU mobilisation); admissibility challenge
Proposed solution	Alternative domestic accountability and reconciliation	Power sharing	Domestic justice process
Location of authority to enable solution	OTP and Security Council	Conflict principals	PTC and Security Council

well as the mediators in the Panel of Eminent African Personalities. In their roles as party leaders, president and soon-to-be prime minister, Kibaki and Odinga were able to authorise the power-sharing agreement and the proposed amendment to the Constitution, with these subsequently blue-stamped by parliament. The Panel could legitimise the deal internationally; it drew formal authority from the AU and the UN and situated power from being 'the only game in town' able to orchestrate the involvement by dominant Western states. In the Ugandan case, by contrast, politico-legal authority to overcome the sticking point had been transferred away from the Juba process and the conflict principals, to decision-makers in New York and The Hague, who saw themselves as external to the peace process.

Linked to a high level of involvement at Stage 4, international delegation to the ICC involved the transfer of politico-legal authority. It was a form of legitimated structural power: the Security Council and the Prosecutor had formal authority by virtue of the legal structures of the Rome Statute, not because they had requested to take a position on the Juba dilemma. The authority to take political decisions in relation to peace and security was vested in the Prosecutor and the Security Council in Articles 16 and 53, respectively. Due to these authority relationships, peace negotiations that take place in the context of high-level ICC involvement will be constrained by the legal and political interpretations of the OTP and the Security Council.

While authority internal to the Kenyan peace process enabled the parties to overcome their Negotiation phase sticking point, the political authority that high-level ICC involvement transferred to the Security Council and the Prosecutor was by these international actors considered inappropriate and irrelevant to efforts to overcome the Ugandan sticking point. In the context of a high level of involvement in Kenya, justice became a sticking point in the Implementation phase, where politico-legal authority had been transferred to international actors. Thus, the government mobilised regional AU allies and launched admissibility proceedings in an effort to reverse the delegation and relocate authority at the national level.

Discursive authority

International delegation to the ICC also entails the transfer of discursive authority to the ICC, which means that the Court obtains the authority to express itself verbally on national matters. In addition, the nature of the Prosecutor's discourse in the Indictment stage relates to whether or not he or she needs to mobilise support for arrest, rather than whether ICC involvement was triggered by invitation or imposition. In Uganda, where ICC involvement was quasi-voluntary on the part of the government, the Prosecutor's discourse was less accommodating and sensitive to local debates than in Kenya, where involvement was imposed.

Chapter 4 examined how international delegation of the LRA problem to the ICC entailed a transfer of discursive authority: while the government used to narrate the conflict, portraying it as apolitical violence by 'criminals' and 'terrorists',

ICC involvement forwarded this discursive authority to the OTP. Using this narrative power, the Prosecutor engaged in an advocacy campaign to render the Juba Peace Talks meaningless, simultaneously reinforcing the militaristic discourse of government hardliners opposed to negotiations with the LRA. Arguing that Kony's real intentions were to rearm and regroup, the Prosecutor made the Talks seem futile; within this discourse, military capture was the only means of removing the LRA. This discourse supported hardliners against moderates within the Ugandan political establishment, a faction that succeeded in terminating the Negotiation phase in December 2008 by launching Operation Lightning Thunder.

The Prosecutor's discourse in Kenya was of a very different kind, focusing not on capture and culpability, but on prevention and protection. His statements narrated a straightforward causal relationship between criminal accountability and peace, equating his investigation with a peaceful next election. Kenya epitomised the many countries where perpetrators of political violence act without being held to account and its fight against impunity was therefore to be an 'example to the world' and 'to the [African] region'. He built a narrative of community, togetherness and inclusion, emphasising that Kenyans were supported internationally and even globally. Visiting regions affected by the post-election violence, he promised to 'listen to all Kenyans' (OTP 2010). In marked contrast to his engagement in Uganda, the Prosecutor felt part of Kenya's peace process; in his own words, 'The AU Panel for Kenya chaired by former Secretary-General Kofi Annan has made the ICC part of a comprehensive solution for Kenya' (OTP 2009a, 6).

The different Ugandan and Kenyan discourses – of capture and protection, respectively – are puzzling, given the fact that the Uganda intervention was invited while the Kenya involvement was imposed: invitation could be expected to inspire sensitivity towards local agendas, while imposition could be expected to encourage a disregard for local processes. The discourses also reflected poorly the vulnerabilities of affected communities, as Northern Ugandans arguably were in greater need of international protection, while most Kenyans desired capture and at most experienced a non-military mobilisation against the ICC.

The OTP discourses are explained by the fact that the Ugandan indictees were wanted, while their Kenyan counterparts were summoned. In contrast to his case against the LRA, the Prosecutor and the ICC did not need to mobilise Kenyan, regional or international support for the arrest of the Ocampo Six. A logic of consequences thus influenced the nature of the Prosecutor's discursive involvement: the need to mobilise state cooperation for arrest to secure a trial necessitated a set of narratives about evil. As a result, Uganda's Kony, Libya's Saif Gaddafi and Sudan's al Bashir were constructed as the personification of evil, to the extent that elections in Sudan were like 'Hitler elections' (Reuters 2010). In situations where there was no need to mobilise international cooperation, that is, when the accused was in detention or summoned to appear, the Prosecutor could focus on forward-looking topics such as prevention and assistance. Table 7.2 summarises the comparative findings on discursive delegation.

Table 7.2 Discursive delegation

	Uganda		*Kenya*	
Peace process	*Pre-Negotiation phase*	*Negotiation phase*	*Negotiation phase*	*Implementation phase*
ICC involvement	*Stage 4 involvement*	*Stage 4 involvement*	*Stage 2 involvement*	*Stage 4 involvement*
Indictment Form	Arrest warrants	Arrest warrants	–	Summons to appear
OTP Discourse	Supportive of peace process (before Museveni's security guarantee); anti-peace process (after the security guarantee)	Anti-peace process	Supportive of peace process	Supportive of peace process

Decontestation of justice

Decontestation refers to the process of seeking to determine the meaning of the political concepts, which are per se contestable (Freeden 1996). It aims to eliminate competing meanings so a concept appears to signify one thing. ICC involvement in the peace processes in Juba and Nairobi interactively and constitutively shaped the meaning of justice in a process of decontestation that related to the level of involvement. As the ICC's involvement moved up the five-stage trajectory of intervention, the two peace processes had to relate to an increasingly narrow justice concept. During the high level of ICC involvement (Stage 4) in the Ugandan Negotiation and Implementation phases and the Kenyan Implementation phase, peace process actors had to negotiate a narrow notion of justice. By contrast, the Kenyan Negotiation phase, which took place in the context of a low level of involvement (Stage 2), experienced a greater degree of freedom to define justice.

In the Juba process, the arrest warrants for the LRA leaders introduced the issue of accountability into peace negotiations, to the extent that it constituted a separate agenda item and in fact became 'the heart of the process'. This focus stood in contrast to all of the NRM government's previous negotiations with insurgents, which had not addressed the issue of accountability. Accountability was, however, framed in a highly specific manner because it had to result in either an agreement that included the LRA leaders' voluntary surrender or an alternative to the ICC, which could serve as the basis for a successful admissibility challenge. With such highly specific requirements, the negotiations over accountability became an exploration of the possibilities of international criminal law by the conflict parties and the three Ugandan lawyers attached to the mediation team. They tried to define the relevant articles of the Rome Statute broadly, to create a 'zone of possible agreement' not between the two conflict parties but between the LRA leaders and the ICC. In this sense, the Rome Statute shaped the conditions of possibility for justice.

In contrast to the experiences in Juba, and in the context of low-level ICC involvement, the negotiators in the Kenya Dialogue did not have to frame their justice response according to the Rome Statute in any particular sense. Instead, they were at liberty to articulate rather general aims on holding perpetrators to account and to delegate the issue of justice to CIPEV. None of the clauses in the peace agreements or the establishment of CIPEV were incompatible with the Rome Statute due to their relatively high level of generality; had the negotiators wanted to stray too far from the idea of individual criminal accountability, Kenya's ICC membership (Stage 1) and the mediator acted as a constraint. According to a member of the mediation team, Annan would not have allowed any kind of impunity-related formulations in the Negotiation phase.[2] Although the negotiations were not framed by the Rome Statute in any significant way, they were legalised; but, as we saw, it was Kenyan laws that framed the negotiations.

After the parliamentary defeat of the STK, and still in the context of Stage 2 involvement, the power-sharing cabinet resolved to opt for the reform of the security forces and justice system rather than to delegate the problem to the ICC. Due to the low level of ICC involvement, the cabinet could do this; it had to consider the ICC system but was not compelled to use it. At higher levels of ICC involvement, however, the Kenyan government had less room for manoeuvre.

At the Indictment stage of both peace processes, two interpretations by the ICC served to narrow the justice concept. First, the Court's interpretation of the 'complementarity test' defined the nature and form to which national justice must conform in order to be considered alternative to an ICC process: there must be domestic proceedings against the same person for having perpetrated the same conduct (Jurdi 2010; Rodman 2009). This test was formulated first in the ICC case against Germain Katanga, a Congolese warlord whose case was found admissible by the ICC Trial Chambers because national courts had not investigated or prosecuted him for the Bogoro massacre for which he was charged at the ICC (ICC 2009). Thus, justice could be seen to be done only if Uganda and Kenya prosecuted specific individuals for particular OTP-defined acts of atrocity. Second, the OTP decoupled the interests of justice from those of peace. This conceptual change reinforced the compulsory power of the complementarity test.

Given the narrow specification of justice, the only alternative to a trial at The Hague seemed to be the establishment of a national criminal justice tribunal: the ICD established in Uganda and the proposed STK. Certainly a justice policy modelled on the South African Truth and Reconciliation Commission would not have met the justice definition. As such, there was a chorus of protests by local and international justice NGOs when the Kenyan Truth, Justice and Reconciliation Commission Bill took an ambiguous position on the granting of amnesty for international crimes.

In a constitutive rather than interactive sense, criminal justice crowded out other notions of justice, such as restorative and social justice, in the Implementation phases of the Juba Peace Talks and the Kenya Dialogue. In the former, and contrary to the agreed-upon justice policy, the government's unilateral implementation of the Agreement on Accountability and Reconciliation and the involvement of European donors and human rights NGOs ensured that the ICD would carry out ordinary retributive justice. In Kenya, implementation of the agreed land reform and a national discussion about the perceived injustices that constituted the underlying conflict were displaced by the compelling idea of ending impunity. This development took place as CIPEV and the ICC Prosecutor formulated the dominant narrative of the post-election violence in Kenya: at the 'heart of the post-election violence' was a 'cycle of impunity' linked to the political use and institutionalisation of violence following the introduction of multi-party democracy in 1991 (Republic of Kenya 2008). CIPEV therefore recommended the establishment of a special tribunal and an anti-impunity mechanism that relied on the threat of ICC involvement. Land reform 'languished' (Kanyinga and Long 2012, 143) and, moreover, was not linked to reconciliation. Table 7.3 summarises the comparative findings on the decontestation of justice.

Table 7.3 Decontestation of justice

	Uganda	*Kenya*		
Peace process	*Negotiation phase*	*Negotiation phase*	*Implementation phase*	*Implementation phase*
ICC involvement	*Stage 4*	*Stage 2*	*Stage 2*	*Stage 4*
Meaning of justice	Criminal justice by the ICC	Criminal justice in an unspecific sense, procedural justice and social justice (land reform)	Anti-impunity and criminal justice by hybrid STK, judicial reform	Anti-impunity and criminal justice by ICC
Scope of justice concept	Narrow	Broad	Less broad	Narrow
Dealing with justice	Alternative accountability and reconciliation enabled by admissibility challenge	Delegation of justice issue to CIPEV	Seeking to establish STK, then opting for judicial reform	Mobilisation of AU and UN Security Council, admissibility challenge, Jubilee Coalition framing ICC as a neo-imperial project

Civil society contestation

The international narrowing of justice was, however, contested by national civil societies. In Uganda, the struggle to define justice centred on the amnesty law, while in Kenya it merged with the 2013 elections. Throughout the ICC's active involvement in Uganda, external actors such as the Prosecutor, the UN High Commissioner for Human Rights, and Amnesty International pressured the government to amend or repeal the Amnesty Act (2000) (OTP 2004; United Nations; Vision Reporter 2005; UN 2012). Having amended the law in May 2006, the government utilised the new provisions for lapsing Part II of the Amnesty Law six years later, ensuring that it could grant no new amnesties. However, following an outcry and parliamentary petition by civil society, Part II was reinstated in May 2013 (Republic of Uganda 2013).

In Kenya, the results of the 2013 general elections signified contestation of the narrow justice of the Indictment stage. Like in Uganda, reactions to the ICC intervention drew primarily from the communities associated with the Prosecutor's indictees. The Jubilee Alliance, led by the two ICC suspects, Kenyatta and Ruto, campaigned against intervention by the supposedly neo-imperial ICC and in defence of Kenya's sovereignty and nationhood. Civil society contestation of the justice defined by the ICC is signified by the Jubilee Alliance's ability to win the elections. Lynch (2014) and Wolf (2013) trace the election results to a combination of ethnic voting, Jubilee discourse and community-related positions on the ICC. Members of the ethnic communities of Kenyatta and Ruto displayed a higher voter turnout, while only 22–28 per cent of them supported the ICC intervention. By comparison, 77–87 per cent of the five other main ethnic communities supported the ICC process.

Table 7.4 displays the comparative findings across the four different effects. In order to illuminate the proposed relationship between involvement levels and their effects, it is organised according to ICC involvement stages rather than in chronological order. The table illustrates the similarities between the Kenyan Implementation phase and the Ugandan Negotiation and Implementation phases, all of which occurred in the context of a high level of ICC involvement. These characteristics are contrasted with the Kenyan Negotiation and Implementation phases, which took place in the context of a low level of ICC involvement.

Part 2 How ICC involvement affects peace processes

By disaggregating the processes of ICC involvement and conflict resolution, the investigation has identified and analysed the interplay between phase-specific peacemaking dynamics and stage-specific ICC activities and discourses. As discussed in Chapter 2, ICC involvement at Stages 1 and 2 represents a low level of involvement, while Stages 4 and 5 indicate a high level of involvement (see Figure 2.1). Stage 3 equates to a medium involvement level.

The remainder of this chapter proposes a set of general findings about the impact of ICC involvement on peace processes, which should nevertheless be

Table 7.4 Summary of selected aspects of judicialisation

	Uganda		*Kenya*		
Peace process	*Negotiation*	*Implementation*	*Negotiation*	*Implementation*	*Implementation*
Level of ICC involvement	*High (Stage 4)*	*High (Stage 4)*	*Low (Stage 2)*	*Low (Stage 2)*	*High (Stage 4)*
Level of legalisation	High	High	High	Low	High
Source of legalisation	ICC	ICC	PEAP, PNU, ODM	CIPEV	ICC
Sticking point	Justice	Justice	Right to rule	Justice	Justice
Nature of sticking point	Legal	Legal	Political	Legal	Legal
Situatedness of politico-legal authority	External: OTP, UNSC	–	Internal: negotiators, principals, PEAP	Internal: GNU	External: AU, UNSC, PTC
Situatedness of discursive authority	External: OTP	External: OTP and PTC	Internal: PEAP (conflict parties)	Internal: CIPEV	External: OTP
Central narrative	Talks are futile and illegitimate; indictees must be marginalised and arrested	Indictees must be marginalised and arrested	Conflict is many-faceted; widespread reform is needed	The problem is impunity	The problem is impunity but ICC is there to help; ICC supports the Dialogue
Scope for justice	Narrow scope: criminal justice; efforts to expand scope failed	Narrow scope: criminal justice (ICC and ICD)	Broad scope: delegation to CIPEV	Semi-broad scope: STK and justice sector reform	Narrow scope: criminal justice
Legal frame for justice	Rome Statute	Rome Statute	Constitution of Kenya	Constitution of Kenya	Rome Statute

understood as non-deterministic and subject to contextual factors. The findings are organised into three sections. The first section discusses the different effects of low and high levels of ICC involvement on the ability to overcome the sticking point of the Negotiation phase. It identifies the move into Stage 4 ICC involvement as a watershed moment for a peace process. The second section summarises three aspects of ICC involvement that change once the ICC moves up the trajectory of involvement. The last section discusses why individual peace process phases have different levels of resilience towards the effects of judicialisation by the ICC.

The difference that involvement levels make

The analysis and comparison of the Juba Peace Talks and the Kenya Dialogue has revealed a pattern: how ICC involvement affects the conditions of possibility for entering into a political settlement depends on the level of ICC involvement during the Negotiation phase. A low level of involvement affects the Negotiation phase differently than does a high level of involvement. In negotiations that occur in a context of low-level involvement, negotiators and mediators are able to resolve the central sticking point on their own terms, without having to rely on the politico-legal authority of international actors to facilitate their solution and are unconstrained by the narrow justice concept of the Indictment stage. This was the case in Kenya, but also pertained to the IGAD Peace Process between the Sudanese government and SPLM/A.

In the Sudanese IGAD process, ICC involvement was completely absent during the Negotiation phase, while individuals from the government were indicted during the Implementation phase.[3] In both the Kenya Dialogue and these Sudan peace negotiations, external third parties were involved as mediators, but issues of justice were given much less importance than governance. The central sticking point concerned political power, with both negotiations agreeing on a power-sharing solution. Accountability issues were displaced to a commission of inquiry in the Kenyan negotiations, while the negotiations over the status of Southern Sudan ignored such concerns altogether (Johnson 2011; Scherr 2016, 191). This was possible because Sudan was not party to the Rome State. Since Kenya had ratified the Rome Statute in 2005, issues pertaining to accountability had to be addressed, given state parties' duty to prosecute ICC crimes: if negotiations leave issues of individual accountability unaddressed, the Prosecutor has the right to launch a *proprio motu* investigation into that country, subject to PTC approval. Kenya's obligations to the Rome Statute allowed some flexibility towards politically defining the appropriate justice forum.

As will be argued in the next chapter, the pattern is confirmed by the ongoing Havana Peace Process between the Colombian government and FARC that has taken place in the context of a low level of ICC involvement (Stage 2). These negotiations had a sticking point in disarmament rather than justice. The justice agreement between the government and FARC operates with a semi-narrow justice notion that nevertheless includes a criminal dimension. The Colombian solution refers conflict-related justice issues to a Special Jurisdiction for Peace, where alleged perpetrators will receive reduced sentences in exchange for truth and guarantees of non-recurrence (Cassel 2015; Olásolo 2015).

In situations with a high level of ICC involvement during the Negotiation phase, in contrast, ICC involvement delegates the authority to solve the central sticking point to international actors. Conflict settlement thus becomes dependent on the way in which these actors interpret the Rome Statute and view the conflict parties and the negotiations, as well as on how much they care. In Uganda, as we saw, the Rome Statute delegated authority to the Security Council and the Prosecutor, equipping them with a mandate to make a discretionary decision. High-level involvement also affected the negotiations in more subtle ways, placing justice issues at the heart of the negotiations and subjecting them to a prosecutorial discourse that discredited the Talks and mobilised for arrest.

In Kenya, the ICC deepened its involvement during the Implementation phase, launching the Indictment stage after the constitutional referendum. Suddenly the government experienced that politico-legal authority to remove the new sticking point – the demand for narrow justice – had been transferred to the international level. It therefore directed its efforts to where this authority was located, launching admissibility proceedings at the ICC and seeking to influence the Security Council to defer ICC proceedings against Kenyan actors.

These findings suggest that Stage 4 involvement, the Indictment stage, constitutes a watershed for any peace process that takes place in the context of an ICC intervention. Until this stage, sufficient authority is retained within the peace process and justice is defined sufficiently broadly to enable a creative treatment of this potentially difficult issue. Keeping in mind the non-deterministic nature of this finding, Table 7.5 maps six peace processes where the Negotiation phase takes place in the context of ICC involvement and conforms to the pattern. The seventh process, in Abuja, failed to settle the conflict in Darfur and thus reminds us that a low level of ICC involvement does not guarantee or facilitate a settlement; rather, it permits a political settlement where conflict parties are able and willing to resolve their sticking point. Table 7.5 highlights the proposed relationship between a high level of ICC involvement and peace process outcomes. The following two sections discuss why this relationship exists.

Changing effects of deepening ICC involvement

As an ICC intervention deepens, moving from the first active stage (Stage 2) up the trajectory of the intervention, Court involvement generates four effects. These effects are to some extent related or overlapping. First, deepening ICC involvement delegates politico-legal authority to external actors, which may or may not be supportive of a political settlement. This is a constitutive effect of ICC involvement in the sense that it is diffuse and informal rather than formally handed over to the ICC and the Security Council. Indeed, the Prosecutor has emphasised his independence from the Juba Peace Talks (ICC 2007, 31).

Table 7.5 Peace processes mapped according to their outcome and level of ICC involvement

		ICC involvement during the Negotiation phase	
		Low-level ICC involvement	*High-level ICC involvement*
Peace process outcome	**Political settlement**	Southern Sudan (IGAD Process, 2002–2005)* Kenya (National Dialogue, 2008–2013) Colombia (Havana Talks, 2010–2017)	
	Return to war	Darfur (Abuja Process, 2005–2006)	Uganda (Bigombe Talks, 2004–2005) Uganda (Juba Talks, 2005–2008) Darfur (Doha Process, 2010–2012)

Note
* In South Sudan, there was no ICC involvement during the Negotiation phase, but high-level involvement during the Implementation phase.

Second, deepening ICC involvement delegates discursive authority to the ICC, a constitutive transfer of authority that entitles the Prosecutor to comment on any relevant situation in a state party. In the context of Stage 2 involvement (Preliminary Examination) in Kenya, the Prosecutor recommended a 'three-pronged' justice policy, while in Colombia, the new Prosecutor de facto approved the negotiated justice policy (OTP 2016). At Stage 4 involvement, the ICC may engage in a discourse of capture or a discourse of support, depending on the form of indictment. Where the indictment takes the form of a warrant of arrest, the Prosecutor faces the imperative of mobilising support for the military arrest of an individual. As a result, high-level involvement introduces a discourse of capture and marginalisation, with adverse effects for a peace negotiation. Where the indictees are summoned to appear, the ICC's discourse may be much more forward-looking, focusing on prevention and assistance.

This finding pertaining to the nature of Court discourse is supported by ICC involvement in Darfur, where the PTC issued an arrest warrant for four government actors and summons to appear for three rebel leaders. These rebels were in principle as 'evil' as Joseph Kony, leading illegitimate armies and using civilian violence to obtain their goals. However, the rebel leaders have not been vilified by the Prosecutor and insurgent violence hardly appears in his advocacy and reporting material (Moreno-Ocampo 2010; OTP 2009b). In contrast, the Prosecutor has often described and deplored the violence perpetrated by indicted government actors.

Third, the scope for defining the meaning of justice becomes increasingly narrow. This is also a constitutive effect. At Stage 4 involvement, given the complementarity test and the decoupling of the interests of justice and peace, justice is a very narrow concept that means criminal prosecution of ICC-identified perpetrators for particular instances of ICC-identified conduct. Other forms of justice become complementary, rather than alternative, and therefore cannot substitute the ICC's narrow justice. At earlier stages, particularly Stage 2, the scope for negotiating a context-appropriate justice solution is much broader. In Kenya, mediators and negotiators judged that any question of responsibility for the violence would fuel the ongoing violence, and the justice issue was therefore 'parked' in CIPEV until the violence had ceased (Elklit 2011).

Last, as justice becomes increasingly narrow, ICC involvement shapes the sticking point. At a high level of ICC involvement, the requirements of the Rome Statute are so narrow that the sticking point becomes justice related. This is partly due to the way in which the Court has interpreted important features of the Rome Statute, such as admissibility and the interests of justice. If peace is negotiated during the early stages of a justice trajectory, the sticking point may be unrelated to justice issues and is likely to stem from the causes or triggers of conflict. Needless to say, if conflict parties overcome a cause-related sticking point, their negotiations are more likely to contribute to a durable peace.

Differentiated resilience of peace process phases

The phases of a peace process have different levels of resilience towards the effects of judicialisation and are affected by ICC involvement in different ways. In the Pre-Negotiation phase, prosecution of one side of the conflict alters the relationship between the conflict parties. It may become more symmetrical or asymmetrical than it was before ICC involvement, but this depends on the conflict dynamics. The justice discourse entails the incentives narrative, which claims that arrest warrants make suspects 'ripe' and willing to enter negotiations. Although the Juba Peace Talks are often cited as an example of this interactive effect, interviews with LRA/M negotiators and mediators did not indicate support for this claim.[4] One interviewee said that the LRA had expressed willingness to talk peace many times before being indicted, while another explained that the LRA had not been in a hurry to negotiate, but had waited to see the outcome of the February 2006 elections (see also Atkinson 2010; Branch 2010).

In the Negotiation phase, a high level of ICC involvement effectively suspends mediation. The different mediation tools – whether coercive, facilitative or incentivising – become irrelevant when decisions to overcome the central sticking point do not depend on the conflict parties. Furthermore, when ICC indictments cannot be negotiated and seemingly cannot be withdrawn, they can be used neither as a stick nor a carrot. When conflict parties have authority to make the most important decisions, different mediation techniques can be usefully employed to secure a political settlement. In Kenya, these techniques included the legalisation, depoliticisation and politicisation of the sticking point.

A successful Negotiation phase depends on politico-legal authority to overcome the sticking point. In theory, this authority can be located outside the peace process, but it needs to be available. This phase is moreover vulnerable to hostile discourses by the ICC, as these can undermine the 'working trust' between conflict parties or negotiators that is required for meaningful negotiations and agreements (Kelman 2005). In Uganda, the hostile ICC discourse produced two narratives, which contributed to the sense of impatience and the international support for the military pursuit of the rebels.

In the Implementation phase, the agreed policies are vulnerable to being either subjected to externally determined deadlines or, in cases of high-level ICC involvement, side-lined by the existential concerns of powerful individuals who are threatened by ICC prosecution. However, the Implementation phase of a successful peace process is more resilient to a high-level involvement than is the Negotiation phase. The Implementation phase commences after the political settlement has been agreed, where the political and economic costs of returning to war are higher than during the Negotiation phase. As the settlement becomes subject to different centrifugal and centripetal forces, the effects of ICC involvement may be balanced by those interested in maintaining the settlement. Furthermore, as dangerous elements are likely to have been demobilised, an arrest warrant is less likely to involve retaliation against civilians or a return to war.

The effects of ICC involvement

The comparison between the Juba Peace Talks and the Kenya Dialogue demonstrates that peace processes that take place in the context of active ICC involvement cannot be empirically separated from the justice processes in their midst because these two processes interact. Justice and peace processes were conceptually separated in order to enable disaggregation and systematic process tracing, but the analysis shows that the Court's justice interventions in Uganda and Kenya affected the peace processes in multiple ways.

This chapter has argued that ICC involvement shapes the sticking point, delegates politico-legal and discursive authority to the international level and decontests justice. However, whether these effects materialise depends on the level of ICC involvement: a high level of involvement is associated with all four effects, while a low level of involvement entails discursive delegation and a broad concept of justice. Given the national retention of politico-legal authority, the possibility of purely political sticking points, and the broader scope for justice, it is possible to reach a political settlement in the context of a low level of ICC involvement. This happened in the Kenya Dialogue and, as we are about to discover, the Havana Process.

The comparison also gave rise to the proposition that the phases of a peace process have different capacities for resilience towards the effects of ICC involvement. This means that the Negotiation phase is more vulnerable to the adverse effects of, say, a justice-related sticking point than the Implementation phase is, while the Pre-Negotiation phase is most vulnerable to the effects of the conflict parties' loss of authority. This set of findings requires further and more fine-grained research, but also lends support to the initial idea of analysing peace processes in terms of their different phases.

The comparison at the centre of this chapter may be open to the objection that the Juba process and the Kenya Dialogue were too different to lend themselves to meaningful comparison, given the nature of their underlying conflicts. As discussed, the conflicts they sought to settle were very different: insurgency and election-related crisis. Two other differences, however, made the comparison meaningful: their peace process outcomes (a return to war and a political settlement) and the level of ICC involvement during the respective peace processes. The next chapter analyses a third peace process that resembles the Juba Peace Talks in terms of conflict nature, while having the same outcome and involvement level as the Kenya Dialogue: the Havana Peace Process between the Colombian government and FARC. The analysis of the Havana Process provides a test of the book's theory. If the theory is correct and relevant beyond East Africa, the patterns of effects identified in the Uganda and Kenya cases will also apply to the Havana Process.

Notes

1 Quoted in Sharma (2012).
2 Telephone interview with member of the mediation team, Geneva, October 2010.
3 The Security Council referred the situation in Darfur to the ICC in Resolution 1593 (2005), thereby enabling active ICC involvement in Sudan although Sudan has not ratified the Rome Statute. Article 13(b) of the Statute permits the Court to exercise jurisdiction when a situation is referred to the Prosecutor by the Security Council acting under Chapter VII of the UN Charter.
4 Interviews in March and April 2011 and February 2013.

References

Abbott, Kenneth W, Robert O Keohane, Andrew Moravcsik, Anne-Marie Slaughter, and Duncan Snidal. 2000. 'The Concept of Legalization.' *International Organization* 54 (3): 401–419.

Atkinson, Ronald R. 2010. '"The Realists in Juba"? An Analysis of the Juba Peace Talks.' In *The Lord's Resistance Army: Myth and Reality*, edited by Tim Allen and Koen Vlassenroot, 205–222. London and New York: Zed Books Ltd.

Bradley, Curtis A, and Judith G Kelley. 2008. 'The Concept of International Delegation.' *Law and Contemporary Problems* 71 (1): 1–36.

Branch, Adam. 2010. 'No Peace without Justice?' Keynote address delivered at 'The Politics of Peace and Justice' panel in the NGO wings of the Rome Statute Review Conference, Kampala, Uganda, 3 June. www-rohan.sdsu.edu/~abranch/Publications/Branch-No Peace without Justice.pdf.

Cassel, Douglass. 2015. *Letter to Juan Manual Santos Calderon*. University of Notre Dame Law School. http://humanrights.nd.edu/assets/177163/spec_jurisd_peace_legal_ltr_9.25.15.pdf.

Elklit, Jørgen. 2011. 'The Role of International Organisations during Electoral Crises: The Case of Kenya 2007–08.' *Representation* 47 (4): 399–415.

Freeden, Michael. 1996. *Ideologies and Political Theory: A Conceptual Approach*. Oxford: Clarendon.

International Criminal Court. 2007. *[Transcript, Status Conference, 11 December 2007]* ICC-02/04–01/15-T-3-ENG ET WT 11–12–2007 1/57 SZ PT. The Hague: International Criminal Court.

International Criminal Court. 2009. *Judgement on the Appeal of Mr Katanga against the Oral Decision of Trial Chamber II of 12 June 2009 on the Admissibility of the Case.* The Hague: International Criminal Court.

Johnson, Hilde F. 2011. *Waging Peace in Sudan: The Inside Story of the Negotiations That Ended Africa's Longest Civil War.* Eastbourne: Sussex Academic Press.

Jurdi, Nidal Nabil. 2010. 'Some Lessons on Complementarity for the International Criminal Review Conference.' *South African Year Book of International Law*, Vol. 34: 28–56.

Kanyinga, Karuti, and James D Long. 2012. 'The Political Economy of Reforms in Kenya: The Post-2007 Election Violence and a New Constitution.' *African Studies Review* 55 (1): 31.

Kelman, Herbert C. 2005. 'Building Trust among Enemies: The Central Challenge for International Conflict Resolution.' *International Journal of Intercultural Relations* 29 (6): 639–650.

Lindenmayer, Elisabeth, and Josie Lianna Kaye. 2009. *A Choice for Peace? The Story of Forty-One Days of Mediation in Kenya.* New York: International Peace Institute.

Lynch, Gabrielle. 2014. 'Electing the "Alliance of the Accused": The Success of the Jubilee Alliance in Kenya's Rift Valley.' *Journal of Eastern African Studies* 8 (1): 93–114.

Moreno-Ocampo, Luis. 2010, July 15. 'Now End This Darfur Denial.' *Guardian*. www.theguardian.com/commentisfree/libertycentral/2010/jul/15/world-cannot-ignore-darfur#start-of-comments.

Office of the Prosecutor. 2004. *President of Uganda Refers Situation Concerning the Lord's Resistance Army (LRA) to the ICC.* Press Release. The Hague: International Criminal Court.

Office of the Prosecutor. 2009a. *The Role of International Judicial Bodies in Administering the Rule of Law. Remarks [by] Luis Moreno-Ocampo, Prosecutor of the International Criminal Court. Qatar Law Forum, Doha, Qatar.* The Hague: International Criminal Court.

Office of the Prosecutor. 2009b. *Statement to the United Nations Security Council on the Situation in Darfur, the Sudan, Pursuant to UNSCR 1593 (2005) [by] Mr Luis Moreno-Ocampo, Prosecutor of the International Criminal Court, New York, 4 December 2009.* The Hague: International Criminal Court.

Office of the Prosecutor. 2010. *ICC Prosecutor to Visit Kenya to Meet Victims and Listen to All Kenyans.* Press Release. The Hague: International Criminal Court.

Office of the Prosecutor. 2016. *Statement of ICC Prosecutor, Fatou Bensouda, on the Conclusion of the Peace Negotiations between the Government of Colombia and the Revolutionary Armed Forces of Colombia – People's Army.* The Hague: International Criminal Court.

Olásolo, Héctor. 2015. 'The Special Jurisdiction for Peace in Colombia and the Cautious Optimism of the Prosecutor of the International Criminal Court.' *Peace Process Online Review* 1 (1): 1–5. www.peaceprocesses.it/images/pdf/h._olasolo_-_the_special_jurisdiction_for_peace_in_colombia.pdf.

Republic of Kenya. 2008. *Report of the Commission of Inquiry into the Post-Election Violence.* Nairobi: Government of Kenya.

Republic of Uganda. 2013. *Report of the Committee on Defence and Internal Affairs on the Petition on the Lapsing of Part II of the Amnesty Act, 2000.* Kampala: Parliament of the Republic of Uganda.

Reuters. 2010, March 23. 'ICC Prosecutor: Sudan Poll like Vote under Hitler.' *Reuters.com.*

Rodman, K A. 2009. 'Is Peace in the Interests of Justice? The Case for Broad Prosecutorial Discretion at the International Criminal Court.' *Leiden Journal of International Law* 22 (1): 99. doi:10.1017/S0922156508005657.

Scherr, Kathrin Maria. 2016. 'Of Justice, Accountability, and Reconciliation: Preliminary Stocktaking on Transitional Justice Efforts in South Sudan.' In *Handbook of Research on Transitional Justice and Peace Building in Turbulent Regions*, edited by Fredy Cante and Hartmut Quehl, 181–200. Hershey, PA: Information Science Reference.

Sharma, Serena K. 2012. 'The 2007–2008 Post-Election Crisis in Kenya: A Success Story for the Responsibility to Protect?' In *Responsibility to Protect: From Principle to Practice*, edited by Julia Hoffmann and André Nollkaemper, 27–35. Amsterdam: Pallas Publications.

United Nations. 2012. *UN Position on Uganda's Amnesty Act, 2000: Submission to the Hon. Minister for Internal Affairs*. Geneva: UN Office of the High Commissioner for Human Rights.

Vision Reporter. 2005, October 22. 'Ban Amnesty Law.' *The New Vision.*

Wolf, Thomas P. 2013. 'International Justice vs Public Opinion: The ICC and Ethnic Polarisation in the 2013 Kenyan Election.' *Journal of African Elections* 12 (1): 143.

8 Conclusion

Understanding the judicialisation of peace

We cannot expect to attain our goals of peace, development and respect for human rights without promoting and supporting a robust system of international criminal justice.... Supporting the tribunals and courts means respecting – and not calling into question – their independence, impartiality and integrity.

UN Secretary-General Ban Ki-Moon, General Assembly thematic debate, 'The Role of International Criminal Justice in Reconciliation', 10 April 2013

This book began by asking how and why ICC involvement in situations of ongoing conflict affects the conditions of possibility for a political settlement. To investigate this question, it built an analytical framework from literature about the relationship between politics and law and a disaggregated, step-wise conceptualisation of ICC involvement and peace processes. The semi-inductive analysis of the Juba Peace Talks and the Kenya National Dialogue and Reconciliation revealed how and why these two East African peace processes were affected by the ICC's justice interventions. The subsequent comparison of these effects brought out the importance of involvement levels and timing as well as the differentiated impact that involvement stages have.

This chapter first tests these findings on a third case, the Havana Peace Process between the Colombian government and Fuerzas Armadas Revolucionarias de Colombia (the Revolutionary Armed Forces of Colombia, FARC).[1] This analysis demonstrates the robustness and relative generalisability of the book's argument. The chapter thereafter summarises and discusses the book's main argument in the light of scholarship on legalisation. The last section provides a discussion of the main policy implication stemming from the research: the idea of sequencing peace processes and international justice interventions. Building on the differences among stages and phases, this discussion engages critically with contemporary scholarly treatment of the policy of sequencing and offers a concrete idea of what sequencing could entail.

The Havana Peace Process

The comparison of the effects of ICC involvement on the Juba Peace Talks and the Kenya Dialogue identified four ways in which judicialisation by the ICC affected the politics of peacemaking: depending on the levels of intervention, it shaped the central sticking points, delegated politico-legal and discursive authority from the local to the international level, and decontested the meaning of justice. To boost the robustness of these findings, this part of the chapter conducts a deductive analysis of the Havana Peace Process between the Colombian government and FARC to end the country's decades-long civil war.

The Havana Process is comparable to both the Juba Peace Talks and the Kenya Dialogue. All three peace processes took place in the context of active ICC involvement. Colombia's conflict has changed over the years, but is currently derived from a left-wing insurgency by FARC and a government-sponsored paramilitary counter-insurgency (Delgado 2015; Leech 2011). Although FARC and the LRA differ in important respects, such as ideological commitment, territorial control, civilian relations and political economy, their insurgencies had become entrenched. The Havana and Juba processes involved ICC member states that engaged in negotiations with their main insurgent armies.

The Colombian and Kenyan cases share two theoretically important characteristics: the level and timing of ICC involvement vis-à-vis the Negotiation phase. The Negotiation phase of the Colombian peace process took place in the context of a low level of intervention by the ICC. Court involvement was at the Preliminary Examination stage when the Kenyan and Colombian conflict parties negotiated their political solutions. Interestingly, both peace processes succeeded in ending the conflicts.

The timing and levels of ICC involvement in the Havana Process

ICC involvement in Colombia began at the Membership stage on 5 August 2002, when Colombia ratified the Rome Statute. The OTP launched a preliminary examination in June 2004, which became public over the course of 2006 (OTP 2011, 14). So far, the Preliminary Examination stage has lasted 15 years, and has consisted of information gathering, monitoring of relevant legislative developments and guiding the government to avoid policies or practices that would trigger ICC admissibility. Due to its relatively long duration, Stage 2 involvement has been led by two Prosecutors, Moreno-Ocampo and his successor, Fatou Bensouda. This change in officers, however, did not affect the OTP's approach, as Bensouda has maintained her predecessor's interpretation of relevant aspects of the Rome Statute, such as the interests of justice and the location of discretionary authority (OTP 2015a, 16).

The Preliminary Examination stage represents an active form and a low level of ICC involvement. The OTP has so far judged that it does not have grounds to move to the Investigation stage, as the principle of complementarity prevents further Court involvement where governments are investigating or prosecuting ICC crimes. To that end, the OTP (2011; 2016a) has found the Colombian authorities to have conducted a large number of relevant proceedings, including judicial action against illegal armed group leaders, paramilitary leaders, state officials, and politicians with links to armed groups; investigation of '*falsos positivos*'; and the prosecution *in absentia* of senior insurgent leaders.[2]

In this context of Court involvement, the Havana Peace Process began in September 2010, representing the conflict parties' fourth attempt to negotiate a political solution. The Pre-Negotiation phase was secret and confidential and had three sub-phases, the first being informal talks between government and FARC representatives (Gomez-Suarez and Newman 2013, 819; Segura and Mechoulan 2017, 10). In March 2011, these were replaced by a series of exploratory meetings, which resulted in the selection of chief negotiators for both conflict parties.[3] Finally, between February and August 2012, the delegations met in negotiations in Havana, which aimed to strengthen the process before it became subject to public scrutiny (HD 2016, 14; Segura and Mechoulan 2017, 13).

The war continued amidst this dialogue, with the death of more than 50 members of FARC, including its commander-in-chief. Nevertheless, nine months later the conflict parties agreed to enter into formal negotiations and signed the pre-negotiation agreement, the General Agreement for the Termination of the Conflict and the Construction of a Stable and Lasting Peace. This agreement located future talks in Havana, Cuba, and designated Cuba and Norway as guarantor observer countries and Venezuela and Chile as 'accompaniers' (Government of Colombia and FARC-EP 2012, sec. iv).

The Negotiation phase was launched in Oslo, Norway, on 18 October 2012. It was structured around six agenda items: integrated agricultural development policy; political participation; end of the conflict (including justice issues); solution to the problem of illicit drugs; victims; and implementation, verification and ratification. According to the pre-negotiation agreement, 'Nothing is agreed on until everything is agreed on' (Government of Colombia and FARC-EP 2012, sec. 3). This meant that agreements on individual agenda items were subject to a comprehensive Final Agreement.[4] Figure 8.1 below illustrates the temporal overlap of the justice intervention and the peace process.

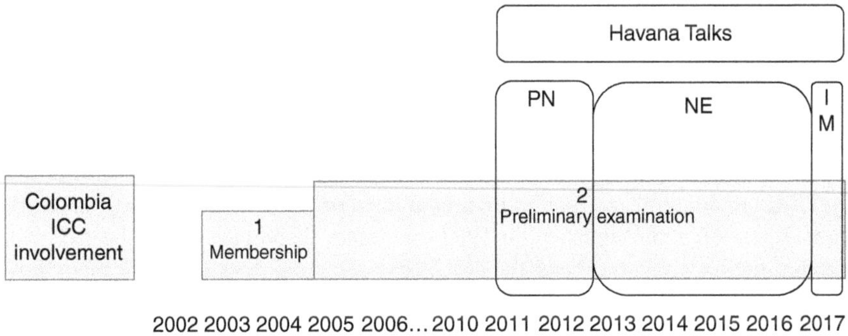

Figure 8.1 The processes of ICC involvement and peacemaking in Colombia.

Note
Peace process phases are abbreviated as Pre-Negotiation (PN), Negotiation (NE) and Implementation (IM) phases.

If the present theory about ICC involvement is correct, the negotiations of the Havana Process will share similarities with those of the Kenya Dialogue because the Negotiation phase of both processes took place in the context of a low level of ICC involvement. Moreover, they will differ from the negotiations of the Juba Peace Talks because the latter was affected by a high level of ICC involvement. As ICC involvement in Colombia remains at the Preliminary Examination stage, the implementation of the Havana outputs is expected to resemble neither the Uganda case nor the second half of Kenya's Implementation phase. To investigate these expectations, the analysis will focus on efforts to overcome the sticking points, the delegation of political and discursive authority, and the decontestation of justice.[5]

The shaping of sticking points

The sticking point in the Negotiation phase of the Havana Process was the disarmament of FARC. This prospect generated deep insecurity in the rebel group and stalled the negotiations for six months although there had been progress on issues at the heart of FARC's insurgency, such as land reform and political participation (Levin 2016). The 'laying down of weapons' – FARC rejected the term 'disarmament' as it implied military defeat – was one of the hardest issues to negotiate in the Pre-Negotiation and Negotiation phases (Segura and Mechoulan 2017, 13; see also International Crisis Group 2016, sec. 5). The government insisted that disarmament should precede the rebels' political rehabilitation, while FARC asserted that weapons surrendering was 'out of the question' although it would refrain from using them in politics (Florey 2015). Disarmament involved the protection of FARC members participating in politics, a sensitive issue because of earlier experiences of violent persecution following political rehabilitation in the mid-1980s.

In 1984, FARC signed the Uribe Accord with the government, led by President Belisario Betancur. This peace agreement created Unión Patrótica (UP), a political party that would enable FARC to transit from an insurgent movement to a democratic political actor. Launched in 1985, the UP became a party for social and leftist activists as well as former FARC members. The government committed to offer protection and reform the political structures to enable UP to participate, but the party quickly became a target for paramilitary and right-wing violence. These forces assassinated 200 demobilised FARC members during the initial campaigns for UP, and cultivated a deep mistrust of government security guarantees. As a consequence, in 1987 the rebels abandoned the Uribe Accords and left the UP to rearm. Over the next six years, more than 2,000 UP members, including two presidential candidates and four elected members of Congress, would be killed by right-wing and paramilitary violence (Gomez-Suarez and Newman 2013, 825). By 1990, Leech (2011, 31) argues, it was clear that a 'political genocide' was taking place.

These prior experiences of demobilisation and political participation were reflected in the annotated agenda, which tabled discussions of rights and guarantees for exercising political opposition, democratic mechanisms for citizen participation, and security guarantees for demobilised FARC members. Furthermore, the pre-negotiation agreement envisaged the end of conflict as a 'comprehensive and simultaneous process', which included the political, economic and social reintegration of FARC as well as government commitments to 'finish off' paramilitary organisations and offer security guarantees (Government of Colombia and FARC-EP 2012, sec. 2 and 3).

To overcome the sticking point, the parties agreed to internationalise monitoring and verification of the disarmament process and the security guarantee. They transcended their sticking point by 'externalising control' and using international involvement to raise the political costs of non-compliance (Wallensteen 2012, 56). Externalisation involved establishing a Tripartite Mechanism composed of the conflict parties and the UN to monitor and verify the cessation of hostilities, the ceasefire and the arms handover. Only the UN would guarantee and verify FARC's disarmament, while all three actors would investigate possible violations (UN Security Council 2016a). UN involvement consisted of a special political mission authorised by the Security Council following a request by the Colombian government and FARC (UN Security Council 2016b).

Dealing with Item 3 of the agenda, the end of the conflict, the conflict parties established a technical sub-commission, which received technical expertise from the UN Departments of Political Affairs and Peacekeeping Operations (Segura and Mechoulan 2017, 22). This technical involvement enabled the parties to produce the specific request for a political mission, at the same time limiting the Security Council's scope for redefining or expanding the UN's role in the Implementation phase. Both the government and FARC had strong feelings about UN involvement stemming from sovereignty concerns, the need to handle the security vacuum without being seen to rely on international force (a nod to military hardliners) and reticence about including a human rights mandate. As a result, mission personnel were to be unarmed.

The issue of disarmament was not resolved 'until everything [was] agreed', but the request for UN assistance represented the transcendence of the sticking point. In the revised Final Agreement signed after the plebiscite, the parties agreed to request the UN General Assembly to establish a second political mission to verify the reintegration of ex-combatants and ensure their protection for three years (Government of Colombia and FARC-EP 2016a).

The Final Agreement was subject to popular approval through a plebiscite six days after it was signed by Santos and FARC leader, Timoleon Jimenez. This democratic provision created a space for hardliners to oppose the settlement. As a result of a vigorous 'No' campaign led by the political opposition, land owners and the Catholic church, the peace agreement was narrowly rejected by 50.21 per cent of the voters. Almost as many voters, 49.78 per cent, approved the peace agreement, while the turnout was a low 37 per cent of those registered to vote. Interestingly, however, Colombians in the war-affected rural zones overwhelmingly approved the deal, while those who opposed it mainly resided in the central and urban areas (Gill 2017, 159; Segura and Mechoulan 2017, 31).

Following the plebiscite, rejectionist parties and organisations presented more than 260 revisions to the peace agreement, which were then re-negotiated between the conflict parties. The result was a new Final Agreement, signed on 12 November 2016. The changes to the original agreement concerned all the substantive agenda items, although changes to the modalities of disarmament were minor. The conflict parties argued that they made changes to 56 of 57 topics, the main exception being FARC's political participation. On 29 November 2016, the new Final Agreement was unanimously approved by Congress.

During the Implementation phase, FARC members demobilised in 26 transitional zones. On 27 June 2017, the UN Mission in Colombia (2017, 1) verified that FARC had handed over its individual weapons, although a number of stored weapons would remain at the group's disposal to secure the transition camps. Accompanying these disarmament activities, President Santos established, by decree, a national commission on security guarantees to design and monitor policy related to the dismantling of criminal organisations, including former paramilitaries threatening FARC's political participation (UN Security Council 2017, sec. 4).

Accountability and justice were difficult issues in the Negotiation phase, but did not constitute its main sticking point. As examined below, the parties developed a common position on justice within the semi-narrow confines of Rome Statute compliance and the threat of high-level ICC involvement. Stage 2 involvement sought to decontest and shape justice, but did not shape the sticking point. To juxtapose the findings from the Juba Peace Talks, Kenya Dialogue and Havana Process, Table 8.1 summarises these processes' sticking points and resolution efforts. To show the relationship between involvement levels and their effects on the peace processes, the tables in this chapter are organised according to ICC stages rather than chronologically.

Delegation of politico-legal authority

In the Havana Process, politico-legal authority was not delegated to international actors, but remained at the level of the peace negotiations, even to the extent of excluding the possibility of having an international mediator. Like in Kenya, authority residing within the conflict parties was central to their ability to transcend the sticking point. During the Negotiation phase, the conflict principals used this authority to commit to the peace agreements and to marginalise hardliners. To the latter end, for instance, Santos re-allocated power within his administration by swapping the portfolios of moderates and hardliners (International Crisis Group 2015, sec. 10). FARC's top leaders delegated authority to the leaders of all major combat units by establishing a rotating peace delegation with 30 members (Gomez-Suarez and Newman 2013, 827; International Crisis Group 2015, 9). The rotation of members enabled combat leaders to learn about the peace process and influence its outcomes, building moderation within the rebel group.

Different actors legitimised this politico-legal authority during the negotiations. For instance, the president of the Congress committed to refraining from

Table 8.1 Sticking points and resolution efforts in Colombia, Kenya and Uganda

	Colombia	*Kenya*		*Uganda*
Peace process	*Negotiation phase*	*Negotiation phase*	*Implementation phase*	*Negotiation phase*
ICC involvement	*Stage 2*	*Stage 2*	*Stage 4*	*Stage 4*
Sticking point	Disarmament and security for FARC	The right to govern the country	The imperative of ICC prosecution of political actors	The imperative of ICC prosecution of LRA leaders
Efforts to overcome the sticking point	Political negotiations aided by technical advice by UN	Legalisation of the negotiations, politicisation of the Constitution	Legal and political mobilisation by the government (AU request, admissibility challenge)	Politicisation of the Rome Statute by Juba participants
Proposed solution	International verification mechanism	Power-sharing	Domestic justice process	Alternative accountability and reconciliation
Location of authority to enable solution	Conflict parties and principals	Conflict principals	PTC and Security Council	OTP and Security Council

legislating on issues that were subject to discussion during the Negotiation phase.[6] Like in Kenya, but unlike in Uganda, the US government adopted a policy of boosting the moderates, as President Obama and Vice President Joe Biden made regular statements of support for the talks (Isacson 2014, 2).

Because the ICC's justice intervention was at a low level, it did not internationalise the politico-legal authority needed to overcome the sticking point. This authority lay with the conflict principals. As the distribution of authority within each conflict party differed, the principals shared authority with their leadership groups to different extents. FARC has a more collective decision-making structure and Jimenez's authority to overcome the sticking point therefore depended on legitimation by the FARC leadership. On the other hand, Colombia's president and High Commissioner for Peace, respectively, were more constrained by political and military hardliners than were FARC negotiators.

Delegation of discursive authority

Active ICC involvement, which begins with Stage 2, delegated some discursive authority to the OTP. The Court's discourse on Colombia was very similar to that on Kenya, emphasising support and assistance. Like in Kenya, the OTP (2015a, 5) also emphasised that the ICC was 'an integral part of the judicial system of Colombia. Colombia made it so, by becoming a State Party to the Rome Statute.' To assert discursive authority, the Prosecutor issued a statement of support after the signing of the first Final Agreement, expressing 'hope that this peace agreement will provide a basis for building lasting peace in Colombia' and pledging her continued support (OTP 2016b).

The Prosecutor's support even included prompt although cautious approval of Colombia's negotiated justice policy. A day after the parties announced their agreement on this difficult issue, the Prosecutor stated that she 'of course welcomed' any genuine and practical conflict resolution initiative that paid homage to justice and noted 'with optimism' that the agreement excludes amnesty for ICC crimes and is designed to end impunity for atrocity (OTP 2015b; see also Olásolo 2015). This discourse of assistance stood in marked contrast with her predecessor's antagonistic reaction, seven years earlier, to the justice policy negotiated in Juba: although it sought to end conflict, paid homage to justice and excluded amnesty for ICC crimes, the Agreement on Accountability and Reconciliation received a hostile reaction by Moreno-Ocampo. As analysed in the Juba case study, the Prosecutor's hostility derived primarily from the fact that the peace agreement involved individuals wanted by the Court and around whom he had created narratives of culpability and ill intention.

A comparison of the nature of OTP discourses in Uganda, Kenya and Colombia illuminates how the OTP's discursive agency relates to the level of ICC involvement. In the absence of narratives of culpability essential for the building of a criminal case, the Court was at liberty to be supportive. It did not have to vilify alleged perpetrators or mobilise domestic or international opinion in favour of marginalisation or arrest. Had the OTP indicted the FARC leadership, it would have been difficult for the Prosecutor to maintain support for the peace process, unless it committed the conflict parties to their surrender or arrest.

Like the Juba Peace Talks, the Havana Process had to deal with the narrative that FARC was negotiating peace to regroup and rearm: FARC 'was only seeking to take advantage of the peace talks in order to regroup and escalate the armed struggle' (Gomez-Suarez and Newman 2013, 820). This narrative reflected Colombian military thinking before and during the Havana Process, as it had reflected Ugandan military discourses before and during the LRA negotiations (Delgado 2015, 831). Linked to this narrative were claims familiar to Ugandans, namely that FARC was a criminal gang without a political agenda (Gomez-Suarez and Newman 2013, 828). Importantly, however, and although it has examined alleged crimes in Colombia, the Court did not advance narratives about FARC's ulterior motives or its criminal, apolitical character. Instead, it maintained support for a peace deal with FARC, implicitly recognising the rebel group as a political actor.

The plebiscite took place in the overlap between the Negotiation and Implementation phases, and was the site for a local peace/justice debate. Many Colombians argued that the peace agreement amounted to a granting of impunity, while others defended the negotiated solution. Others opposed the Final Agreement for other reasons, such as its provisions for land reform or political rehabilitation (Eslava 2016; International Crisis Group 2017). The head of Human Rights Watch's Americas division, José Miguel Vivanco, recommended a popular rejection of the peace deal, arguing that its justice provisions gave FARC 'impunity' (Grandin 2016). In this polarised debate, a statement by the Court's Prosecutor would have received a lot of attention. Yet Bensouda refrained from commenting further on the peace process. Given the discursive environment in Colombia at the time, non-action by the OTP translated into tacit support for the Final Agreement. Table 8.2 juxtaposes the nature of OTP discourses in relation to the Court's involvement in Colombia, Kenya and Uganda.

Decontestation of justice

The ICC delimited the conflict parties' zone of possible agreement on a justice policy, but, due to the Court's low level of involvement, there was room for negotiating a policy that could meet Colombia's obligations to the Rome Statute and FARC's need to continue to exist as a political actor. The process of delimitation took the form of communicating a set of 'red lines' to the government as it negotiated with FARC: amnesty for ICC crimes was out of the question and suspended sentences were unacceptable and 'would amount to shielding persons' from criminal responsibility (OTP 2015a, 11). The result was a justice concept that was semi-narrow: it had to have an element of criminal accountability for ICC crimes, yet the crime of rebellion could be amnestied. Moreover, while reduced or alternative sentences were in theory possible, the assessment of such sentences 'would depend upon the particular circumstances of a given case' (OTP 2015a, 11).

Table 8.2 OTP discourses in Colombia, Kenya and Uganda

	Colombia		*Kenya*		*Uganda*	
Peace process	*Negotiation phase*	*Implementation phase*	*Negotiation phase*	*Implementation phase*	*Pre-Negotiation phase*	*Negotiation phase*
ICC involvement	*Stage 2*	*Stage 2*	*Stage 2*	*Stage 4*	*Stage 4*	*Stage 4*
Indictment nature	–	–	–	Summons to appear	Arrest warrants	Arrest warrants
OTP discourse	Supportive of peace process	Supportive of peace process	Supportive of peace process	Supportive of peace process	Supportive of peace process (before security guarantee), anti-peace process (after security guarantee)	Anti-peace process

The power to delimit justice derived from the OTP's preliminary examination, while the process of delimitation preceded the Havana Process's Pre-Negotiation phase. Having established in 2005 that Colombia had been the site of crimes against humanity and war crimes by state and non-state actors (Easterday 2015, 439), the complementarity principle became the only thing that could keep a medium or high-level justice intervention at bay. As a result, since 2005 Colombia has created, codified and implemented a range of justice policies targeting paramilitary leaders, investigating their links with the government, investigating 'false positives', providing reparations to victims and prosecuting rebel leaders *in absentia*.

These processes were tailored to the country's transitional context by means of special legislation, such as the Justice and Peace Law (2005), the Victim's Law and Property Restitution (2011) and the Legal Framework for Peace (2012). Since 2005, dialogue between the government and the OTP ensured that these policies and laws complied with Colombia's obligations to the ICC. Stage 2 involvement interactively decontested justice to the extent that it came to mean ordinary criminal accountability. Indeed, Easterday (2015, 445) concludes that the ICC had 'significant input' into and 'helped to shape' Colombia's justice project.

During the Negotiation stage, the Prosecutor identified the area of sentencing as a site of some flexibility, arguing that states have 'wide discretion' in sentencing and that effective penal sanctions could 'take many different forms' although not suspension (OTP 2015a, 10). At the same time, she made clear that a peace agreement would not cut the government any favours, stating, 'How a peace agreement affects national proceedings will have an impact on the Office's assessment of the admissibility before the ICC of [Colombian] cases' (OTP 2015a, 8).

Like in the Juba Peace Talks, Havana negotiators had to forge an overlap between the ICC's definition of justice and FARC's need to politically survive the transition. This made the issue of justice one of the most difficult challenges during the negotiations. Indeed, FARC consistently maintained that it would not accept a deal that included imprisonment; as FARC negotiator Ivan Marquez reminded the government and, perhaps, the ICC, 'No peace process in the world has ended with leaders of the insurgency behind bars' (Florey 2015). Commenting on this challenge, Santos (2015, 14) explained, 'We are entering unexplored terrain: there are no examples of successful peace negotiations in the era of the Rome Statute.' As ICC involvement incidentally was at a low level, it did not threaten particular FARC leaders' future prospects, thereby allowing them to envisage their rehabilitation. To help the negotiations, Norway convened an informal international advisory group on transitional justice, the seven-member 'New York group' (Segura and Mechoulan 2017). Subsequently, negotiators established a legal sub-group on transitional justice, which explored the possibilities for a negotiated justice policy that sat conceptually within Colombia's semi-narrow justice space.

Havana's negotiated justice policy was the Agreement Regarding the Victims of the Conflict: Comprehensive System for Truth, Justice, Reparations and

Non-Recurrence (Government of Colombia and FARC-EP 2016b, chap. 5). Based on a joint declaration of principles for the victims' approach (signed 7 June 2014), this Agreement established five different justice programmes: the Special Jurisdiction for Peace (SJP) (signed 23 September 2015); the Truth, Coexistence and Non-Recurrence Commission; the Special Unit for the Search for Persons Deemed as Missing in the context of the conflict; a specific reparations system; and Guarantees of Non-Recurrence. Through these, the Comprehensive System combines judicial and extra-judicial mechanisms, with the SJP representing the judicial approach. Thus, it was incumbent on this SJP to provide measures of justice that met the Prosecutor's expectations for a 'genuine' domestic regime and thereby kept ICC involvement at a low level.

The SJP provides amnesty to political crimes such as rebellion and sedition, but excludes amnesty for ICC crimes. The latter are instead subject to a special procedure consisting of confessions and guarantees of non-recurrence followed by five to eight years of 'effective restrictions on freedoms and rights for their implementation, such as freedom of residency and movement' (Government of Colombia and FARC-EP 2016b, sec. 5(1)(2)(I)(60)). Those who refuse to acknowledge their responsibility will face ordinary sanctions of 15–20 years of imprisonment.

To bolster the SJP's implicit complementarity claim, Douglass Cassel (2015, 6) of the technical sub-group argued that the Special Jurisdiction 'me[t] applicable international standards to respect victims' rights to truth, reparations, justice and non-repetition with regard to serious international crimes allegedly committed by the FARC'. The Prosecutor initially appeared to agree, 'not[ing] with optimism' that the Special Jurisdiction appeared to exclude amnesty for ICC crimes and aimed to end impunity (OTP 2015b). The following year she adopted a more cautious position, promising continued engagement (OTP 2016a, sec. 59).

Table 8.3 below displays the concepts of justice in the Havana Process, Juba Peace Talks and Kenya Dialogue. Had there been a perfect correlation between involvement stages and the scope of justice, ICC involvement in Kenya and Colombia would have allowed equally broad scopes for justice. However, due to the OTP's extensive involvement and ongoing dialogue with the government in Colombia, it had developed a more fine-grained definition of justice in Colombia than in Kenya. The higher level of legal precision narrowed the scope in Colombian relative to Kenya.

The analysis of the Havana Process bolsters the findings from the Juba Peace Talks and the Kenya Dialogue. ICC involvement was found to have affected peacemaking in all three cases, but how it affected the conflict parties' ability to settle their conflicts varied according to the level of involvement. Conflict parties in Havana and Juba faced the same justice dilemma, but only the Colombians reached a political solution. Like their Kenyan counterparts, they relied on the exercise of politico-legal authority to settle the conflict. At the time, this authority was maintained at the national level. Due to the Court's involvement levels during the Negotiation phases, Colombian and Kenyan politico-legal authority

Table 8.3 Decontestation of justice

	Colombia	*Kenya*			*Uganda*
Peace process	*Negotiation phase*	*Negotiation phase*	*Implementation phase*		*Negotiation phase*
ICC involvement	*Stage 2*	*Stage 2*	*Stage 2*	*Stage 4*	*Stage 4*
Meaning of justice	ICC compliant criminal justice; social justice (land reform, etc.)	Unspecific criminal justice; social justice (land reform)	Criminal justice by hybrid STK; judicial reform	Criminal justice by ICC	Criminal justice by the ICC
Scope of justice concept	Semi-narrow	Broad	Semi-narrow	Narrow	Narrow
Dealing with justice	Establishment of Special Jurisdiction for Peace	Delegation to Commission of Inquiry into Post-Election Violence	Seeking to establish Special Tribunal, then opting for judicial reform	Mobilisation of AU and UNSC, admissibility challenge	Agreement on alternative accountability and reconciliation policy

had not been delegated to international actors. In the Juba negotiations, by contrast, politico-legal authority to solve the sticking point was unavailable to the conflict parties because the obstacle concerned justice. ICC indictments introduced a demand for a particular, narrow conception of international justice, which was unacceptable to the LRA leaders.

Besides sticking points and politico-legal authority, the Havana case shows similar patterns of discursive and semantic involvement. The nature of OTP discourse in relation to Colombia resembled its discursive involvement in Kenya. In both cases, the Prosecutor expressed support and offered capacity-building. The ICC altered and narrowed the meaning and scope for justice in all three cases, while justice was most decontested in the Juba Peace Talks where the ICC's involvement level was high. Across the cases, the ICC advanced the same interpretations of the Rome Statute, delimiting the zones of possible agreement on justice.

The argument

This book argues that ICC involvement in situations of ongoing conflict affects the peace processes that take place in its midst and that the nature of this impact depends on the level and timing of the intervention. A high level of ICC involvement shapes the nature of the sticking point, delegates politico-legal and discursive authority away from the conflict parties and decontests the meaning of justice. These effects are likely to adversely affect the ability of conflict parties and/or principals to commit to a political settlement during the Negotiation phase, but may not be detrimental to the politics of the Implementation phase.

By contrast, a low level of ICC involvement retains politico-legal authority at the level of the peace process, co-exists with a broad or semi-narrow notion of justice and has no effect on the nature of the sticking point. If the Negotiation phase occurs in the context of a low level of ICC involvement, therefore, conflict actors have authority to commit to solutions that resolve or transcend their sticking point. A low level of ICC involvement is also associated with the international delegation of discursive authority, but the Prosecutor is unlikely to advance hostile discourses given his or her institutional interests during the Membership or Preliminary Examination stages.

These effects pertain to the ICC's judicialisation. They derive from the Rome Statute and the Court, as well as from interpretations of the Rome Statute by international actors who derive agency in judicialised peace processes from their structural positions. Across all levels of involvement beginning from the Membership stage, the Rome Statute imposes a duty to prosecute ICC crimes, which delimits the justice provisions of a peace agreement. At the Indictment stage, criminal accountability is likely to become a sticking point because the Statute advances a very particular and ambitious notion of justice. Moreover, given the ICC's reliance on state cooperation for enforcement, the Rome Statute creates the conditions for advancing discourses of capture and marginalisation, which are likely to destabilise or undermine the peace process.

The adverse effects also derive from a set of narrow and legalistic interpretations of relevant provisions of the Rome Statute by Court actors, such as complementarity, admissibility and the interests of justice. Outside the Court, the Rome Statute has provided the Security Council with discretionary deferral powers pertaining to matters of international peace and security. These powers are, however, also subject to interpretation about when it is necessary, wise and/or legitimate to invoke them. Framed by the justice discourse, dominant Security Council actors have interpreted their referral and deferral powers in ways that have hindered rather than helped peace processes in intervention countries.

The theory goes beyond rationalist concepts of precision, obligation and delegation (Abbott *et al.* 2000; Kelley 2007) by conceptualising judicialisation critically: it is largely subject to legal and political interpretation; constitutes a structuring element that redefines meaning, relocates authority and imposes importance and irrelevance on actors and entities; and generates effects that are mostly informal and constitutive and, perhaps, unintentional. Had the present analysis used definitions of delegation that require the formal granting of authority (Abbott *et al.* 2015; Bradley and Kelley 2008), it would have missed important aspects of how ICC involvement affected the peace processes in Uganda and Kenya. At the same time, rationalist theories are an indispensable point of departure because they approach the elements of judicialisation conceptually and systematically.

The theory relies on constructivist notions of constitution and influence without assuming that legalisation and judicialisation entails persuasion, commitment or internalisation. Much constructivist scholarship on human rights and international justice articulates the justice discourse because it assumes a priori that legalisation makes the world a better place (e.g. Risse *et al.* 2013; Sikkink 2011). However, as a high level of ICC involvement contributed to the continuation of the LRA's insurgency, life has become less secure in areas affected by rebel violence in CAR, DRC and South Sudan.

Implications: Sequencing

International justice is based on the idea that it is possible to stop conflict and violence by judicial means. At the Rome Conference, the former Nuremberg prosecutor Benjamin Ferencz (1998) invoked this idea, speaking powerfully of 'the dream of a more humane world order under law': 'Without clear international laws, courts and effective enforcement there can be no deterrence, no justice and no world peace.' The Rome Statute reflects this idea by not disallowing the ICC to intervene during ongoing conflict.

As has been presently demonstrated, however, in certain conditions peace processes and justice interventions are at odds: a high level of judicial involvement is likely to have adverse effects on conflict parties' ability to make peace. Thus, it is only partially correct to assert that peace and justice are 'mutually reinforcing' (International Center for Transitional Justice 2011). Societal peace may enable and facilitate the pursuit of formal accountability, but criminal justice cannot be said to reinforce a peace that is not already there: judicial bodies institutionalise non-violent conflict resolution in peaceful societies, but in contexts of ongoing conflict, judicialisation may diminish the conditions of possibility for making peace. One solution to this problem is to sequence justice and peace interventions.

Sequencing means that implementers plan accountability and peace interventions to follow each other rather than to take place coterminously. The idea relies on the assumption that 'the order in which things happen affects outcomes by opening up some possibilities and closing off others' (Dukalskis 2011, 438). As a high level of ICC involvement in the Negotiation phase closes off the possibility of transcending the conflict's incompatibility, the order of involvement stages vis-à-vis peace process phases affects the outcome of conflict settlement. To safeguard the conditions of possibility for a political settlement, a sequence of interventions should place the Indictment stage after the Negotiation phase. This enables conflict parties to retain a sufficient amount of politico-legal authority and allows for political sticking points that are susceptible to negotiation.

It is not always politically desirable and legally sound to commence the justice process after the peace process has ended. This book shows that this is not necessary. Given the relative resilience of the Implementation phase and the effects of the Preliminary Examination stage, a temporal overlap between implementation and examination would not necessarily endanger the political solution: the Prosecutor could monitor dialogue and guide the conflict parties while the settlement is being implemented. This would likely result in the narrowing of the justice concept, but if ICC involvement stayed at this level for, say, five years (longer than Stage 2 involvement in Uganda and Kenya, but eight years shorter than in Colombia), the conflict parties would have time to demobilise and enter a process of finding an acceptable criminal accountability format.

The idea of sequencing justice and peace processes forefronts the temporal aspect of politics by acknowledging its contingent nature. As we saw, temporal expectations and evaluations shaped the politics of peacemaking in both Uganda and Kenya. More generally, turning points may become possible at one particular moment and impossible the next. Mediators and third-party actors are often aware of the role of time. In Sudan, the US Special Envoy, Scott Gration (quoted in Bosco 2013, 159), stressed the importance of introducing (and imposing) justice 'when the time is right':

> That's why we're continuing to talk with the government of Khartoum, the Government of Sudan. That's why we continue to negotiate with them to be able to save lives, to be able to bring peace, and then when the time is right, we'll ensure there's accountability and justice.

Gration's approach to peace and justice in Sudan implicitly articulates a sequencing approach. It also highlights the linear conception of time entailed by a sequencing policy – a linearity that may not be borne out by the politics of peacemaking.

Transitional justice scholars have been discussing the idea of sequencing for some time, yet it remains 'an important but understudied aspect of transitional justice that may have an impact on peace and democracy' (Skaar *et al.* 2015, 49). The idea of sequencing is mentioned, but rarely researched at length (Fletcher *et al.* 2009, 217; Murithi 2015, 95). In one of the first substantial discussions of sequencing, Dukalskis (2011) provides a theoretical investigation of sequenced truth and accountability processes, but does not focus on peacemaking. Kersten (2016, 31) dismisses the sequencing of peace and justice processes because it is 'difficult, if not impossible to imagine a dictator, tyrant or rebel leader accepting an amnesty that they knew would subsequently be revoked'. In an earlier discussion, Kersten (2011) elaborates on this scenario:

> [The] parties enter inclusive peace negotiations to achieve a power-sharing agreement and peaceful transition. The parties discontinue active conflict ... [and the] leaders are guaranteed amnesties as an incentive to cease violent activity. Once stability is assured and the time for accountability is ripe, those amnesties are revoked and the leaders of the conflict are brought to account, ushering in positive peace and justice.

The problem with Kersten's account is that it relies on the dichotomised and undifferentiated categories of peace and justice, which he criticises the peace/justice debate for applying. He equates peace with amnesty and justice with bringing leaders to account, presumably in a trial. However, for countries with active ICC involvement, amnesties are 'off the table'. The Kenyan and Colombian cases show that peace can be achieved if justice is at a low level. This level of judicialisation enabled Kenyan negotiators to defer the justice issue to a future process and allowed Colombian negotiators to develop a justice scheme that offers substantially reduced sentences for perpetrators of ICC crimes. In these two processes, peace was equated with ending violence and justice signified broad or semi-narrow criminal accountability.

Kersten's discussion premises sequencing on two logically incompatible institutions: amnesty and trial. If this is the only form that peace and justice can take, then sequencing is perhaps a 'fallacy' (Kersten 2011). However, it could also mean a sequencing of the Negotiation phase and the Preliminary Examination stage or a sequencing of the Implementation phase and the Investigation stage, to the extent that investigations may only be commenced a number of years after a political settlement has been concluded. This idea may not be very far off the early OTP interpretation of justice; indeed, in early 2005 the Prosecutor (quoted in *The New Vision* 2005) told Ugandan actors, 'Timing is possible but immunity is not possible.' As documented in Chapter 3, however, the Prosecutor changed his view on timing. Indeed, in the ICC's first decade, calls for sequencing were approached as a rejection of justice, a defence of impunity.

During the past few years, in part due to the contemporary African and AU critique of the ICC, the issue of sequencing has been somewhat rehabilitated. Hellmüller *et al.* (2015, 5) argue that 'different norms should not be seen as incompatible in general. Rather, it is a question of how to sequence them'. They imply that normative entrepreneurship should play a smaller role in the Negotiation phase, arguing that by focusing too much on the mediation phase 'we risk imposing overly high expectations on the mediator and forgetting that norms can also be sequenced'. More controversially, the Malabo Protocol, which provides the African Court on Human and Peoples' Rights with an international criminal jurisdiction, sequences power and justice. Once entered into force, the Protocol grants temporary immunity to 'any sitting AU heads of state or government or anybody acting or entitled to act in such capacity, or other senior state officials during their tenure of office' (Assembly of the African Union 2014). For this provision to enhance the conditions of possibility for a negative peace, however, it would need to be linked to peace negotiations rather than incumbency.

Conclusion: Beyond peace versus justice?

People in Uganda, Kenya and Colombia experienced and participated in localised peace/justice debates. In Uganda, the debate became relevant following the indictment of the LRA commanders and lasted throughout the peace process, while in Kenya it was sparked by the CIPEV report and its recommendations to establish the Special Tribunal or call in the ICC. In Colombia, the debate became prominent when the government and FARC asked people to approve their final peace agreement in a plebiscite. In all these debates, ordinary people, politicians, power-holders, academics, local and international NGOs and, sometimes, mediators and international organisations considered the merits and consequences of implementing justice in relation to peace.

These localised peace/justice debates demonstrate the global and unsettled nature of the empirical relationship between justice and peace. Yet the debate is at an impasse. Hanssen-Bauer (quoted in HD 2015, 27) spoke for many when remarking that 'transitional justice and the implications for mediation have been subject to debate for many years, but the debate is not really solved'. The debate has been difficult to solve because of its dichotomous approach to justice – as either present or absent, desirable or undesirable, helping or hindering. Furthermore, deliberative progress is stalled when the debate is declared 'settled' (OTP 2015a) or even 'a relic of the past' (Drumbl 2013, 537). By insisting that peace and justice always go hand in hand, actors like the EU and UN prevent policymaking that takes the challenge of judicialisation seriously.

This book not only re-opens the debate, it also offers a theory about how, when and why active ICC involvement affects conflict resolution. According to the theory, the level and timing of ICC involvement shape whether judicialisation helps or hinders the settlement of conflict. These findings invite actors to nuance the peace/justice debate by discussing how much international judicialisation to promote and when. Policy actors that want to give peace processes the best possible conditions for ending conflict should pay attention to the level of ICC involvement during the Negotiation phase. They should seek to keep politico-legal authority at the level of the peace process and only pressure the

ICC to issue indictments if the peace process has moved into the Implementation phase. They should adopt a critical approach to the role that Court officials play in advancing narratives about the conflict and its parties.

The book shows that politico-legal authority is essential to achieve a conflict settlement and that a high level of ICC involvement delegates this authority away from peace process actors. While in principle this authority could be returned to the local level, the depoliticising ways in which the Court and the Security Council interpret their Rome Statute mandates has made delegation largely irreversible. The Court has redefined the interests of justice to be irrelevant to conflict resolution, while the Security Council approaches its deferral powers as impossible to deploy in conflicts with ICC involvement. These interpretations take place although states created a limited space for political agency within the Rome Statute regime by means of permitting two conditional, discretionary actions: time-limited deferrals of prosecution based on a Security Council request as well as interests-of-justice-based decisions to refrain from investigating or conclude a prosecution.

The analysis demonstrates that justice was approached as fate by the world's states: although the Rome Statute, including the provisions of Articles 16 and 53(1)(c) and (2)(c), was a result of international negotiations, state parties permitted the OTP to institutionalise a narrow understanding of the interests of justice. While many of them have experience of past or present internal conflict, they accepted an interpretation promoted by NGOs with no such experience. UN members also accepted Western resistance to invoking the Security Council's rights to make deferral requests. To paraphrase de Waal (2009), states acted as if 'the mantra "no peace without justice"' is a substitute for political analysis.

The book also documents the OTP's different discursive approaches to peace processes, from seeking to delegitimise the Juba Peace Talks to supporting the Havana Process. The difference relates to the level of ICC involvement and the form that the indictment takes, rather than the provisions of the Rome Statute. The narratives served the Court's institutional interests and should be understood politically rather than legally.

If armed conflicts were on the wane, perhaps it would not be a problem that judicial involvement by the ICC in some conditions creates obstacles to their resolution. However, since 2010 the world has witnessed a rise in the number of wars and battle-related deaths and displacements. This trend poses a problem to the 'new world' of peace and justice, given the impact of high-level ICC involvement. It may thus be necessary to consider how new interpretations and policies can minimise the adverse effects of a high level of ICC involvement on peace negotiations. It may also be useful to discuss how the ICC can play a positive role when peace processes take place in its midst, beyond stubbornly asserting that justice is essential to achieve peace.

Notes

1 FARC's full name is Fuerzas Armadas Revolucionarias de Colombia – Ejército del Pueblo, officially shortened as FARC-EP. This book uses the shorter acronym, FARC.
2 'False positives' are cases of killed civilians staged to look like combat deaths.
3 'Timeline', FARC-EP website, http://farc-epeace.org/index.php/peace-process/timeline; 'Exploratory Meetings', FARC-EP website, http://farc-epeace.org/index.php/peace-process/news/item/262-exploratory-meetings.
4 The Final Agreement as well as English and French translations of the Agreement are available on the website of the Colombian government's High Commissioner for Peace: www.altocomisionadoparalapaz.gov.co.
5 Given the novelty of the political settlement, the analysis will primarily focus on the Pre-Negotiation and Negotiation phases of the Havana Process.
6 'Members of Congress Visit Peace Delegation', FARC-EP website, http://farc-epeace.org/index.php/peace-process/timeline.

References

Abbott, Kenneth W, Philipp Genschel, Duncan Snidal, and Bernhard Zangl. 2015. 'Two Logics of Indirect Governance: Delegation and Orchestration.' *British Journal of Political Science* 46: 719–729.

Abbott, Kenneth W, Robert O Keohane, Andrew Moravcsik, Anne-Marie Slaughter, and Duncan Snidal. 2000. 'The Concept of Legalization.' *International Organization* 54 (3): 401–419.

Assembly of the African Union. 2014. *Decision on the Draft Legal Instruments*. Doc. Assembly/AU/Dec.528(XXIII). African Union.

Bosco, David. 2013. *Rough Justice: The International Criminal Court in a World of Power Politics*. Oxford: Oxford University Press.

Bradley, Curtis A, and Judith G Kelley. 2008. 'The Concept of International Delegation.' *Law and Contemporary Problems* 71 (1): 1–36.

Cassel, Douglass. 2015. *Letter to Juan Manual Santos Calderon*. University of Notre Dame Law School. http://humanrights.nd.edu/assets/177163/spec_jurisd_peace_legal_ltr_9.25.15.pdf.

Centre for Humanitarian Dialogue. 2015. 'Preserving the Peacemaking Space: A Frank Conversation with Mark Bowden, Lakhdar Brahimi, Jimmy Carter, Alastair Crooke, Elisabeth Decrey Warner, Jon Hanssen-Bauer and David Harland.' In *The Oslo Forum. The Search for Peace: Perspectives on Mediation 2010–2015*, 18–27. Geneva: Centre for Humanitarian Dialogue.

Centre for Humanitarian Dialogue. 2016. *Oslo Forum 2016: Adapting to a New Conflict Landscape*. Geneva: Centre for Humanitarian Dialogue.

de Waal, Alex. 2009, September 5. 'The ICC, Sudan, and the Crisis of Human Rights.' *African Arguments*. http://africanarguments.org/2009/03/05/the-icc-sudan-and-the-crisis-of-human-rights/.

Delgado, Jorge E. 2015. 'Colombian Military Thinking and the Fight against the FARC-EP Insurgency, 2002–2014.' *Journal of Strategic Studies* 38 (6): 826–851. doi:10.1080/01402390.2015.1005610.

Drumbl, Mark. 2013. 'The Future of International Criminal Law and Transitional Justice.' In *The Ashgate Research Companion to International Criminal Law: Critical Perspectives*, edited by William A Schabas, Yvonne McDermott, and Niamh Hayes, 531–545. Farnham: Ashgate Publishing Limited.

Dukalskis, Alexander. 2011. 'Interactions in Transition: How Truth Commissions and Trials Complement or Constrain Each Other.' *International Studies Review* 13: 432–451.

Easterday, Jennifer. 2015. 'Beyond the "Shadow" of the ICC: Struggles over Control of the Conflict Narrative in Colombia.' In *Contested Justice: The Politics and Practice of International Criminal Court Interventions*, edited by Christian De Vos, Sara Kendall, and Carsten Stahn, 432–455. Cambridge: Cambridge University Press.

Eslava, Luis. 2016. 'Colombia: Counter/Revolution in Present Tense (6 October 2016).' *Critical Legal Thinking: Law and the Political*. http://criticallegalthinking.com/2016/10/06/colombia-counterrevolution-present-tense/.

Ferencz, Benjamin B 1998. *Address by Benjamin B. Ferencz, Pace Peace Center*. United Nations. www.un.org/icc/speeches/616ppc.htm.

Fletcher, Laurel E, Harvey M Weinstein, and Jamie Rowen. 2009. 'Context, Timing and the Dynamics of Transitional Justice.' *Human Rights Quarterly* 31: 163–220.

Florey, Rebecca. 2015, February 23. 'FARC Guerrillas Will Neither Go to Prison nor Surrender Weapons: Rebel Negotiator.' *Colombiareports.com*.

Gill, Lesley. 2017. 'Another Chance for Peace in Colombia?' *Journal of Latin American and Caribbean Anthropology* 22 (1): 157–160.

Gomez-Suarez, Andrei, and Jonathan Newman. 2013. 'Safeguarding Political Guarantees in the Colombian Peace Process: Have Santos and FARC Learnt the Lessons from the Past?' *Third World Quarterly* 34 (5): 819–837.

Government of Colombia, and FARC-EP. 2012, August 26. *General Agreement for the Termination of the Conflict and the Construction of a Stable and Lasting Peace [Translated by Crisis Group]*. Bogotá: Government of Colombia.

Government of Colombia, and FARC-EP. 2016a. *Acuerdo Final Para La Terminación Del Conflicto Y La Construcción de Una Paz Estable Y Duradera*. Bogotá: Government of Colombia.

Government of Colombia, and FARC-EP. 2016b. *Final Agreement to End the Armed Conflict and Build a Stable and Lasting Peace*. Bogotá: Government of Colombia.

Grandin, Greg. 2016, October 3. 'Did Human Rights Watch Sabotage Colombia's Peace Agreement?' *The Nation*.

Hellmüller, Sara, Julia Palmiano Federer, and Matthias Siegfried. 2015. *Norm-Pushers or Deal-Brokers? Normative Challenges of Modern-Day Mediators*. Bern: Swisspeace/NOREF.

International Center for Transitional Justice. 2011. *Peace versus Justice: A False Dilemma*. New York: International Centre for Transitional Justice. http://ictj.org/news/peace-versus-justice-false-dilemma.

International Crisis Group. 2015. *On Thinner Ice: The Final Phase of Colombia's Peace Talks. Latin America Briefing No. 32*. Bogotá/Brussels: International Crisis Group.

International Crisis Group. 2016. *Colombia's Final Steps to End the War (7 Sept 2016)*. Bogotá/Brussels: International Crisis Group.

International Crisis Group. 2017. *In the Shadow of 'No': Peace After Colombia's Plebiscite (31 January 2017)*. Bogotá/Brussels: International Crisis Group.

Isacson, Adam. 2014. *Ending 50 Years of Conflict: The Challenges Ahead and the US Role in Colombia*. Washington, DC: Washington Office on Latin America.

Kelley, Judith. 2007. 'Who Keeps International Commitments and Why? The International Criminal Court and Bilateral Nonsurrender Agreements.' *American Political Science Review* 101 (3): 573. doi:10.1017/S0003055407070426.

Kersten, Mark. 2011. 'The Fallacy of Sequencing Peace and Justice.' *Justice in Conflict*. https://justiceinconflict.org/2011/09/30/the-fallacy-of-sequencing-peace-and-justice/.

Kersten, Mark. 2016. *Justice in Conflict: The Effects of the International Criminal Court's Interventions on Ending Wars and Building Peace*. Oxford: Oxford University Press.
Leech, Garry. 2011. *The FARC: The Longest Insurgency*. London and New York: Zed Books Ltd.
Levin, Jamie. 2016, June 28. 'For Colombia's Peace Process, Disarmament Was a Sticking Point. Here's Why.' *Washington Post*.
Murithi, Tim. 2015. 'Ensuring Peace and Reconciliation While Holding Leaders Accountable: The Politics of ICC Cases in Kenya and Sudan.' *Africa Development* 40 (2): 73–97.
Office of the Prosecutor. 2011. *Report on Preliminary Examination Activities, 2011*. The Hague: International Criminal Court.
Office of the Prosecutor. 2015a. *Transitional Justice in Colombia and the Role of the International Criminal Court. Speech by James Stewart, Deputy Prosecutor of the International Criminal Court*. The Hague: International Criminal Court.
Office of the Prosecutor. 2015b. *Statement of the Prosecutor on the Agreement on the Creation of a Special Jurisdiction for Peace in Colombia*. Press Statement, September 24. The Hague: International Criminal Court.
Office of the Prosecutor. 2016a. *Report on Preliminary Examination Activities, 2016*. The Hague: International Criminal Court.
Office of the Prosecutor. 2016b. *Statement of ICC Prosecutor, Fatou Bensouda, on the Conclusion of the Peace Negotiations between the Government of Colombia and the Revolutionary Armed Forces of Colombia – People's Army*. The Hague: International Criminal Court.
Olásolo, Héctor. 2015. 'The Special Jurisdiction for Peace in Colombia and the Cautious Optimism of the Prosecutor of the International Criminal Court.' *Peace Process Online Review* 1 (1): 1–5. www.peaceprocesses.it/images/pdf/h._olasolo_-_the_special_jurisdiction_for_peace_in_colombia.pdf.
Risse, Thomas, Stephen C Ropp, and Kathryn Sikkink. 2013. *The Persistent Power of Human Rights: From Commitment to Compliance. Cambridge Studies in International Relations, 126*. Cambridge: Cambridge University Press.
Santos, Juan Manuel. 2015. 'Colombia: A Ray of Hope. Keynote Address by H.E. Mr Juan Manuel Santos, President of the Republic of Colombia.' In *Peacemaking in the New World Disorder: Oslo Forum 2015 Meeting Report*, 12–15. Geneva: Centre for Humanitarian Dialogue.
Segura, Renata, and Delphine Mechoulan. 2017. *Made in Havana: How Colombia and the FARC Decided to End the War*. New York: International Peace Institute.
Sikkink, Kathryn. 2011. *The Justice Cascade: How Human Rights Prosecutions Are Changing World Politics*. New York: W.W. Norton & Company.
Skaar, Elin, Camila Gianella Malca, and Trine Eide. 2015. 'Towards a Framework for Impact Assessment.' In *After Violence: Transitional Justice, Peace, and Democracy*, edited by Elin Skaar, Camila Gianella Malca, and Trine Eide, 29–66. Abingdon: Routledge.
The New Vision. 2005, April 18. 'Court Rules out Kony Immunity.' *The New Vision*.
UN Mission in Colombia. 2017, June 30. *Statement to the Security Council by Jean Arnault Special Representative of the Secretary General and Head of the United Nations Mission in Colombia*. Press release. United Nations.
UN Security Council. 2016a. *Identical Letters Dated 19 January 2016 from the Permanent Representative of Colombia to the United Nations Addressed to the Secretary-General and the President of the Security Council*. UN Doc. S/2016/53. New York. United Nations.

UN Security Council. 2016b. *Resolution 2261 (2016) Adopted by the Security Council at Its 7609th Meeting, on 25 January 2016.* UN Doc. S/RES/2261. New York. United Nations.

UN Security Council. 2017. *Report of the Secretary-General on the United Nations Mission in Colombia (24 March 2017).* UN Doc. S/2017/252. New York. United Nations.

Wallensteen, Peter. 2012. *Understanding Conflict Resolution.* 3rd edn. London: SAGE Publications.

Index

Page numbers in *italics* denote tables, those in **bold** denote figures

For Product Safety Concerns and Information please contact our EU representative GPSR@taylorandfrancis.com
Taylor & Francis Verlag GmbH, Kaufingerstraße 24, 80331 München, Germany

www.ingramcontent.com/pod-product-compliance
Ingram Content Group UK Ltd.
Pitfield, Milton Keynes, MK11 3LW, UK
UKHW011011180926
475701UK00004B/683
* 9 7 8 0 3 6 7 5 9 3 3 5 3 *